Bitcoin, Blockchain, and Cryptoassets

Bitcoin, Blockchain, and Cryptoassets

A Comprehensive Introduction

Fabian Schär and Aleksander Berentsen

The MIT Press
Cambridge, Massachusetts
London, England

This book was set in Stone Serif and Stone Sans by Westchester Publishing Services. Printed and bound in the United States of America.

This book was originally published in German as *Bitcoin, Blockchain und Kryptoassets: Eine umfassende Einführung*, BoD Norderstedt, 2017.

Library of Congress Cataloging-in-Publication Data

Names: Schär, Fabian, author. | Berentsen, Aleksander, author.
Title: Bitcoin, blockchain, and cryptoassets : a comprehensive introduction /
    Fabian Schär, Aleksander Berentsen.
Description: Cambridge, Massachusetts : MIT Press, [2020] |
    Includes bibliographical references and index.
Identifiers: LCCN 2019046399 | ISBN 9780262539166 (paperback)
Subjects: LCSH: Bitcoin. | Cryptocurrencies. | Blockchains (Databases)
Classification: LCC HG1710 .S335 2020 | DDC 332.4–dc23
LC record available at https://lccn.loc.gov/2019046399

10 9 8 7 6 5 4 3 2 1

Contents

Preface

The most important contribution in monetary economics in the twenty-first century is the paper "Bitcoin: A Peer-to-Peer Electronic Cash System." It was published via a mailing list for cryptography in 2008 under the pseudonym *Satoshi Nakamoto*. The basic idea of the paper was to create "a purely peer-to-peer version of electronic cash that would allow online payments to be sent directly from one party to another without going through a financial institution."

The Bitcoin developers have linked several technological components together to create a virtual asset that is substantially different from any other asset. For the first time, ownership of virtual property is possible without the need for a central authority—a development with the potential to fundamentally change the current financial system and many more areas in business and government.

As with any fundamental innovation, the true potential of this new technology will become apparent only many years—or possibly decades—after it is widely adopted. As of now, the most apparent application is Bitcoin as a virtual asset. It is likely that cryptoassets will emerge as their own asset class and develop into an interesting investment and diversification instrument. Bitcoin itself could, over time, assume a role similar of that of gold.

The aim of this book is to introduce the reader to cryptocurrencies and blockchain technology. The focus is on Bitcoin, but many elements are shared by other blockchain implementations and alternative cryptoassets. As with any fundamental innovation, it is amazing how difficult it is to put the concept into simple words. The question "What is Bitcoin?" opens up a whole spectrum of possible explanations. If Bitcoin is reduced to a monetary asset, such as digital cash, false expectations arise, and Bitcoin may appear uninteresting or even irrelevant. To capture the complexity and potential of Bitcoin and blockchain technology, the reader must be willing to apprehend knowledge from the disciplines of economics, cryptography, and computer science (figure 0.1).

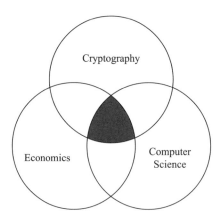

Figure 0.1
Interdisciplinarity of Bitcoin

Bitcoin does not belong to any person or company, nor is it controlled by any single entity. Rather, Bitcoin is an autonomous construct with a multitude of different stakeholders, which shape the system through complex interactions and incentive structures. This independence enables the technology to establish virtual property without the need for a central authority for the first time in history. This achievement is a technological breakthrough.

Before the invention of the Bitcoin blockchain, a consensus about ownership of a virtual asset could only be reached through centralization. In centralized systems, an institution is exclusively endowed with the right of record keeping and hence is responsible for maintaining and establishing property rights. Our current financial infrastructure, for example, relies on centrally managed accounting systems. Centralization creates several problems. With every transaction, user data is collected and centrally stored. This leads to a lack of privacy and creates a central point of attack (so-called data honey pots) as the many recent data breaches show. Further, centralized records can be easily manipulated (internal as well as external), and these play such an important role that they quickly become systemically relevant. Finally, in centralized systems individuals can be excluded from participation, and their assets can be easily confiscated. The decentralized nature of the Bitcoin system makes it immune to many of these problems.

The Bitcoin developers have provided a basic framework which serves as the foundation for a large number of new applications. Analogous to the TCP/IP protocol that enabled the prospering of the internet, Bitcoin technology can be used to represent virtual property in the broadest sense. Virtual claims to real estate, bank money, and company shares are just as conceivable as claims to postal stamps, domain names, or intellectual property rights. Any real asset can be tokenized and traded worldwide 24/7 without intermediaries on decentralized exchanges. Other applications include smart contracts and autonomous organizations. Finally, because it is very difficult to change records retroactively, the Bitcoin blockchain can be used to serve as proof that a specific data file existed in a particular form at a specific point in time.

The book consists of three parts and eight chapters. The first part of the book is a nontechnical introduction which requires no previous knowledge. Bitcoin was developed with the goal of creating a new kind of monetary unit. Therefore, in chapter 1 we focus on monetary theory to better understand the original motivation behind the Bitcoin system. We discuss the role of money for an economy and analyze the components of value of a monetary unit. We then distinguish between different types of money and study their basic characteristics and control structures. This chapter will help set the stage to understand how cryptocurrencies like Bitcoin are a radical departure from existing monetary instruments. In chapter 2 we begin our analysis of the Bitcoin system, and we introduce blockchain technology by presenting the main building blocks in a nontechnical way. This chapter serves as an overview of the Bitcoin technology that aims to highlight the innovative character of the Bitcoin system.

Part II includes the most challenging chapters of the book and deals mainly with the technical aspects of the Bitcoin system. Chapter 3 introduces the Bitcoin network and differentiates between various types of network participants. We consider the Bitcoin communications protocol, analyze various types of messages, and explain how network participants interact. Chapter 4 explains how Bitcoin units can be assigned to an individual and which principles of mathematics enable a decentralized validation of a transaction's legitimacy. For this purpose, we introduce pseudonyms and expand on the necessary cryptographic foundations. We also present the various transaction types as well as the specific conditions that have to be fulfilled for Bitcoin units to be transmitted. Finally, we look at signature hash types and more recent protocol changes such as Segregated Witness. Chapter 5 explains how transactions find their way into the Bitcoin blockchain and show how the network is able to reach consensus on the current state of the ledger. We study the data structure of blocks; discuss how these blocks are linked together; and analyze the basics of Bitcoin mining, the underlying game theory, and the proof-of-work consensus mechanism.

Part III of the book is dedicated to specific issues and applications. The Bitcoin technology is fascinating and has the potential to radically change the current financial system and many other sectors. Nevertheless, one has to admit that the technology still faces many hurdles. In chapter 6 we take a closer look at some of these challenges and discuss potential solutions. The challenges include high price volatility, scalability, energy consumption, and regulatory uncertainty. Further, we discuss hot topics such as central bank cryptocurrencies and stablecoins. The Bitcoin blockchain provides an infrastructure that enables numerous non-monetary applications. Chapter 7 discusses alternative applications and is intended to provide an outlook outside the purely monetary area. The applications discussed are decentralized verification and attestation, tokens, smart property, and blockchain contracts (smart contracts). Finally, chapter 8 provides some practical advice on how to get started using Bitcoin. It considers several possibilities for procuring and safeguarding Bitcoin units and indicates some of the risks and errors that users should avoid. It also discusses how to make and receive Bitcoin payments.

Our book is aimed at students and practitioners who would like to familiarize themselves with the subject. The interdisciplinary approach and the technical completeness ensure that it is equally interesting and worth reading for beginners and advanced readers.

We would like to take this opportunity to thank the Förderverein des Wirtschaftswissenschaftlichen Zentrum der Universität Basel and the Federal Reserve Bank of Saint Louis for supporting this project. Further thanks go to the following persons and to all those who supported and accompanied us in the development process of this book: Florian Bitterli, George E. Fortier, Pascal Gantenbein, Stefan Gehrig, Brigitte Guggisberg, Raphael Mani, Marina Markheim, Matthias Mohler, Remo Nyffenegger, Edith Schär, Michèle Schär, Joachim Setlik, and Christopher Waller.

I Introduction

1 The Context of Monetary Theory

Bitcoin was developed with the goal of creating a new kind of monetary unit. As we shall show in the course of this book, the possible applications of Bitcoin technology extend far beyond that of a monetary unit. Nevertheless, to grasp the special features of Bitcoin technology, one must be adequately acquainted with the roots of Bitcoin and thus with the topic of money.

In modern monetary theory, money is described as *memory*. [130] The origin of this definition stems from the observation that people do each other favors on a daily basis without being reciprocated. For example, "gifts" of this kind are exchanged within the family, among friends, or at work among colleagues. Undertaking housework at home, accepting an undesirable task at the office, or issuing the next dinner invitation to friends are only a few examples of such behavior. Every day, we enter into dozens of such *gift-giving* relationships. [26]

The factor that characterizes these relationships is that all the individuals involved keep an account of their current indebtedness. The accounts are not recorded in writing; instead, they are recorded in the subconscious ledger of the participants' memory. Nonetheless, each participant has a rough idea about whether the exchanges of gifts and favors are approximately balanced.

If, in a household relationship, tasks are always carried out by one person, and the other person profits from this work without carrying out other tasks, this will cause disruptive arguments that destabilize the relationship. In an office, if the same person is always left to carry out the team's loathsome tasks, this will also lead to arguments. If dinner invitations in a friendship are very one-sided, the invitee will be seen as selfish, and the friendship will be threatened.

For a system of *gift-giving* to function, there must be a mechanism for reaching consensus. Agreement is usually reached when the participants talk together and settle their differences. In practice, we see that the exchanging of gifts and favors functions smoothly where the participants know each other well and the group is small. In large groups, or in groups where participants are anonymous, the system tends to break down, because it becomes difficult to reach consensus. In such groups, *gift-giving* is replaced by the exchange of money. Money usurps the role of memory in complex societies with complicated trading relationships. Money keeps an account of the global trade in favors. Money is *memory*.

A payments system regulates how its money is represented, how it is produced, and how the transfer of ownership of monetary units takes place. To gain a better understanding of how the Bitcoin system operates, it is worthwhile taking a quick look at traditional payment systems.

Let us start by looking at cash; that is, coins and banknotes. Coins and banknotes are physical objects. This has a great advantage, as the ownership rights are always clearly defined. The ownership of a banknote or a coin is transferred as payment from the buyer to the seller of a good. This allows people who do not know each other to trade anonymously with each another. Further, any agent can participate in a cash payment system; nobody can be excluded. There is a permissionless access to it.

Cash has a major disadvantage because it requires the physical proximity of the buyer and the seller. This restriction has become particularly apparent with the rise of the internet. In addition, it is unappealing to hold larger sums of cash due to safety and expense. For these reasons, the idea of replacing physical cash with digital money soon emerged. In a naïve implementation, a buyer would send a digital coin to a seller in the form of a text file. The problem is that this digital coin can be copied any number of times. A buyer could thus send the same digital coin to several sellers or even retain additional copies of the coin.

This "copy" dilemma is referred to in the literature as the *double spending problem*. Two solutions exist for this issue.

The first solution consists in an institution being appointed to monitor all electronic payments. This involves, in particular, verifying that a buyer is the rightful owner of the digital coins that will be used to pay for the good. Worldwide, the prevailing electronic payment systems rely on the first solution. Users of these payment systems pay with electronic money, which is also called *deposit money*, *bank money*, or *book money*. Electronic money is virtual money because it does not exist in a physical form. It has been created by commercial banks, which are responsible for accurate bookkeeping. It therefore depends on a central authority.

The Bitcoin system provides the second solution, as it solves the problem of *double spends* without a central authority (see chapter 2). To ensure that this system functions, there is a mechanism that establishes consensus and is very similar to the exchange of favors among family members, friends, and colleagues. In contrast to the simple subjective consensus rules governing *gift-giving*, the Bitcoin system guarantees an objective, globally verifiable consensus so that at any point in time, the property rights associated with every Bitcoin unit are firmly established. Thus, the Bitcoin system fulfills the function of *memory* in complex societies but needs no central authority to manage it.

To fully understand the value of a cryptocurrency such as Bitcoin, we must first understand monetary theory. The rest of this chapter will provide an understanding of the fundamentals of monetary theory. We will discuss the role of money for an economy and analyze the components of value of a monetary unit. We will then distinguish the different types of money and study their basic characteristics and control structures. This information will help set the stage to understand how cryptocurrencies like Bitcoin are a radical departure from existing monetary instruments, which we will discuss in more detail in chapter 2.

1.1   Origin of a Monetary Unit

The economic theory of Carl Menger[154] suggests that money may evolve without government intervention. He proposed that a monetary unit emerges spontaneously from a process in which a good that is frequently traded incrementally becomes a generally accepted medium of exchange. Such a social coordination does not require any formal decision making or legislative decisions but can instead be induced by demand that already exists.[94] Further, there are strong network effects. The more market participants there are who use a specific medium of exchange, the greater is the utility that this medium offers; that is, the dominance of the medium of exchange has a self-reinforcing effect.[128,129]

It can be assumed that early monetary units originated in this way. In different regions and in different eras, various goods and abstractions have been used as money. Many of these early examples share the same factor: they served as a basic foodstuff or as a (ceremonial) item of jewelry, generating a constant demand.[153] Although this is not a comprehensive list, some examples of this include stones, livestock, whales' teeth, shells, and feathers.[15]

1.2   Functions of a Monetary Unit

Monetary units fulfill three functions (analogous to figure 1.1). As a *medium of exchange*, they facilitate trade and improve the allocation of goods and services. As a *unit of account*, they serve as a universal reference and simplify the comparative valuation of

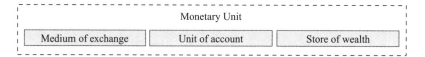

Figure 1.1
Functions of monetary units.

goods and services. As a *store of wealth*, monetary units can be used to save. These functions are described comprehensively in the following sections.

1.2.1 Medium of Exchange

A medium of exchange is indispensable in a modern economy typified by the specialization of labor; that is, when economic actors specialize and only produce a small subset of goods. Such specialization is only possible if all other goods can be acquired through trade and so an economy with division of labor must necessarily be an exchange economy.

In an economy that does not use money, goods and services can only be bought through barter.[1] A person who owns a loaf of bread but who would prefer to consume a jug of milk would therefore first have to find a person who owns a jug of milk and would prefer to consume a loaf of bread. Only then will both parties be willing and able to trade goods. Consequently, a simple agreement is not sufficient. A barter transaction can only be concluded if one party has what the other party wants and vice versa. This problem, known in the literature as the *double coincidence of wants*, makes it difficult to find a suitable trade partner.[53,164]

Another impeding factor is the progressive number of possible pairs of tradable goods. Given an arbitrary number n of different goods and services, there will be $\frac{n(n-1)}{2}$ different pairs of tradable goods. In economies which have a moderate number of different goods and services, direct barter is likely to have a few disadvantages. As soon as an economic system is more complex, it will consist of millions of subjects, goods, and services. The search for suitable trade partners (or a specific pair of tradable goods) will then entail considerable costs.[2]

---

1. If an established relationship of trust exists between the trade partners, loans would be a feasible alternative. Mutual favors are then given on a credit basis, summed up over time, and settled.[104]
2. Increasing economic specialization increases the complexity of barter trade and the associated transaction costs. Higher transaction costs again lead to greater potential savings and promote the primacy of the generally accepted medium of exchange. Conversely, a generally accepted medium of exchange fosters economic specialization or even can be seen as a prerequisite for it.

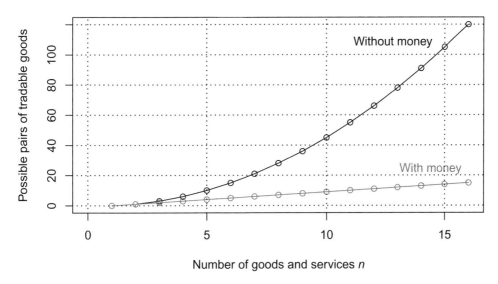

Figure 1.2
Number of pairs of tradable goods with and without monetary units.

If, however, one good is accepted by all members of the economy, then all trades can be settled using this good as a medium of exchange. A simple coincidence of wants is sufficient for the transaction, and therefore the number of relevant pairs of tradable goods is immediately reduced by the factor n so that only $n - 1$ potential pairs of goods remain.

Figure 1.2 shows the number of possible pairs of tradable goods in the economy with and without using money. It illustrates how the number of potential pairs of tradable goods surges when the number of goods increases.

1.2.2 Unit of Account

A unit of account allows the values of all goods and services to be expressed in units of the same reference scale and to be compared. The amount of information required for a comprehensive overview of the market is thereby substantially reduced. Instead of having to dynamically adjust the respective ratios of $\frac{n(n-1)}{2}$ pairs of tradable goods, a unit of account provides a universal reference for evaluating different types of goods and services. Once the prices for all goods and services are expressed in monetary

---

Although the direction of a causal dependency cannot be identified clearly, it is well established that specialization and money are closely linked and are positively correlated. [139]

units, then only one single monetary-exchange value is needed per good (that is, $n - 1$). This simplification ensures more transparency in the market and reduces the search and transaction costs of trading.

Most often, monetary units combine the functions of a medium of exchange and a unit of account. These two functions, however, can be easily separated (see box 1.1).

Box 1.1
Outsourced Units of Account

In most economies, the medium of exchange assumes the function of a unit of account. This is not always the case, as shown by the following examples.

In the Middle Ages, the diversity of coins and the continual changes in their precious metal content[a] led to pounds, shillings, and pence being used as units of account, where a pound corresponded to 20 shillings or 240 pence. This made it possible to use a universal price and take account of the changes in value of a specific coin without adjusting the stated prices of goods. [132]

There are still examples today of cases where the function of a unit of account is split off from the medium of exchange. The *Unidad de Fomento* in Chile (CLF) is an inflation-adjusted national price index that is determined vis-à-vis the national currency (peso) and is published every day. The shopping prices in Chile are expressed in CLF. This avoids the administrative expense of making price adjustments when the peso depreciates. To calculate the peso's price, agents only need to apply a single exchange rate. [131]

---

a. Coins were filed and clipped, and metals were dissolved in acid baths. Sometimes coins were officially "called up" and reminted with a lower precious-metal content.

1.2.3 Store of Value

The store of value function of money enables agents to self-insure against liquidity shocks. This permits consumption smoothing and protection against unexpected expenses. A medium of exchange is always a store of value because there is an interval of time between receiving money and spending it. In contrast, there are many assets that are used to store savings, such as gold or real estate, which are not used as a medium of exchange.

1.3 Fundamental Properties of Money

To fulfill the three functions of money presented in section 1.2, monetary units must be storable, transferable, divisible, homogeneous, verifiable, scarce, and price stable.

Storability. The monetary unit's use as a *medium of exchange* and a *store of value* is conditional upon its storability. Perishable or sensitive goods are not suitable. The same applies to goods that are difficult to store and consequently generate high storage costs.

Transferability. For an object to be used as a *medium of exchange* or a *store of value*, it must be possible to transfer the property rights to it without substantial impediments or costs.

Divisibility. The *medium of exchange* function demands that the monetary unit (of a fractional amount of it) may be exchanged for any chosen quantity of goods or services. Consequently, money must either be divisible or available in sufficiently small denominations. Indivisible money introduces sizable inefficiencies into an economy. [29,192]

Homogeneity. Monetary units (with the same nominal value) must be homogeneous; that is, fungible and exchangeable. Nonhomogeneous goods have to be individually evaluated every time they are traded, which entails high transaction costs and a failure to function as a *medium of exchange*.

Verifiability. Both the function of a *medium of exchange* and that of a *store of value* require that the authenticity of the units can be verified and potential counterfeits identified.

Scarcity. A monetary unit's limited availability is an essential property for using it as a *medium of exchange*. If a monetary unit is available in unlimited quantities, it will have no value.

Stability of value. *Store of value* and *unit of account* depend on a certain price stability of the monetary unit. Goods with high seasonal and random supply fluctuations (e.g., agricultural products) are not suitable.

1.4   Monetary Value

The market value of a monetary unit is based on three components: the intrinsic value, the value of an attached promise of payment, and a liquidity premium (see table 1.1).

The *intrinsic value* relates to the material, inherent value of the object. This value stems from the utility that results from the consumption or ownership of the good or its usefulness as a factor of production. The intrinsic value of a monetary unit is independent of the monetary function of the object.

A *promise of payment* is a component of value that is not materially embedded in the monetary unit. In contrast to the intrinsic value, this component of value is subject to the issuer risk. If the issuer of the promise does not fulfill his obligation, then this value component becomes void.

Table 1.1
Components of a monetary unit.

	Intrinsic value
+	Promise of payment
+	Liquidity premium
=	Market value of the monetary unit

Table 1.2
Types of money according to value components.

	Intrinsic	Promise	Premium
Commodity money	+		(+)
Credit money		+	(+)
Fiat money			+

The liquidity premium is the outcome of the option to flexibly trade the monetary unit for goods and services. This option has a positive effect on the monetary unit's market value.

These three value components form the market values of the three types of monetary units shown in table 1.2. Monetary units are assigned to these categories depending on the composition of value components that form their market value.

1.4.1 Commodity Money

Commodity money has an intrinsic value and often contains a liquidity premium. The market value may be higher than the intrinsic value as a result of the liquidity premium. The intrinsic value remains if the good loses its function as a medium of exchange since in this case, the good may be consumed or may be used as a factor of production.

The following items are examples of objects used as commodity money: shells in Africa and China, rings and pieces of jewelry in New Guinea, and garments (furs) in North America as well as metal money in many other regions of the world. Cattle and basic foodstuffs have often also been used as commodity money.

1.4.2 Credit Money

Credit money is a promise of payment and possesses no intrinsic value. Generally, it is a piece of paper or a digital record which states that the issuer will make a payment at a specific future date. This type of promise of payment is called an IOU (I owe you).

Basically, promises of payment may have any number of forms; for example, "I owe individual × a cow on July 1, 2090" or "I owe individual × a sleigh ride on

January 30, 2030." Most often, the liability is expressed in the prevailing unit of account.

Default risk plays an important role in determining the market value of the promised payment. In this regard, the reputation of the issuer has to be considered since a promise to deliver one ounce of gold made by individual A may have a completely different market value from the same promise made by individual B.

A promise of payment becomes money when it is generally accepted in trade. In most countries, bank deposits, which are liabilities of the respective deposit-taking bank, are used for making electronic payments. A bank deposit is nothing other than a promise made by a commercial bank that it will exchange the deposit for government-issued currency (banknotes and coins) at any time (on sight).

Box 1.2
The Origins of Paper Money

Early examples of paper money were similar to other promises of payment because they were secured by a real asset (usually gold). These notes bore a pledge of convertibility into a previously agreed amount of precious metal or into other commodities. The credit character of these bills becomes particularly evident when their origin is considered. The first banknotes/bills originated in China during the Tang Dynasty (the years 618–907) as a credit agreement between private individuals. Depending on the reputation and the creditworthiness of the issuer, this bill could circulate and serve as a monetary substitute for the *Kai Yuan* bronze-coin chains. [42]

Analogous to other types of money, credit money may also include a liquidity premium. The liquidity premium can cause the market value of the credit money to be higher than the market value of the associated promise of payment.

1.4.3   Fiat Money

The expression "fiat money" derives from the Latin term *fiat* (let there be), illustrating that fiat money possesses neither intrinsic value nor a promise of payment and that its value therefore has no fundamental basis: it arises out of nothing (let there be money). Its value indeed derives from its liquidity premium alone, and if it ceases to have a monetary function, its value can fall to zero.

Currencies, such as the US dollar, the euro, or the Swiss franc, belong to the category of fiat money. The banknotes can neither be consumed nor integrated in a production process, nor are they secured by gold or any other fundamentally valuable good. The stability of the currency's value is guaranteed uniquely by the central banks, which have an exclusive right to issue the currency and the legal duty to ensure its value remains stable.

In Switzerland and in many other countries, banknotes, and to a certain extent also coins, are legal tender. Article 3 of the Federal Act on Currency and Payment Instruments (CPIA) stipulates an "obligation to accept"; that is, "everyone must accept Swiss banknotes in payment without restriction." [199] This legal basis ensures that there is a demand for Swiss banknotes and that it promotes the liquidity premium of the Swiss monetary unit. Further, state support can have a stabilizing effect on a fundamentally very volatile category of money.

Fiat money is a relatively young phenomenon. Up until the 1970s, paper money was backed by gold, either implicitly or explicitly, and therefore represented credit money. However, owing to its loss of gold backing and the negligible material intrinsic value of a paper bill, the category of fiat money arose. As we shall see later, Bitcoin also belongs to this category.

Box 1.3
Decision to Accept a Fiat Currency as a Coordination Game

The value of a fiat currency and, as we will see, the value of a Bitcoin unit, is based exclusively on expectations regarding its future market acceptance and marketability (liquidity premium). The greater the likelihood is that a person will meet a market participant who will accept it as payment, the more willing he or she will be to accept it today.

This situation is illustrated in the following graph. Consider an agent who is contemplating whether to accept fiat money as payment. Suppose that Π represents the probability that a future trade partner will accept the monetary unit as payment and that π is the agent's acceptance probability. The correspondence $\pi = \pi(\Pi)$ is the agent's best response to a given expectation regarding the value of Π. For low values of $\Pi < \hat{\Pi}$, the best response is to not accept the monetary unit; that is, $\pi(\Pi) = 0$. For high values of $\Pi > \hat{\Pi}$, the best response is to accept the monetary unit with certainty; that is, $\pi(\Pi) = 1$. Finally, for $\Pi = \hat{\Pi}$, the best response is $\pi(\Pi) \in [0, 1]$; that is, any acceptance probability yields the same payoff.

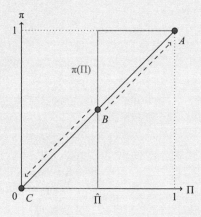

Every intercept of $\pi(\Pi)$ with the 45° axis represents a Nash equilibrium. There are exactly three Nash equilibria: A, B, and C. The two outer equilibria represent situations in which no participant (C) or all participants (A) are willing to accept the monetary unit. The market value of the currency in equilibrium C is zero, and the value in equilibrium A is strictly positive. A third mixed-strategy equilibrium (B) arises at the threshold $\hat{\Pi}$. Above this value, reinforcing forces are at work, which bring the economy into the monetary equilibrium. If the probability is below $\hat{\Pi}$, then the level of acceptance will diminish and completely disappear. Situations with these characteristics are also termed *coordination games* in microeconomics (more precisely, in game theory).[24]

1.5   Monetary Control Structures

Monetary units display different control structures, which can be roughly captured by three dimensions: *creation*, *representation*, and *transaction processing*.

The term "money creation" refers to the process by which new monetary units can be produced. The term "representation" relates to whether the value of a monetary unit is tied to a physical object or whether the unit is traded solely as a virtual abstraction. The term "transaction processing" relates to whether the transmission of a monetary unit can be processed on an independent, decentralized basis or whether this must be carried out by a central authority.

1.5.1   The Creation of Money

For money to be valuable, its quantity must be *scarce*. Scarcity is usually achieved by means of the money creation process, which can take place under either competition or monopoly.

In a competitive framework of money creation, every economic subject can create new monetary units. Every individual assesses on the basis of pure self-interest whether it is worthwhile to produce a new monetary unit, given the associated production costs. An economic subject will have an incentive to produce another monetary unit up until the point at which the production costs of an additional unit (marginal costs) correspond to the current market price for that monetary unit (marginal revenue); in other words, production will be continued as long as the production process delivers a positive return.

Competitive money creation requires a technological restriction that brings the creation process into equilibrium. Figure 1.3a presents a diagram of this relationship and visualizes the equilibrium, which is situated at the intersection of the marginal cost and

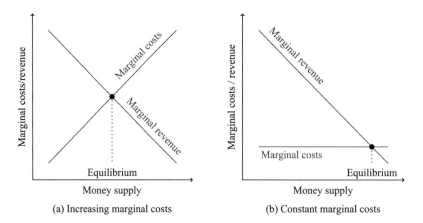

Figure 1.3
Competitive money creation.

the marginal revenue curves. The negative slope of the marginal revenue curve is due to a larger total amount of the money supply (with demand being constant) leading to a fall in the market value of the monetary unit and thereby reducing marginal revenue. The positive slope of the marginal cost curve is due to the assumption that the production of a monetary unit requires factors of production, which become scarcer and thus more expensive with increasing production. The cost of producing a further unit thereby increases with the expansion of the money supply.

A classic example of money creation under competition is prospecting for gold. Basically, every person can engage in this activity and bring new gold into circulation. Individuals will, however, only engage in this activity as long as their efforts are remunerated. The more gold that has already been discovered, the more difficult, and thus the more cost-intensive, the process becomes. At the same time, an increase in supply—all things being equal—leads to falling prices for gold so that with every additional unit of gold, the marginal costs of production increase and marginal revenue decreases. Above a specific production amount, the marginal costs for producing an additional unit of gold exceed the value of the gold unit, entailing that creation is halted.

On the other hand, low, constant marginal costs, analogous to figure 1.3b, lead to large amounts of the monetary unit being produced. If the marginal costs are small or even zero, individuals will then have an incentive to create new monetary units until the market price for these units falls to zero.

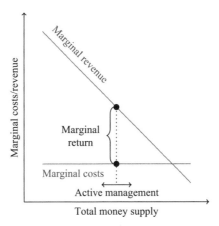

Figure 1.4
Monopolistic money creation with constant marginal costs.

The marginal cost of producing banknotes are small, and for this reason, an artificial restriction has to be established by monopolizing the right to create money. Normally, a state-controlled institution is awarded the exclusive right to issue and manage the national currency. It is also possible for this monopoly right to be privatized.[25] The monopoly right to create money allows the production costs to be kept lower than the market price.

Monopolized money creation is illustrated in figure 1.4. The money-issuing monopolist chooses the total supply, and the market price of the monetary unit is determined by aggregate demand. Monopolized money creation allows for a monetary unit with a positive market value even when the marginal production costs are zero.

An illustrative example of monopolistic money creation is the production of the physical Swiss franc. The Swiss National Bank has the exclusive right to issue banknotes and thereby possesses a monopoly over the creation of currency. The cost of producing a banknote amounts, on average, to thirty cents (called "Rappen").[47] For the one-hundred franc note, the cost is only 0.3 percent of its market value. Under perfect competition in the production of money, the market would be flooded with banknotes until the real value of a note equaled the cost of producing it. This also means that far more resources would have to be given up to produce a given total value for the medium of exchange. From a societal viewpoint, this leads to an inefficient allocation of resources and an efficiency advantage for the monopolistic money-issuing process.

Box 1.4
Relative Production Costs of Monetary Units

The following table shows an example of the production costs for the Swiss franc. The data include the costs of development and production and relate to a notification issued by the Swiss Federal Council in 2013. [47] The first column shows the denomination in CHF, the second column includes the production costs in CHF, and the third column gives the relationship of production costs to value as a percentage ratio.

Denomination	Production costs	Percentage ratio
0.05	0.0422	84.40%
0.10	0.0663	66.30%
0.20	0.0847	42.35%
0.50	0.0710	14.20%
1.00	0.0993	9.93%
2.00	0.1940	9.70%
5.00	0.3630	7.26%
10.00	0.3000^a	3.00%
20.00	0.3000^a	1.50%
50.00	0.3000^a	0.60%
100.00	0.3000^a	0.30%
200.00	0.3000^a	0.15%
1,000.00	0.3000^a	0.03%

As an example of competitive money issuance, we will look at data on gold digging. The production costs of the ten largest gold producers are estimated to be between US$825 and US$1,071 per ounce of gold and thus are relatively close to the current price for gold.[b] This corresponds to a ratio of production costs to market value of between 70 percent and 95 percent. [21]

---

a. Average value across all banknotes.
b. An exact correspondence between the production costs and the price of gold cannot be observed in practice because (a) gold digging presents substantial barriers to entry in spite of its generally competitive nature and (b) the data relates to the ten most cost-efficient producers and therefore excludes a part of the market.

In addition to the mentioned efficiency considerations, there is a further important difference between competitive and monopolistic money creation. Under competition, the money supply is determined by production costs and aggregate demand. In contrast, a monopoly-issuer can actively influence the money supply and respond to changes in demand. Since economic activities are often of a cyclical nature, a money-issuing monopolistic institution has the capacity to stabilize the value of money by expanding or contracting the money supply.

> **Box 1.5**
> **Money Creation**
>
> Central banks are creating new money by granting loans to commercial banks or buying foreign exchange and securities. When a central bank grants a loan to a commercial bank, the loan is shown on the assets side of its balance sheet. In contrast, the newly created money is booked on the liabilities side of its balance sheet. This process is called balance sheet extension. Since the newly created money is potentially circulating in the economy, new "money" has been created through this balance sheet extension. In the commercial bank's balance sheet, the loan is shown on the liabilities side and the newly created money on the assets side.

Providing a central bank with the discretionary power to adjust the money supply to stabilize the price level can be of great benefit to society. Nevertheless, a high degree of trust must be placed in any monopoly supplier of money. If the independence of the institution is not guaranteed, the exclusive right to create money can lead to abusive financing of public expenditure through the "printing press," which has often resulted in the complete destruction of the respective currency. Monetary history covers numerous examples of such cases (see box 1.6 and box 1.7). Figures 1.5 and 1.6 display the real value of money for various currencies from 1960 until 2018.

Consider, for example, the path for the real value of money for the Argentinian peso in figure 1.5. In this graph we have normalized the real value of money to one in 1960. This means that one Argentinian peso could buy one unit of a standardized basket of goods and services at that time. About seventeen years later, the same unit of money would buy only 0.0001 units of the same standardized basket of goods and commodities. Roughly thirty years later, one Argentinien peso would buy 0.0000000000001 units.

The price history of the Argentinian peso is not an outlier. In fact, it would be difficult to find a developing country that has not experienced a destruction of the real value of its currency in the last sixty years. Further, figure 1.6 shows that even for developed

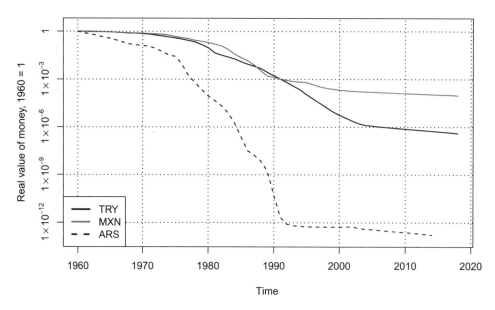

Figure 1.5
Development of the real value of money of the Argentine peso, the Mexican peso, and the Turkish
lira. Logarithmic scale, normalized to one in January 1960.
Source: FRED Economic Data.

countries the real value of money has been melting like ice in the Sahara over the last
sixty years. Consider, for example, the British pound and the Japanese yen. The currencies of these two countries lost about 90 percent of their purchasing power between
1960 and 2018. The Swiss franc is the best in the cohort displayed in figure 1.6. Between
1960 and 2018 it only lost about 70 percent of its value.

Box 1.6
Central Banks Are Honey Pots

What is the reason for the mediocre and sometimes even catastrophic performance of the
government-issued fiat monies documented in figures 1.5 and 1.6? The reason is that central banks are centralized institutions. They are honey pots: the financial assets of a central
bank are easily located and confiscated for political or personal gain. Moreover, in countries with weak political institutions, monetary policy is often misused to benefit the ruling
political party's chance of reelection.

   Centralized institutions are not censorship resistant and create a single point of failure. The people involved in monetary policy decisions are well known. They can be

manipulated, pressured, and coerced. The assets managed by a central bank are easily located and can be confiscated. In general, censorship resistance means that an institution can withstand outside interference. This is unfortunately not the case for central banks and is historically the main reason for the failures in the history of government-issued fiat money.

In contrast, the main attraction of Bitcoin is its censorship-resistant governance. There is no single point of failure, and its decentralized structure makes Bitcoin very resilient.

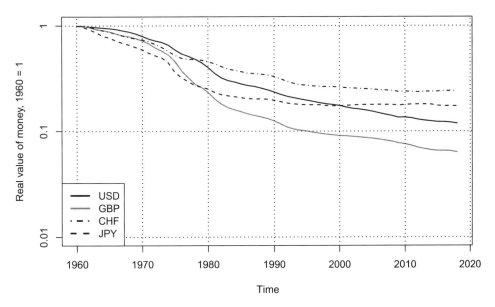

Figure 1.6
Development of the real value of money of the US dollar, the British pound, the Swiss franc, and the Japanese yen. Logarithmic scale normalized to one in January 1960.
Source: FRED Economic Data.

Figures 1.5 and 1.6 do not consider the nominal interest rates paid on money-like assets of the various national currencies. Taking such interest payments into account will dampen the loss in the real value of money for the respective currencies. However, one also needs to bear in mind that, in many developing countries, a large fraction of the population (typically the poor) has no access to the financial system and can only save by storing cash.

Box 1.7
Hyperinflation

A common threshold value that separates inflation from hyperinflation is a monthly inflation rate (price increase) of 50 percent, which amounts to an annualized inflation rate of just under 13,000 percent. Hyperinflation occurs most often when a state finances a public deficit for a longer period of time by printing money. [35,50]

Since World War II, fifty-six cases of hyperinflations have been documented. The highest monthly rates range between 50.8 percent (Taiwan, 1947) and 4.19 percent $\times 10^{16}$; that is, 41.9 quadrillion percent (Hungary, 1945–1946). More recently, Zimbabwe's hyperinflation (2007–2008) caused a sensation. On bad days, the purchasing power of the Zimbabwe dollar fell 50 percent in just over twenty-four hours. [108]

Such extreme values are possible because the respective institutions can change the denomination of their banknotes. If the marginal cost of banknote production exceeds the current value of the note, the money-creating institution can adjust the nominal value of the note and thus reduce the relative production costs per monetary unit. This results in absurd banknotes such as the 100 trillion mark note, which was issued in 1924 in Germany.

Today's monetary order cannot be described by a purely monopolized money-creation process. Commercial banks create bank deposits which, although not legal tender, are in most cases considered the equivalent of legal tender and are circulated in a similar manner. Bank deposits are nothing else than promises of the respective commercial bank to redeem the legal tender on demand. For example, if a person has a US$100 banknote, he or she is in possession of the legal tender. However, if the same person has a deposit account with a commercial bank with a balance of US$100, the balance is a promise of payment—in other words, credit money as described in section 1.4.2.

Commercial banks create money in a similar way to the central banks (see box 1.5). Commercial banks generate money (i.e., demand deposits) when they issue loans to private individuals and companies. When commercial banks issue loans to their clients, they increase the clients' demand deposits and book the loans as their clients' liabilities.

Technically, a commercial bank can create any amount of money (demand deposits) by granting loans. In practice, the profitability of this business limits money creation. In addition, there are minimum reserves and other regulatory restrictions that limit private money creation. Nor is it in the bank's interest to create so many demand deposits that it cannot keep the promise to exchange them for legal tender. In this case, the bank would become illiquid.

The prospect of commercial bank illiquidity has precipitated many financial crises in the past and is one of the main reasons for the rigorous regulation of financial intermediaries. Efficient interbank markets, where commercial banks can loan each other legal tender, as well as a central bank as the *lender of last resort* reduce these risks.

> **Box 1.8**
> **Fractional Reserve Banking**
>
> In the current monetary system, commercial banks create more money than they hold in reserves in the form of central bank money. For this reason, the system is named *fractional reserve banking*. This is seen in certain circles as a shortcoming of the existing monetary order. In particular, there are demands that commercial banks must hold 100 percent in reserves or that client deposits should be kept as off-balance sheet accounts.

In spite of the risk involved with fractional reserve banking, the importance of demand deposits for payments should not be underestimated.[191] In many countries, demand deposits are the only option that individuals have to hold and transfer money in a virtual form.[3] Although there is no legal obligation to accept private money, electronic transfers and card payments are so ubiquitous that acceptance is widespread. For this reason, most people assume incorrectly that demand deposits are central bank money. This false assumption is promoted by the at-par trading of demand deposits and central bank money in normal times. If a commercial bank is no longer in the position to fulfill its promise to deliver central bank money on demand, only bank clients will notice the difference between central bank money and commercial demand deposits.[4]

1.5.2 Representation

There are two ways that money can be represented—monetary units either can have a physical representation or can have a virtual representation.

Physical monetary units are linked to an object. The physical control of the object also implies possession of the corresponding value. For example, if someone controls a physical gold coin, then he basically has the right to use it.

Physical monetary units are particularly attractive because of their simple handling. Since the holder of a physical monetary unit is automatically the owner of the corresponding value, the ownership rights to the units, which are circulating freely

---

3. Today, there is no possibility for private individuals to hold central bank money in virtual form.[34]

4. In Switzerland, commercial bank deposits up to CHF 100,000 per client are protected by insurance (see Art. 37 ff. of the Swiss Federal Act on Banks and Savings Banks).[198]

in the economy, are always clearly defined without anyone having to keep records. This feature allows for a decentralized payment system where physical monetary units can change hands between agents without the involvement of a third party. Therefore, physical monetary units allow agents to remain anonymous (see box 1.12) and protect the owner against systemic dependencies since the transfer of the unit of value does not require any additional infrastructure or trust.

Physical monetary units have some disadvantages, which are described below.

Restricted to a geographic location. Physical monetary units are limited to transactions in which the parties (or representatives) stand face-to-face to make the exchange.

Safekeeping and transport. Money in physical form generates costs of safekeeping and transport. The monetary units have to be professionally stored, secured and often insured. A large portion of these costs are directly related to the relative physical bulk of the stored amounts as well as the distance of a transport.

Physical integrity. Regardless of whether money creation is competitive or monopolized (see section 1.5.1), the monetary unit must be resistant to forgery. With monopolized money creation, it is necessary to ensure that the monetary units can only be produced by the dedicated monopoly. Under competition, it is necessary to ensure that objects with similar appearance and lower production costs are prevented from entering circulation as money substitutes. The integrity of a physical monetary unit is often guaranteed by placing security features on them.

Denomination and divisibility. Physical monetary units are not fully divisible. Dividing a physical monetary unit can be expensive (precious metals) or impossible (banknotes). Fiat money systems create different denominations, and central banks guarantee, for example, that a banknote with the number 100 printed on it is exchanged for ten banknotes which have the number 10 printed on them.

Virtual money is an alternative to money in physical form. Virtual monetary units include all types of monetary units that *do not* have a physical representation. More precisely, a monetary unit is virtual if it can be transferred to a new owner without the transfer involving a change in control over a physical object.

Box 1.9
Definition of Virtual Monetary Units

At this point, it should be mentioned that the European Central Bank (ECB) has published a definition of a virtual monetary unit that conflicts with our definition. The ECB holds the position that virtual currencies must strictly be of a digital nature. (Excerpt from the ECB

Report[90] on the topic "Virtual Currencies": "A virtual currency is a type of unregulated, digital money, which is issued and usually controlled by its developers, and used and accepted among the members of a specific virtual community").

Although the words *virtual* and *digital* are used in most cases interchangeably, their use as synonyms should be avoided. The adjective "virtual" is the antonym of "physical" and does not derive from any association with "digital."

Moreover, the ECB's requirement that the word "unregulated"—a feature of the definition—as it applies to the term excludes some monetary unit substitutes which clearly ought to be assigned to the range of virtual monetary units. To mention one example, demand deposits used in the classical financial system are clearly regulated and are nevertheless purely virtual in nature.

Virtual money shares many attributes of physical money without the disadvantages of a physical representation, but there are also downsides. While the ownership of a physical object is clearly established by the whereabouts of the corresponding object, ownership of a virtual claim is contestable. To counteract this problem, the legitimization and proof of virtual claims takes place via implicit or explicit ledgers that keep a record of all economic subjects' holdings.[5]

Box 1.10

A Digital Banknote

A naïve attempt to represent value virtually would be to use "cash" data files. This type of data file could be used as a digital banknote and circulate freely in a manner analogous to physical banknotes. As long as the ownership of the data file can be clearly proven, no ledger is necessary.

This idea, however, has one major problem. In distinction to physical objects, virtual objects can be easily copied. Such "cash" data files therefore lack the most essential fundamental characteristic of money, namely scarcity, and cannot establish itself as money.

---

5. *Stored value cards* (SVC) offer an alternative to using a ledger. The monetary units can be loaded onto the chips of these cards without it being necessary to record the card balances in a central ledger. The chip prevents any unauthorized adjustment of the balance. Equally, the validation of a payment requires no connection with a ledger. Common examples of this virtual payment method are telephone cards[60] or the *Mondex* and *Cash* functions[59] on Swiss debit cards. SVCs have become less important today, and most projects have been terminated. A major reason for the lack of success is that although SVCs fall into the area of virtual monetary units, their use requires the physical presence of the user and special chip readers.

Implicit ledgers are solely based on the oral agreement of the participants who use them and are therefore limited to small, well-networked communities. Box 1.11 deals with an example of a virtual monetary unit based on an implicit ledger. Larger social groups produce complex systems and complicated ownership relationships that make the use of explicit ledgers compulsory. For such cases, databases are used to store records in written or digital form.

Box 1.11
On Virtual Millstones

An impressive and very vivid example of a virtual (but not digital) money based on an implicit ledger is provided by the American anthropologist William Henry Furness III. At the beginning of the twentieth century, he spent several months on the German Micronesian island of Yap to study the Yap natives' way of life and culture. He was particularly impressed by the monetary system of the island's inhabitants. In his report,[101] he writes of large millstone-like formations that were extracted from the island of Palau, just 280 miles away, and then rafted to Yap. Once there, the stones were used as money.[a]

But instead of laboriously moving the stones—each with a diameter of up to thirteen feet—to the property of the new owner with each transaction, the inhabitants agreed to leave the unwieldy objects at their respective place. The only decisive factor was that the community would recognize the change of ownership. News about the transactions that had taken place and the consequent changes in ownership would be communicated among the island's inhabitants until all had been informed.[b]

Although the millstones are physical objects, the claim to their ownership was detached from them and was traded independently. This dissociation has the consequence that physical control over the stone no longer entails ownership of the physical object's value. According to the reports of Furness, the process of virtualization was well advanced, such that even the unit value of a stone which sank in the sea when being transported from Palau to Yap was still accepted as a medium of exchange, even if the stone itself had been lying at the bottom of the ocean for generations.[100] The physical stones were of secondary importance and were not relevant to establishing actual rights of ownership—this separation being the characteristic according to which the monetary unit satisfies our definition of virtuality.

---

a. This corresponds to the competitive money creation analogy to section 1.5.1 since theoretically every island inhabitant is in the position to haul new stones to the island. The marginal costs principally consist of production costs, transport costs, and opportunity costs. The marginal revenue is determined by the market value of the stone.
b. The Yap monetary system has a few commonalities with Bitcoin technology but is nevertheless distinct from it in essential respects. For a comparison, see the *Economist*[214] as well as box 2.1.

Today's financial system is based on a multitiered architecture of explicit ledgers. The central banks keep ledgers of the assets of the commercial banks. The commercial banks in turn keep ledgers of their clients' assets. As we shall see in the following chapters, Bitcoin is also managed on the basis of an explicit ledger, namely the Bitcoin blockchain.

Box 1.12
Monetary Units and Anonymity

Trading with physical monetary units provides a very high level of anonymity.[a] Usually, there are no data, or only rough approximations, that indicate where the physical monetary units are actually located. For this reason, it is difficult to track down individual monetary units, and this is generally only possible if the physical monetary unit is not completely homogeneous or if it has a serial number or bears another specific feature.

Systems with virtual monetary units are much more transparent. The existence of a ledger means that at least one party is always informed about the current distribution of all monetary units as well as about all the transactions, thereby undermining anonymity. Regardless of whether the record is in written, digital (explicit register) or verbal (implicit register) form, it is inevitable that at least one restricted group of people will have access to some of the information relating to the ownership relationship and the executed transactions.[b] This fact raises certain concerns about privacy because there may also be good reasons for not disclosing payment and ownership information.

---

a. The need to protect privacy in payments has many different legitimate and lawful origins. [122]
b. Bitcoin counteracts this problem by using one-way pseudonyms so that, although the pseudonyms are recorded in the Bitcoin ledger, they may only be assigned to an individual under specific circumstances (see section 4.1.4).

1.5.3 Transaction Processing

Transaction processing may be centralized or decentralized. Decentralized transaction processing means that the holder of a monetary unit can transfer its ownership rights independently without any obligation to enlist the aid of a third party. In contrast to this, with centralized processing, a central authority is responsible for processing the transactions, and its agreement is mandatory for the monetary unit to be transferred.

Independent of whether transaction processing is centralized or decentralized, the three following transactional requirements must be fulfilled.

Transactional capacity. This requirement ensures that transactions can be initiated and value units transferred.

Transactional legitimacy. This requirement ensures that there is a control mechanism to guarantee that transactions may only be initiated by the rightful owner(s).

Transactional consensus. This requirement ensures that there is a process which establishes an unambiguous distribution of ownership of all monetary units at all times.

Physical monetary units are, by definition, processed in a decentralized manner. The current owner of a physical monetary unit can freely determine where they wish to keep the physical object and where they can consequently hand it over, along with its unit value, to a new owner. All three requirements are thereby automatically satisfied: the physical object can (transactional capacity) only (transactional legitimacy) be transferred by the current owner and is always owned by the individual who has control over the physical object (transactional consensus).

The elimination of physical representation undermines the inherent transactional consensus and leads to the need for ledgers (see section 1.5.2). When ledgers are used, the question of who should manage them must be addressed.

It would cause substantial problems if every participant had the right to manage the ledger. In comparison to the example in box 1.11, a general right to adjust the ledger would be a feasible option for small, well-networked groups, but as soon as the system reaches a specific size and the payment flows become more complex, the use of an implicit public ledger would inevitably trigger disputes about the true state of the ledger. Moreover, bad actors could scatter false reports by communicating manipulated transactions. In information technology, these issues are known as the *Byzantine Generals' Problem* (see box 1.13).

Box 1.13
The Byzantine Generals' Problem

The Byzantine Generals' Problem describes a fundamental challenge that faces decentralized information systems. Corrupted parts of the system may disseminate false information and consequently cause contradictions. It is therefore essential that the system has a certain level of fault tolerance and can reach a common agreement by applying a specific algorithm.

In the paper that first introduced this topic, [136] the problem was illustrated in the context of a descriptive story. Several divisions of the Byzantine army lay siege to an enemy city. The divisions are only able to communicate with each other using messengers and have to agree on a common strategy—say, to continue the siege or to attack. Only if the loyal divisions choose the same strategy will the plan be successful and the Byzantine force be victorious.

The problem is that a minority of traitors exist among the members of the army and will attempt to thwart the strategy aimed at coordinating the military divisions by propagating false reports. The following two examples illustrate the difficulties involved in identifying the division of traitors and in coordinating a common strategy.

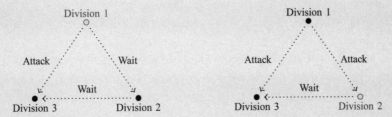

In both examples, Division 1 takes the initiative and communicates a strategy. Division 3 receives contradictory information and has to try to identify the traitors (depicted as gray in both examples). The problem is that from the standpoint of Division 3, both situations look exactly the same [attack/wait], although from its position in the left diagram the treachery is viewed as stemming from Division 1, while in the right diagram Division 2 is viewed as having the treacherous intentions. It is therefore impossible for Division 3 to distinguish truth from lies and to coordinate a strategy with the other loyal division.

Most virtual monetary units are based on ledgers that use a centralized system of transaction processing where a predefined set of agents is given an exclusive authority to manage the ledger. Generally, these agents are commercial banks, which in return provide the necessary payment infrastructure. These institutions establish a network of branches, accept written payment orders, and facilitate client-sponsored interaction via electronic communication channels (transactional capacity). At the same time, they verify the legitimacy of the payment orders to ensure that only legitimate transactions find their way into the ledger (transactional legitimacy). Exclusivity ensures that, at all times, only one version of the ledger exists, automatically satisfying the requirement of transactional consensus.

The existence of a central authority helps to simplify the transactional process and achieve consensus. At the same time, the establishment of such a monopoly is vulnerable to the risk of malpractice. In theory, a central authority can arbitrarily alter the ledger or refuse to process transactions that are fundamentally legitimate. Even in states where such an overt abuse of this position is not expected, a number of questions ought to be addressed: to what extent should and may an economy become dependent on central infrastructures? Who decides on the allocation of the record-keeping privilege, and how is it prevented that a central instance is corrupted or extracts monopoly rents? In addition, a central infrastructure increases the risk of criminal attacks and confiscation of funds by third parties. Examples include hacker attacks; dictatorial, coerced conversions of balances into newly created currencies; or arbitrary confiscations of monetary units. In particular, a pressing philosophic question that needs to be addressed is whether the term "property" has any relevance if the respective unit of value is only transferrable and usable subject to another entity's agreement.

We are facing a dilemma. On the one hand, from an efficiency perspective, a virtual monetary unit is optimal. On the other hand, virtual representation requires centralized transaction processing with all the negatives described above. It would therefore be desirable to design a virtual monetary unit that features decentralized transaction processing. In 2008, the Bitcoin developers proposed a virtual monetary that does not rely on centralized institutions.

1.6 Exercises

Exercise 1.1: Explain the three functions of a monetary unit. For each of these, name at least one basic monetary characteristic that is relevant to its function. Give the reason for your choice.

Exercise 1.2: In a simplified model economy, twenty-six different products are traded directly against each other. Using a quantitative example and reasoning, show what effect the introduction of a generally accepted medium of exchange (or monetary unit) has on the number of exchangeable pairs of products.

Exercise 1.3: Given same marginal costs, explain why the aggregate costs of producing a given, real quantity of money under competitive money creation will never be less than the aggregate costs under monopolistic money creation.

Exercise 1.4: Calculate the equilibrium quantity of money q if the value of a monetary unit created under competition is determined by the inverse demand function $MR(q) = \max[50 - 2q, 0]$ and if the marginal costs for producing a monetary unit have the following form:

  a) $MC(q) = 3q$,

  b) $MC(q) = 10$.

Exercise 1.5: Illustrate the solution from exercise 1.4 in a diagram in comparison to figure 1.3.

Exercise 1.6: Read the Wikipedia article about M-Pesa [225] and evaluate the monetary unit with regard to its control structures.

Exercise 1.7: Describe to what extent the Byzantine Generals' Problem can thwart the decentralized transaction processing of virtual monetary units.

2 Bitcoin Overview

In this chapter, we begin our analysis of Bitcoin. We discuss the term, demarcate the Bitcoin system from the classical financial system, and elucidate the consequences of not having a central authority. We show how the three transactional requirements discussed in section 1.5.3 are satisfied and create a basis for the second, more technical part of this book. After this, we concentrate on the origins, the development, and the political characteristics of the Bitcoin system. The present chapter serves as a short synopsis and rough overview that aims to highlight the innovative character of the Bitcoin system.

Bitcoin is an ambiguous term. It is used to describe both the overall system and some of the subcomponents. The latter category includes the Bitcoin network, the Bitcoin (communication) protocol, and the Bitcoin (monetary) unit. The ambiguity of the term causes a lot of confusion and presents the first obstacle that has to be overcome to understand the system. We are therefore going to use a strict definitional boundary among the various notions. The term Bitcoin, on its own, will be used to refer to the Bitcoin system or the Bitcoin technology. When we refer to the subcomponents, we will always use the terms *network*, *protocol*, or *unit*.

2.1 Classification of Bitcoin

Bitcoin is a comprehensive concept that links several technological components together in such a way that the units of value are issued under competition and have both a virtual representation and decentralized transaction processing. In this way, the Bitcoin system has created money that is substantially different from any other money—such as commodity money, cash, or commercial bank deposits (see figure 2.1).

To understand why Bitcoin is unique, it is useful to revisit different forms of money according to their control structures as shown in figure 2.1. There are three dimensions.

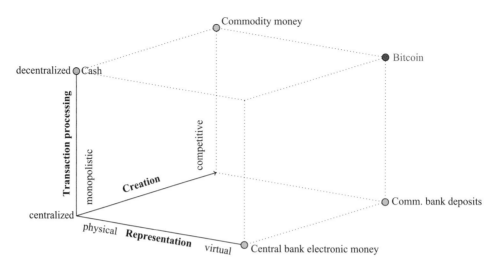

Figure 2.1
Matrix of control structures for monetary units.

The first dimension is representation. Money can be represented in virtual form or physical form. The second dimension is transaction handling. Money can be transacted in centralized or decentralized networks. Finally, the third dimension is money creation. Some monies are created by a monopoly while others are issued under competition.

Cash is represented by a physical object, usually a coin or bill—meaning that its value is inseparable from the object. The holder of a cash unit is automatically the owner of the corresponding value. As a result, the ownership rights to the cash units, circulating freely in the economy, are always clearly defined without anyone having to keep records. This feature allows for a decentralized payment system where cash can change hands between two agents without the involvement of a third party. In most countries, the central bank or the treasury is the monopoly issuer of cash.

Commodity money, such as gold, is also represented by a physical object, and again, the current holder of a unit is by default assigned ownership of the value unit. Consequently, no record-keeping is needed to use it as a payment instrument, leading to decentralized transaction processing by default. Gold differs from cash by its competitive creation process because anyone can enter the business of extracting gold and thereby create new gold units.

Commercial bank deposits is virtual money. It exists only as a record in an accounting system. When a payment is made, the accounts are adjusted by deducting the payment amount from the buyer and crediting it to the seller. There are many ways to initiate payments; the most common are debit cards, checks, and online banking. Commercial banks compete for deposits; that is why we consider the creation of money in the form of commercial bank deposits as competitive (see figure 2.1). The banks are responsible for keeping records, and so any transaction between a buyer and a seller requires a commercial bank or several commercial banks to update the respective accounts. For that reason, commercial bank deposits are transacted in a centralized payment system.

Central bank electronic money is also virtual money. In most countries, public access to electronic central bank money is restricted to financial intermediaries. They use the funds in these accounts for settlement purposes and to fulfill reserve requirements. In contrast to commercial bank deposits, central bank reserves can be created solely by the central bank.

Figure 2.1 demonstrates that Bitcoin's fundamental innovation is the decentralized management of ownership of a virtual asset. The special feature of Bitcoin is that it combines the transactional advantages of a virtual monetary unit with the systemic independence of decentralized transaction processing. As we will see throughout the book, this innovation has the potential to disrupt the current financial infrastructure and many other sectors.

2.2 Bitcoin Components: An Overview

To achieve the unique combination of controls depicted in figure 2.1, Bitcoin uses several components displayed in figure 2.2.

Bitcoin unit. Bitcoin units are the virtual monetary units of the system. They do not exist in physical form. Bitcoin units are merely ledger entries that are assigned to a specific individual.[1]

Bitcoin network. The Bitcoin network is fully decentralized. It comprises participants and their connections and serves as a primary channel of communication for exchanging information and building consensus.

Bitcoin protocol. The Bitcoin protocol stipulates the ways and means by which communication within the Bitcoin network must take place. It primarily contains standardized guidelines on how messages of all types should be formatted.

---

1. More precisely, the transfer of specified Bitcoin units is linked to a condition that only a specific individual or group of individuals can satisfy.

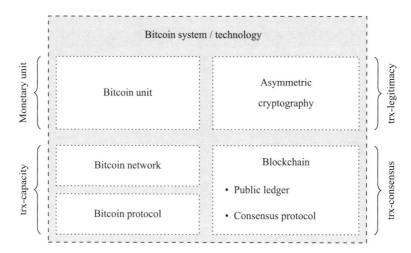

Figure 2.2
Overview of Bitcoin technology (trx = transaction).

Asymmetric cryptography. Asymmetric cryptography (also public key cryptography) is employed for verification purposes. It enables all users of the Bitcoin network to conclusively verify the legitimacy of any transaction message.

Bitcoin blockchain. The Bitcoin blockchain is a public ledger. Every individual can inspect the ledger, download a copy, and change it. However, the network will only consider the version of the ledger that (1) contains only transactions that are verifiably legitimate and (2) is considered to be the most recent version of the Bitcoin blockchain. The latter criterion is guaranteed by a consensus protocol. For this, the Bitcoin blockchain utilizes a procedure known as *proof of work*.

2.3   Bitcoin's Unique Selling Proposition

The use of a ledger is not a novelty attributed to Bitcoin technology. Commercial bank deposits are, for example, nothing other than a ledger-based virtualization of claims to physical monetary units (cash). Here, the ledger is managed exclusively by a central authority that guarantees transactional capacity, transactional legitimacy, and transactional consensus.

Transactional capacity relates to securing the owner's capacity to initiate a payment. In a classical banking system, clients can talk to their client adviser or submit their payment instructions via the bank's online banking platform. The infrastructure provided by the commercial bank and other central service providers ensures that the transaction will be executed. In the absence of a central authority, executing a payment order in this traditional way is not possible. In the Bitcoin system another possibility must therefore exist that allows participants to initiate transactions.

Transactional legitimacy is checked when the transactions are initiated. In a classical banking system, the central authority identifies the initiator of the transaction and ensures that this individual is the rightful owner of the referenced balance. The identification is usually achieved by examining passports, handwritten signatures, and pin codes or by using biometric identification methods. All these control mechanisms rely on a central authority to manage the access criteria. In the absence of a central authority as for the Bitcoin system, transactional legitimacy has to be implemented by other means.

If a single entity is exclusively authorized to manage all payment records, then only one ledger exists which ensures *transactional consensus* by default. In the absence of a central authority as for the Bitcoin system, then different, potentially equally legitimate versions of the ledger will exist. In this case, some other method will have to be used to achieve transactional consensus by determining which version of the ledger represents the true state.

The key innovation of Bitcoin is its refusal to engage a central authority. Without a central authority, it is more difficult to guarantee transactional capacity, establish transactional legitimacy, and achieve transactional consensus. How these requirements are met in the Bitcoin network is described in the following section.

Box 2.1
Differences Compared to the Yap System

With regard to the control structures, the Yap monetary system falls into the same category as Bitcoin (see figure 2.1). The units of value are virtual, they are created under competition, and the transactions are settled in a decentralized system (see box 1.11).

The major difference between the two systems is that Bitcoin can be used in a context that does not require trust. The Yap system, on the other hand, relies on the close relationships between the participants and the threat they face of being socially excluded for misconduct.

Bitcoin ensures that all transactions and the state of the ledger can be mathematically verified by all participants who use the system. It functions without the need for relationships of trust. It is, therefore, clearly different from the Yap system, despite several similarities.

2.4   Bitcoin's Technology: A Primer

In this section, we summarize how Bitcoin satisfies the three transactional requirements described previously.

2.4.1   Transactional Capacity

The Bitcoin network is the foundation of the system. It allows for the exchange of information and is based on *peer-to-peer* technology. The term peer to peer means that all the network participants are equal, without exception, and that communication can take place between any two participants. There is no central structure, and no participant has any exclusive privileges.

Transactions and other messages are sent within the Bitcoin network to establish consensus. For instance, if Edith wishes to send Daniel a Bitcoin unit, she creates a transaction message that contains the respective payment order. The message must be composed according to the standards of the Bitcoin protocol and sent to at least one of the other network participant.

In our example in figure 2.3, the transaction message reaches Tony, who keeps a copy of the message and relays it to his direct connections; namely, Marcia and Michèle. Marcia and Michèle do the same. The message gets forwarded until all network participants have received a copy of it.

Although the payment order is in favor of Daniel, the transaction message does not have to be sent directly to Daniel. Whether and when Daniel learns of this message is initially irrelevant. As we will see later, Daniel does not even have to belong to the (immediate) group of network participants at this point. It is only important that the transaction is acknowledged by a majority of the network participants.

The decentralized and dynamic topology of the Bitcoin network is the reason for the system's outstanding robustness. If individual participants disconnect from the network, this can be compensated for without a problem, and the communication can be

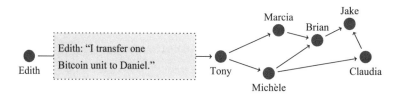

Figure 2.3
Initiation of a transaction.

continued via alternative channels. If someone wishes to initiate a transaction, then it is sufficient to relay the transaction message to any network participant and wait for it to be spread by forwarding. This principle guarantees that the requirement of transactional capacity is satisfied at all times.

Communication within the Bitcoin network functions without any reliance on trust. There are no restrictions on admission, and participants can create any number of pseudonyms, making it impossible to exclude individual participants from the system. Consequently, participants have to assume that every message they receive has been fraudulently altered by the sender and must therefore be conclusively checked for its truth content.

2.4.2   Transactional Legitimacy

If a network participant receives a transaction message, he has to ensure that the transaction was initiated by the rightful owner of the respective Bitcoin units. For this purpose, Bitcoin employs proven cryptographic methods. The same cryptographic principles are used for e-commerce, online banking, and many other applications.

Ownership of Bitcoin units requires the exclusive possession of a private key that is used to cryptographically encrypt transaction messages before they are relayed to the network. For each private key, there is a corresponding public key. This public key can be used to decrypt any message that has previously been encrypted with the corresponding private key.

In contrast to the private key, the public key is public. Anyone who receives a transaction message can therefore decrypt it. The terms encryption and decryption are somewhat misleading in this context. Obviously, the process is not designed to hide any information. After all, everyone is in possession of the public key and can therefore decrypt the transaction message. It is rather used to verify the origin and the legitimacy of the transaction message.

The transaction message can only be successfully decrypted with the public key if it was initially encrypted using the corresponding private key. Since only the rightful owner is in possession of the corresponding private key, this serves as proof of the transaction's legitimacy. If, for example, someone succeeds in decrypting a transaction message using Edith's public key, this serves as clear proof that the messages has been encrypted with Edith's private key. Since Edith is the only person who knows her private key, this procedure allows anyone to mathematically verify that the transaction message was actually composed by her.

Figure 2.4 illustrates the procedure using an example. Edith encrypts the transaction message with her private key before sending it to Tony. Tony receives the message

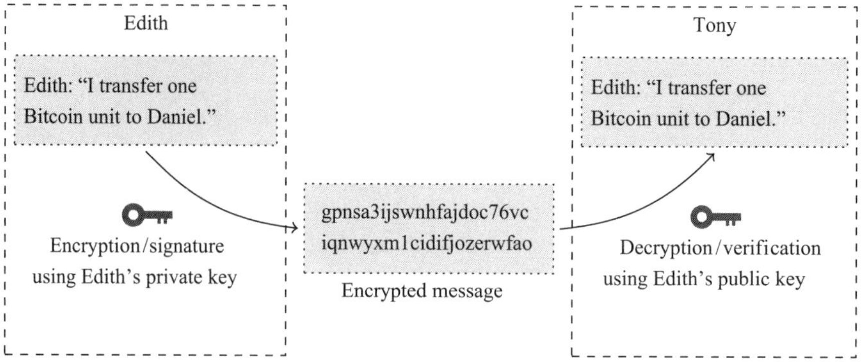

Figure 2.4
Encryption and decryption of the transaction message.

and tries to decrypt it using the corresponding public key. If Tony is able to do so, he then knows that the message was previously encrypted using Edith's private key.

An initial verification of the transaction is not sufficient. Recall that the transaction message is relayed and forwarded through an untrusted network. Every recipient has to verify it. If Tony forwards the transaction message to Marcia and Michèle, then both recipients must independently verify that the transaction message is legitimate. In particular, they have to check whether it was really initiated by Edith and whether none of the transaction parameters have been changed. If this second verification step would not take place, then Tony could modify the message (see figure 2.5) and relay the altered transaction message on behalf of Edith.

To prevent such a manipulation, Marcia and Michèle will only accept the original encrypted message. They will then use Edith's public key to verify the message's authenticity. Tony, who is not in possession of Edith's private key, cannot alter and re-encrypt the transaction message. Marcia and Michèle have therefore no difficulty identifying any fraudulent behavior. An example of a manipulation attempt is illustrated in figure 2.5. Michèle and Marcia fail to decrypt the message and can therefore immediately reject the manipulated transaction message.

If a transaction message is legitimate, it is allocated to the network participants' collections of verified transactions. That is basically a queue for verified messages waiting to be entered into the Bitcoin blockchain.

2.4.3 Transactional Consensus

Owing to the decentralized nature of the network, there will inevitably be situations in which the various transaction queues of the network participants are out of sync or may even contain contradictory transactions.

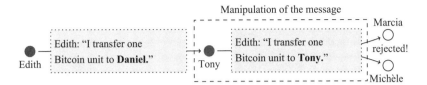

Figure 2.5
Attempted manipulation of a transaction message.

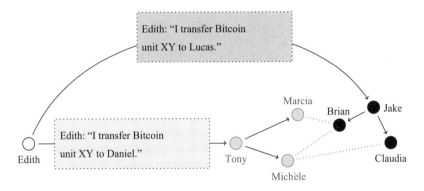

Figure 2.6
The propagation of conflicting transactions.

Let us assume, for example, that an individual simultaneously issues and relays two transactions, trying to transfer the same Bitcoin units to different network participants. In a centralized system, when a conflict like this arises, the transaction that is held to be valid is the one that reaches the central authority first. The Bitcoin system, however, explicitly refuses to employ a central authority. As a consequence, there is no clear leader, and it is possible that one part of the network first hears about the first transaction while the rest of the network first hears about the second transaction. Both transactions are legitimate because they have both been issued by the rightful owner of the corresponding Bitcoin units. However, because both transactions relate to the same Bitcoin balance, only one of the them can be valid.

Figure 2.6 shows a concrete example of such a situation. Edith simultaneously sends messages to Tony and Jake. In her message to Tony, she states that she wishes to transfer a specific Bitcoin unit to Daniel. In her message to Jake, she refers to the same Bitcoin unit but replaces the beneficiary (Daniel) with Lucas. Both messages have been encrypted using Edith's private key and are therefore legitimate. The messages are relayed and remain in the respective transaction queues of the two groups. At this point,

Tony, Marcia, and Michèle think that Edith wishes to transfer the Bitcoin unit to Daniel while Brian, Jake, and Claudia believe that she wants to send it to Lucas.

For the network as a whole, it is irrelevant which of the two competing transactions prevails. However, to prevent double-spending and to achieve consensus among all network participants, only one of the two transactions must be permitted to enter the consensus version of the Bitcoin blockchain.

Bitcoin Mining   To understand the consensus mechanism of the Bitcoin system, we first have to discuss the role of a *Bitcoin miner*. A Bitcoin miner collects pending Bitcoin transactions, verifies their legitimacy, and assembles them into what is known as a block. A block is a data structure that includes at least one transaction. The process of assembling blocks and performing the necessary computations is called *Bitcoin mining*. A miner's goal is to earn newly created Bitcoin units through this activity as explained below.

Bitcoin mining is permissionless but requires computational resources. Every network participant is free to decide how much money he or she wishes to spend on computational resources. To become a Bitcoin miner, a network user needs the most recent copy of the Bitcoin blockchain and a software package that automates the process.

To assemble a block, a Bitcoin miner selects transactions that are waiting in his queue (mempool).[2] For a block to be generally accepted, it must fulfill a specific set of predefined criteria. For example, the included transactions must be legitimate and cannot be in conflict with any other transactions in the current block or in any one of the previous blocks of the Bitcoin blockchain. If a miner violates any of these conditions, his block will be rejected by the rest of the network.

Another important criterion is the so-called identification number of a block. The identification number is obtained by computing the block header's hash value using the SHA256d hash function. We will explain the technical details in part II of the book. Here, we want to emphasize that the identification number is important for two reasons. First, any new block must reference the identification number of a previous block, thereby generating a chronological chain of blocks or a *blockchain*. Figure 2.7 presents the structure of such a chain. Second, the identification number is an important criterion for the acceptance of a block into the Bitcoin blockchain as explained below.

---

2. The number of transactions that can be included in a block is limited by the maximal block size.

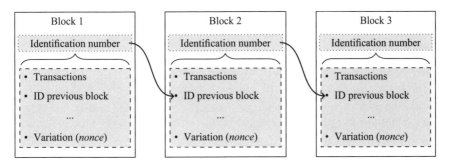

Figure 2.7
Example of a blockchain.

Immutability of the Blockchain   The identification number is unique[3] and is dependent on the contents of the block header. Any modification of a block header's
contents will inevitably cause the identification number to change. This will introduce
inconsistencies into the chain structure so that all subsequent blocks will have to be
recreated.

If someone modifies, for instance, a transaction in block 1 of figure 2.7, the identification number of this block will change. Because the identification number of block
1 is referenced in block 2, this reference will also have to be adjusted. This adjustment
corresponds to a change in block 2 and will cause its identification number to change,
which, then again, leads to the necessity to reassemble block 3, and so on.

A miner obtains the identification number by computing the block header's hash
value using the SHA256d hash function. For example, consider the hash value for the
text, "This block includes transactions 1, 2, and 3." The identification number of this
text, which was calculated using the hash function SHA256d, is

80ac1f5e36cefbdde5d58dbe7379e8532335583b79ab805737e7b4de0bf78ffc.

Now notice the small change in the original text to "This block includes transactions
1, 2, and 4." It will cause an unpredictable change of the identification number, which
can be seen from the corresponding new hash value:

3b72098d7f49bf8912010cb87afe0a64d824803d2bf6490cf95b7a198c6dc146

---

3. As we will see later on, the hash value (see section 4.2) is not unique in a strict mathematical sense. However, since the probability that two blocks have the same identification number is
extraordinarily small, this possibility is unproblematic in practice.

Owing to the special characteristics of the hash function that is used to generate identification numbers, it is impossible to guess what inputs lead to a desired target value. This characteristic is employed in the mining process as follows. For a block candidate to be accepted by all network participants, its identification number must possess an extremely rare feature: The number must be below a certain threshold value, that is, it must display several zeroes at the beginning of the identification number. An example of a identification number of a block that was added to the Bitcoin blockchain in 2010 is given in the following example:

`000000000a93f114165c1c6940dc5a55ea20a5651af1e9ef0415319ad7458fc9`.

Since it is impossible to guess what inputs lead to a desired identification number, the only option the Bitcoin miners have is to try out different block contents until they encounter, by pure chance, an input combination that yields a sufficiently small identification number. For this purpose, a block includes a data field (called the *nonce*) that contains arbitrary data. Miners modify this arbitrary data to gain new identification numbers. These modifications do not affect the set of included transactions.

If a miner succeeds in creating a block candidate with an identification number below the current threshold value, he or she broadcasts the block candidate as quickly as possible to the network. All the other network participants can then easily verify that the identification number satisfies the threshold criterion by computing it themselves.

Consensus   The consensus among miners is that every miner who receives a block that includes only valid transactions and has an identification number that is below the current threshold adds this block to their own copy of the Bitcoin blockchain. From a game theoretical perspective, a strategy profile where all miners add valid blocks to their own copies of the Bitcoin blockchain is a Nash equilibrium. If a miner believes that all other miners are acting accordingly, then the best response for that miner is to add a valid block candidate to his or her own copy of the Bitcoin blockchain. A deviation is not worthwhile because it is not profitable to work on a version of the Bitcoin blockchain that is not generally accepted. Any reward for finding blocks on a version of the chain that is not accepted by anyone else is worthless. Thus, although there is no authority enforcing this rule and miners are free to modify their copy of the Bitcoin blockchain as they wish, there is a strong incentive to follow this rule. This self-enforcing rule allows the network to maintain consensus about the ownership of all Bitcoin units.

Mining is expensive as the computations use large amounts of electricity and are increasingly dependent on highly specialized hardware. The consensus mechanism is therefore called "proof of work." If a miner finds a valid identification number for a block, then this is proof that he or she has, on average, performed a large number of costly computations. Adding false information (e.g., illegitimate transactions) to a block would render the block invalid and essentially waste all the computations. Finding a valid identification number is therefore proof that the miner helped to maintain the Bitcoin system.

An individual block can be calculated in fractions of a second using a conventional computer. At first glance, this speed could be viewed as an advantage. However, generating blocks at such a high speed would make it impossible to achieve consensus. New blocks would be significantly more quickly generated than they could be exchanged over the Bitcoin network. To counteract this issue, the difficulty to find a valid identification number restricts the production rate of valid blocks artificially. The Bitcoin system calibrates the threshold number after every 2,016 blocks (roughly every fourteen days) in order to maintain a ten-minute average per block, independent of the overall computational resources employed in mining.

The asymmetry in costs between finding a solution and verifying it plays a particularly important role. It is extremely rare to find a valid block. In contrast, it is easy to verify that a given block has a valid identification number. It takes the network participants a fraction of a second to do so. Since all miners know that a proposed block will get checked by all other participants, they only include legitimate transactions in their blocks. A block containing illegitimate transactions would not be accepted by the rest of the network even if it had a valid identification number. Anyone not playing by the rules would therefore waste computing resources.

By consensus, network participants accept the longest chain as the current state of the ledger. The logic behind that agreement is that the longest chain is the one that requires the highest amount of resources to be computed, making it the one with the broadest support and, even more important, very expensive to change. In particular, it is only possible to make a change if a miner had the resources to assemble blocks with a higher probability than the rest of the network. Only a network participant who controls more than 50 percent of the system's overall computational resources would be in a position to achieve this.[4]

If a network participant wishes, for example, to change the third block of the chain in figure 2.8, he must reference the second block in the chain and generate a sufficient amount of new blocks to be able to overtake the dominant consensus version of the

---

4. It is important to note that even if someone controls a large part of the network's computational resources, the requirement for cryptographic signatures still holds.

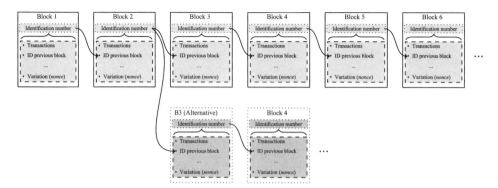

Figure 2.8
Attack on blockchain from block 3.

chain. All the other miners will simultaneously generate new blocks on the basis of
block 6 of the longest chain. The attacking network participant therefore has to generate
new blocks more quickly than all the other network participants. The farther back in
the consensus chain a block is located, the more difficult it will become to change this
block. A block's integrity is therefore protected by the chain.

If we now turn once again to our example in figure 2.6, it should be clear how consensus is achieved. Jake, Brian, and Claudia will include the transaction in favor of
Lucas into their block candidate. Tony, Marcia, and Michèle will instead include the
transaction in favor of Daniel. Which of the two transactions prevails will depend on
which miner is the first to generate a valid block. Once a valid block including one of
the two conflicting transactions has been generated successfully, the other miners have
an incentive to follow the longest chain and continue to work on this new version of
the blockchain. Knowing that the other transaction would be rejected, miners will discard the transaction. As shown in figure 2.9, the chain can develop in several directions
depending on which miner generates the next block.

Mining Reward   Mining is costly. The hardware has to be procured and maintained,
and there are electricity costs. These costs are carried individually by the miners. On
the other hand, maintaining the Bitcoin blockchain benefits all network participants.
In this respect, mining provides a public good: no one can be excluded from using
the network, and all network participants profit from the mining activity. No miner,
however, would have an incentive to contribute and to bear the cost of maintaining
the network if there were no compensation.

The Bitcoin system solves this incentive problem by allowing miners to add a so-
called *coinbase transaction* to every block. This transaction generates new Bitcoin units

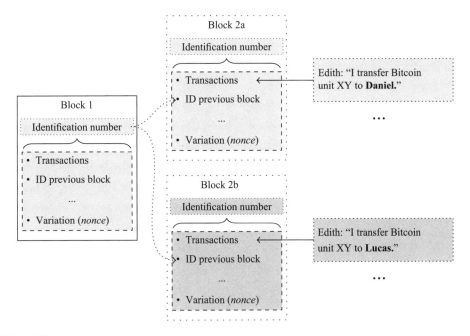

Figure 2.9
Various transaction candidates for blocks.

that can be claimed by the miner who has successfully added the block to the Bitcoin blockchain. Since everyone is following the longest version of the chain, the coinbase transaction will only be accepted by the network if the block is indeed part of the longest version of the blockchain.

In our example, if Brian generated a valid block, then this block would contain Edith's transaction to Lucas as well as the coinbase transaction in favor of him. If Marcia succeeded in generating a valid block, then the transaction would, instead, contain Edith's transaction to Daniel as well as the coinbase transaction in favor of her. The two transactions contained in Marcia's and Brian's block candidates are illustrated in figure 2.10.

As is the case with all other transactions, the coinbase transaction is valid only if it is recorded in the longest version of the chain. This process motivates miners to always reference the last block of the longest blockchain and thereby continue working in the consensus version of the ledger. If a miner decides to reference a block that does not correspond to the last block of the consensus chain, this miner faces a high risk of losing the block reward.

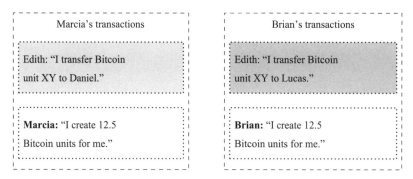

Figure 2.10
Different transactions of the block candidates.

In addition to the solution to the incentive problem, the mining mechanism guarantees that Bitcoin units are created by a competitive process. Every time a new block is added to the Bitcoin blockchain, new Bitcoin units are created. In the first four years of the Bitcoin system, this reward amounted to fifty Bitcoin units per block. The reward is halved after 210,000 blocks (i.e., approximately every four years) and currently amounts to 12.5 Bitcoin units. Due to this "halving," the total number of Bitcoin units will converge to twenty-one million. Figure 2.11 shows this asymptotic growth path. It is expected that the final fractions of Bitcoin units will be created somewhere around the year 2140.[5]

2.5 Origin and Governance

In this section, we will look at the origins of the Bitcoin system as well as its unusual governance structure.

2.5.1 The Dream of Virtual Cash

The first step toward Bitcoin occurred in 1982 with David Chaum's invention of *Digi-Cash*.[55] Chaum argued that existing electronic payment systems would considerably restrict personal privacy and would generate traceable payment flows of sensitive data. This problem motivated him to develop a virtual monetary unit that would imitate the anonymity of cash. Although DigiCash is based on monopolistic money creation and

---

5. Transaction fees are the second reward component that is paid out to miners. Once all the twenty-one million Bitcoin units have been created, the system will be carried solely by fees.

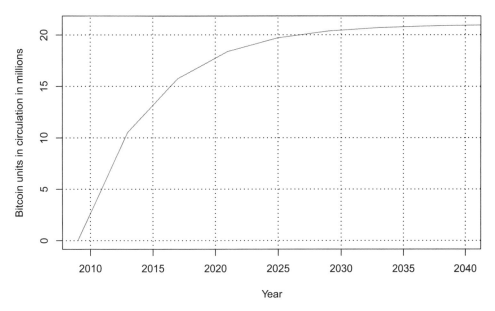

Figure 2.11
Time schedule for the creation of new Bitcoin units.

centralized transaction processing, the commutativity[6] of the applied cryptographic processes facilitates a system in which the central bank *blindly signs* the monetary units and thus has no information about the serial numbers of outstanding monetary units. As a result of this, the serial numbers cannot be assigned to individuals, and the monetary units are used anonymously.

Transactional consensus is achieved by means of a centralized ledger. If a monetary unit is used, then its serial number must be presented to the central bank. If the number is not in the central bank's ledger, it is assumed that the monetary unit is being used for the first time and is therefore valid. If the serial number is already registered by the central bank, it is considered to be an attempted *double spend* and accordingly blocked. While this approach certainly provides some degree of anonymity, it still has a central point of attack and is not censorship resistant.

The aspiration to develop an anonymous virtual monetary unit was further strengthened by Timothy C. May's Crypto Anarchist Manifesto.[151] The manifesto was first presented at the CRYPTO '88 Conference but published in print later. He predicted a

---

6. Given two encryption steps, the order of decryption can be chosen arbitrarily.

social change that would be driven by the technological possibilities of cryptography that would allow a new kind of economic interaction, which would be independent of the possible restrictions and reprisals of an omnipotent state. To achieve this, it would be particularly necessary to have virtual monetary units and binding contracts that function in an anonymous (or pseudonymous) context.

In 1998, the computer scientist Wei Dai, who was clearly influenced by the Crypto Anarchist Manifesto, published a short essay presenting the idea of *b-money*, a pseudonymous virtual monetary unit.[73] In the b-money system, public keys were used as pseudonyms, to which credit or debit transactions could be assigned. Transactional legitimacy is guaranteed by a signature using the corresponding private key of the debited individual. All (or alternatively a subgroup) of the participants manage separate ledgers that contain the records of the current balances of all pseudonyms. The essay contains no concrete proposal on how to achieve transactional consensus. Instead, b-money is presented as a thought experiment that postulates the existence of a synchronous communication channel. The money creation follows a competitive process, using numeric puzzles that can only be solved by means of intensive computation but that can be verified simply. The costs incurred by the money creation process are arbitrarily determined by the system's parameterization.[7]

The concept of making otherwise trivial tasks artificially expensive dates back to the contributions of Adam Back[17,18] as well as Cynthia Dwork and Moni Naor[85] and was originally developed to combat *denial-of-service* (DoS) attacks and spam email. These contributions are the basis for the proof-of-work consensus protocol that is used in the Bitcoin system.

In 2005, Hal Finney presented the idea of the reusable proof-of-work system.[96] His approach combined the ideas of Wei Dai and Adam Back. Later, Hal Finney became one of the first Bitcoin users and the recipient of the first Bitcoin transaction.[97]

It was also in 2005 that Nick Szabo published a blog post on *Bit Gold*.[208] The article describes the application of the proof-of-work algorithm for competitive money creation while at the same time securing a public ledger. Although Szabo's blog post was not quoted in the Bitcoin publication,[158] it can be assumed that *Bit Gold* contributed substantially toward Bitcoin's development.

---

7. Wei Dai was aware that reaching agreement on the system's parameterization would create substantial problems.

2.5.2 Satoshi Nakamoto

Bitcoin was published on October 31, 2008, by an author, or team of authors, under the pseudonym Satoshi Nakamoto.[8] The publication[158] appeared in the style of an academic article on a mailing list for cryptography. It is, however, still unclear today whose identity or identities are hidden by the pseudonym.

Apart from the author's identity, the article (and the reference implementation) discloses complete, detailed information about the Bitcoin technology.[9] The inventor has no privileges within the system and has become irrelevant owing to the disclosure of the information as well as its subsequent technological development by other people. Nevertheless, this should by no means diminish the achievement of the originator. It should be noted here that the anonymous author was nominated for a Nobel prize in economics by UCLA Professor Bhagwan Chowdhry.[10] [58,183]

Box 2.2
Who Is Satoshi? Speculations

In March 2014, the *Newsweek* journalist Leah McGrath Goodman caused a commotion when she reported on the alleged solution to the identity of Satoshi Nakamoto in a major cover story. In an evidently inadequately researched report she claimed that the inventor of Bitcoin was a then sixty-four-year-old American man of Japanese descent. As it turned out, the man with the name Dorian Satoshi Nakamoto had no experience with peer-to-peer networks or cryptographic systems. Ten days after the publication of the *Newsweek* article, Dorian published a written statement in which he negated having ever worked or collaborated on the Bitcoin project.[103]

In fact, only a few individuals are worth considering as the development of Bitcoin required highly specific knowledge and skills. A much-discussed candidate is Nick Szabo. This computer scientist and lawyer is behind the invention of *Bit Gold*, among other things.[208] In addition to many other clues,[107] textual analysis[106] has shown that Nick Szabo's writing style is very similar to that of Satoshi Nakamoto. Nick Szabo denies that he was directly involved in the Bitcoin project.[176] Irrespective of whether he is Satoshi

---

8. Because the pseudonym is masculine, we will subsequently use the masculine singular pronoun. This must not be understood as a presumption of gender. We stress that neither the gender nor the number of individuals who are behind the pseudonym Satoshi Nakamoto is known.

9. Github Repository with versions and complete source code can be found at https://github.com /bitcoin/bitcoin.

10. Since the prize cannot be awarded to anonymous individuals, the nomination can only be made once the secret of Satoshi's identity is unveiled.[147]

Box 2.2 (continued)

Nakamoto or not, he has made substantial contributions to Bitcoin with his research. Another individual that possessed the necessary knowledge and skills to design the Bitcoin system in 2008 was Hal Finney. He is known to have received the first Bitcoin transaction in 2009. [97]

   After the increase in Bitcoin's popularity, there have been many people who claim to be Satoshi Nakamoto, including the Australian Craig Steven Wright. However, since much of the provided "evidence" is highly questionable and, in some cases, has even been disproven, [82,150,105] we see no need to further discuss these claims.

2.5.3   The Governance of Bitcoin

Bitcoin has a decentralized structure and is completely open source. There is no centralized authority, no company, and no individual who has special privileges to determine its future development. Bitcoin is a construct that is brought to life by the collective action of all participants. Its independence from any tangible entity is a deliberate design choice and a possible explanation for why the inventor wishes to remain anonymous.

However, the absence of leadership poses numerous questions and harbors the danger that the system could fall into chaos. In particular, the two following questions arise.

1. What happens if the technology is copied and someone creates his or her own "Bitcoin" units?

2. Who will determine the future development of the Bitcoin system and how should potential problems be handled and the technology be adapted?

Bitcoin Copies: So-Called Altcoins   Bitcoin's source code is public. This has the consequence that every person can copy it, modify it in any way desired, and publish an alternative version of the system.

This does not mean, however, that additional Bitcoin units can be created. Bitcoin clones establish new, clearly separate monetary units, which have their own ledgers. Such copies are termed altcoins. For instance, we could create *Bookcoin*; a new cryptocurrency, heavily inspired by Bitcoin, for the readers of this book. Bookcoin could represent an exact copy of the Bitcoin technology or be parameterized differently. Examples of parameters that could be changed are the total supply of coins or the average time to generate a valid block. To create a new altcoin, the creator modifies a copy of the Bitcoin source code and recompiles it.

Box 2.3
Altcoins and Football: An Analogy

A simple analogy that explains this principle is the sport of football. Just as with the Bitcoin technology, the rules for football are freely available and can basically be modified in any way. Common adaptations made by amateur players regard the size of the field, the number of players, and the nonenforcement of some of the more complicated rules.

No one would stop children in a schoolyard from calling their game "Super Bowl" or from playing it with altered rules. Yet no one would ever consider equating the "Super Bowl" played in the schoolyard with the National Football League's multibillion dollar business. The appreciation and the popularity of a given form of football is established by the players, the fans, and sponsors.

In the case of Bitcoin, this works very similarly. Everyone can create new offshoots and alternative coins. The original rules can be kept or be partially modified. From an economic perspective, alternative versions only become important when a certain valuation and willingness to pay arises.

Over the course of time, thousands of such altcoins have come into existence. Some of them have an extended range of functions or differ significantly in parameterization, but many are simply Bitcoin copies that bear another name. In spite of this competition, Bitcoin is clearly the leader among cryptocurrencies. It has a first-mover advantage and name recognition. Further, due to network effects the market capitalization of Bitcoin monetary units is substantially higher than all the other cryptocurrencies.[11]

Administration and Evolution of the Bitcoin System   The incentive structures within the Bitcoin system are set in such a way that each participant's personal payoff is maximized by following the current rules. Vitalik Buterin explains this phenomenon in the first issue of the *Bitcoin Magazine*.[48] He argues that Bitcoin is the first computer network where fraud is hindered not because of proprietary restrictions but instead because no one can gain an advantage by deviating unilaterally from these rules.

One must, however, be aware that Bitcoin involves software, and that software can be modified. Changes are implemented if a sufficiently large portion of network participants agree on the changes and profit from the modification.

The decentralized management of the Bitcoin system involves a multilayered democratic process of the highest complexity. A conclusive analysis is not possible, and an attempt would exceed the scope of this book. Nevertheless, we would like to discuss

---

11. The service CoinMarketCap.com lists cryptocurrencies, including price and market capitalization.

this topic in a short introduction and highlight some of the system's most important determinants.

Before we begin our analysis, we would like to stress the fundamental importance to have a system that allows for some evolution over time. A strictly static system could have catastrophic consequences and even lead to system failure. If, for example, a security breach is identified that can only be repaired if the technology is modifiable, most users might consider this a legitimate reason to adjust the software. However, there may be subtler reasons that make it worthwhile to change the Bitcoin system, such as a wish to extend its range of functions, to secure long-term stability, or to integrate new features.

Inputs and proposals for such changes are introduced via various decentralized channels and can be submitted by anyone. Questions regarding how these ideas should be implemented are usually debated publicly. Forums and mailing lists are popular discussion platforms used for this purpose. The *Bitcoin Improvement Proposals* (BIP) process is by far the most important instrument that is employed to formalize abstract ideas. [209] BIPs must be formulated using a mandatory structure and must include a justification stating why the improvements are necessary. Moreover, they must provide technical specifications.

If a proposal is so strongly contested that no general consensus can be reached, it can then be voted on. Only miners are able to participate in these votes. A miner submits a vote whenever he successfully generates a valid block.[12] A proposal will be accepted if it achieves a prescribed percentage number of "yes" votes within a previously specified interval (e.g., within the last 1,000 blocks). Usually, a majority approval rate of 55 percent, 75 percent or 95 percent is required for a proposal to be adopted.

However, in a decentralized system, no one can be forced to honor or implement a vote outcome. Without such obligation, any disagreement will threaten to split the system and allow a fork to develop where one part of the network chooses to implement the change and the other part of the network chooses to continue to run the old version. Forks produce competing ledgers that can each represent the longest version of the ledger, in accordance with their respective rules.

To gauge the severity of such disputes and the chance of returning to a consensus, one has to distinguish between *soft forks*, *hard forks*, and *forced forks* (see figure 2.12a, b, and c, respectively). A soft fork refers to a fork where the new software tightens the

---

12. Votes are integrated in the input of the *coinbase transaction* (transaction with the miner's reward). Because the reward is created anew and the transaction thus needs no input, then arbitrary data can be included, instead of referring to a previous transaction.

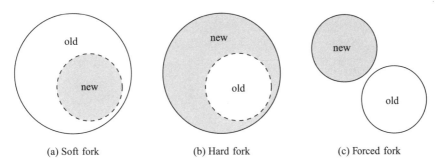

(a) Soft fork   (b) Hard fork   (c) Forced fork

Figure 2.12
Compatibility after a split in the software (fork).

rules of acceptance such that the new rules are a subset of the old rules. As a result, blocks that are valid under the new software will also be accepted as valid under the old software, but most often, not vice versa. A hard fork refers to a fork where the new software broadens the acceptance criteria such that the old rules represent a subset of the new rules. This has the consequence that blocks created using the new software can be rejected by the old software. Conversely, the new software will always consider blocks that are generated with the old software as valid.

A forced fork uses a completely different rule set where the old software will never accept blocks in accordance with the new rules and vice versa. It therefore will always lead to two separate versions of the blockchain.

> **Box 2.4**
> **Examples of a Soft Fork and a Hard Fork**
>
> The difference between a soft fork and a hard fork can be easily explained by discussing changes in the block size limit.
>
> A decrease in the block size limit is a soft fork because the old software version considers blocks that are generated by the new version of the software after the update as valid. Consequently, the chain of blocks generated by the new version of the software is considered valid by the old software.
>
> An increase in the block size limit is a hard fork because the old software version considers some block that are generated by the new version of the software after the update as invalid. Consequently, the chain of blocks generated by the new version of the software is considered invalid by the old software.

As shown in the illustration in table 2.1, a soft fork will dissolve if the new software is dominant; that is, if the majority of network computational resources adopt

Table 2.1
The development of the ledger versions with soft, hard and forced forks in dependency on allocated computational resources.

	New dominant	Old dominant
Soft fork		
Hard fork		
Forced fork		

Notes: White = blocks generated with old software. Gray = blocks generated with new software. Forks occur respectively at the fourth block.

it.[13] If the ledger is extended by a block that has been generated with the old software, this may indeed temporarily cause several versions of the ledger to be generated; however, the dominance of the new software usually ensures that the ledger grows more quickly, applying the new rules. Because this ledger is also valid under the old rules, all the participants will migrate to this version as soon as it becomes the longest version of the blockchain. A hard fork, on the other hand, can only be resolved via the dominance of the old software. If the new software is able to prevail, then two versions of the ledger will persist: one according to the old rules and one according to the new rules. Forced forks are neither forward- nor backward-compatible and cannot be dissolved.

> **Box 2.5**
> **Hard Fork Owing to a Software Update**
>
> On February 19, 2013, version 0.8.0 of the reference-client *Bitcoin Qt* (today called *Bitcoin Core*) was published.[a] The update corrected a mistake that had caused valid blocks to be rejected in rare instances in the previous version. The new version thus extended the scope of acceptance.
>
> Because not all miners migrated to the new software version, a hard fork occurred on March 11. A block was generated that was accepted as valid by the new software but was simultaneously rejected by the old software. The chain of the new version was dominant but was considered invalid by the old software version. To undo the hard fork, some of the

---

13. Soft forks dissolve automatically as soon as the new software attracts the majority of the network's computational resources.

big miners migrated back to version 0.7.0, whose chain consequently grew more quickly than the competing version 0.8.0. [230] As explained in table 2.1, it was possible to avert the hard fork by artificially allowing the old version to achieve dominance and subsequently inducing a coordinated migration to the software version 0.8.0. [135]

---

a. Release notes are available at BitcoinCore, "Bitcoin-Qt version 0.8.0 released," February 19, 2013, https://bitcoin.org/en/release/v0.8.0.

Software upgrades are much easier to achieve if they can be implemented using a soft fork. With a soft fork, even nonupdated network resources can be used in tandem with the new software. With a hard fork, however, each resource must be updated individually. Anyone who is running infrastructure that has not been updated will be unable to participate in the network.

Figure 2.13 shows a time line of some of the best-known Bitcoin forks. Although there have been many forking events, the alternative ledger versions enjoy a relatively low popularity.

Only the miners are directly involved in the previously considered decision processes regarding the further development of the Bitcoin system. Other participants in the Bitcoin system, such as merchants, users, or investors, have no direct influence

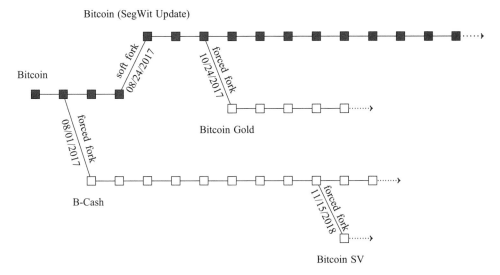

Figure 2.13
Bitcoin fork timeline.

either by explicit voting or by resolving forks. One might therefore argue that the political process is dominated by a select group of stakeholders. In particular, the fact that miners can have their very own goals that may not necessarily be in the interest of the whole Bitcoin system may raise concerns about the sustainability of the process.

In part, these criticisms are justified. However, it would be false to assume that the Bitcoin system is exclusively controlled by miners. Other user groups have a number of ways in which they can influence development and shape the future of the Bitcoin system.

First, all participants have the opportunity to submit proposals, to participate in the political discourse, and to influence public opinion.

Second, an implicit form of veto right exists. If a change is implemented against the will of other groups of stakeholders, systematic uncertainties and instabilities can develop. This will then have negative repercussions on the acceptance and the market price of the Bitcoin unit, which is tantamount to a fall in the miners' real economic reward. An example of a change that failed despite the support of more than 80 percent among miners is SegWit2x. The forced fork was declared canceled in a joint statement by the six initiators due to fears of dividing the community. [23]

Third, many changes require a hard fork. As discussed above, a hard fork requires that each resource has to be updated individually with the new software. Only then will merchants, users, network nodes, and all other resources support the changed version of the consensus protocol and consider transactions and blocks based on it to be valid. [7] Because of this, even with broadly based approval, it is extremely difficult to implement a hard fork. In particular, if a hard fork is forced against the will of the nonmining network participants, the miners are at risk of running an alternative ledger without any users or infrastructure.

The previous discussion is by no means conclusive. Rather, it is intended to highlight the complexity of decision making and to show that significantly more stakeholders are involved in this process than a superficial examination suggests. In particular, miners cannot force the system to evolve against the will of the rest of the network. This complexity leads to relatively few changes and a very robust base layer.

2.5.4 Important Events in Bitcoin's History

2009 The first Bitcoin transactions were carried out exclusively for testing purposes. The Bitcoin units were little more than electronic play money without any real economic value and were often transferred free of charge to new users.

During the course of the year, the user base grew and with it the number of transactions. In mid-2009, approximately two hundred transactions per day were recorded, and although the Bitcoin unit has no fundamental value a price increase was achieved because of its limited number and the fascination for the underlying technology.[14]

A first price estimate was made on October 5, 2009. Based on the then average electricity costs for the creation process, the price of a Bitcoin unit was approximated to be US$0.000764.[160]

2010 On February 6, 2010, *Bitcoin Market* was the first platform to allow Bitcoin units to be exchanged for local currency. The first market trades were carried out on March 17, 2010.[84] The service, together with forums and an internet relay chat (IRC) channel, was instrumental in determining the market price.

The first documented purchase of goods with Bitcoin units dates back to May 22, 2010. The bitcointalk user *laszlo* agreed in an online forum[137] to pay 10,000 Bitcoin units for two pizzas.[15] A direct purchase was not possible at this time because the delivery service did not want to accept any Bitcoin units. Four days after the invitation to tender, *laszlo* was able to find a counterparty. The user *jercos* paid approximately US$25 for the pizzas, using his credit card and receiving the Bitcoin units in return.

The *laszlo pizzas* have now gained cult status and are an important reference point in Bitcoin's price history. This transaction marked a historic exchange rate of US$0.0025 (or one quarter of one cent) per one Bitcoin unit and laid the foundation for further commodity purchases using this cryptocurrency.[16]

In July 2010, prices rose to US$0.08 per Bitcoin unit. At the same time, the infamous Japanese Bitcoin exchange market *MtGox* began operating.[157] MtGox was originally planned as a trading platform for an (online) fantasy card game,[17] but it was converted into a website for trading Bitcoin units in July 2010.[18][163] The platform soon had a relatively high volume and enabled a more or less representative market price formation.

The price finally rose again and reached the US$0.5 level for a short time on November 7 but soon fell back to values between US$0.2 and 0.3.

---

14. Camera, Casari, and Bigoni (2013) show, in controlled experiments, how monetary units that are intrinsically worthless can become valued barter objects. [51]

15. User *laszlo* must surely have regretted this deal later.

16. At the time of the pizza offer, the price on the *Bitcoin Market* was almost double the amount. The varying prices indicate a highly fragmented market with very small exchange and trading volumes. [137]

17. MtGox is an acronym for "Magic: The Gathering Online-Exchange."

18. It is possible to follow the curious development of MtGox in a number of "snapshots" that can be found in the Website archive under the URL https://web.archive.org/web/http://mtgox.com/.

2011   This was followed by a further sharp price increase so that the US$ parity was breached for the first time on February 10, 2011. The upswing in price was overlapped with the launch of the darknet platform *Silk Road*, which likely had a significant impact on the early price development of the Bitcoin unit. The website was launched in February 2011 and allowed anonymous trading of goods and services. Silk Road evolved into a thriving market for all kinds of illegal substances and dubious services where Bitcoin was used as the exclusive method of payment. [56]

June 10, 2011, the Bitcoin unit reached a new peak of just under US$32. The price increase came to a temporary end with the hacking of the MtGox platform in that same month. The attackers succeeded in taking over user accounts on MtGox and created sales orders with deliberately low prices. [163] This had a significant negative impact on confidence and was likely one of the deciding factors for the price slump in the following months. This price development later became known as The Great Bubble of 2011.

At the same time, Wikileaks launched a Bitcoin donation option that allowed like-minded people to support the platform with Bitcoin units. This event had a very important impact on Bitcoin's price development in that it displayed a decisive advantage of using Bitcoin units. At the end of 2010, the online payment service Paypal terminated its business relationship with Wikileaks and thereby seriously hampered their fundraising campaign. Bitcoin transactions cannot be blocked. This opened up an independent source of income for Wikileaks while it allowed Wikileaks' supporters to allocate their donations as desired.

2012   On May 9, a report by the Federal Bureau of Investigation (FBI) [93] was published pointing out the dangers of Bitcoin. At the same time it stated that Bitcoin units are just another option for criminals and that one should not expect Bitcoin to replace existing options to finance illegal activities. The report also explained that Bitcoin transactions are not anonymous and in many cases would allow the criminals to be identified. The report caused a major media response.

In the course of the year, the number of acceptance points for Bitcoin units increased significantly. Bitpay, a large payment service provider, announced on September 11, 2012, that it started working with more than 1,000 companies worldwide, including many restaurants as well as a number of unusual companies such as dentists and funeral homes. [39] On November 15, WordPress, a large and internationally active company, followed with its blog hosting service. [12]

On November 28, an important milestone was achieved: Block 210,000 was created, and for the first time a reward of 25 Bitcoins was paid out instead of the usual 50 Bitcoin units. The so-called Block Reward Halving Day marked the beginning of a period of rising prices, and some voices are heard saying that this event was the cause of the sudden price increase. From an economic point of view, however, this hypothesis is questionable as it was foreseeable that the growth rate would be halved and that the expectation should have been priced in already.

2013   The year 2013 was one in which Bitcoin attracted a great deal of media attention because of its extreme price volatility. The market price of the Bitcoin unit rose steadily at the beginning of the year and broke through the previous high of US$35 around the beginning of March.

In mid-March, a software error culminating in a temporary fork in the register led to a short-term (intraday) price fall of more than 20 percent (see box 2.5).

However, the negative price effects were short-lived. The political situation in Cyprus[19] fueled the demand for alternative investments beyond government reach, and the price peaked above the US$200 mark on April 9. When the situation in Cyprus calmed down again, the Bitcoin price dropped significantly.

At the beginning of May, rumors emerged that the first fully functional Bitcoin Automated Teller Machine (ATM) had been installed in San Diego. According to a report from *NEWS10 ABC*, the machine allowed the purchase and sale of the cryptocurrency against US$.[1] As it transpired shortly afterward, the ATM was only presented at a press conference.[204] The first publicly accessible stationary Bitcoin ATM became operational in Vancouver on October 28, 2013. The introduction was extremely successful; on the first day a turnover was achieved amounting to a five-digit sum in (Canadian) dollars.[223]

On October 2, Silk Road was shut down by the FBI and Ross Ulbricht, the alleged site administrator, was arrested in a public library in San Francisco.[185] Since then, reincarnations of the website have appeared from time to time. The Bitcoin price recorded a short-term decline of around 20 percent but recovered within one day and began to rise again.

A little over a month later, the U.S. Senate held a hearing titled "Beyond Silk Road: Potential Risks, Threats, and Promises of Virtual Currencies."[65,66] Various experts were invited, and the risks and potential of virtual currency units were discussed. In the days following the hearing, the Bitcoin price rose dramatically and reached US$1,216.39 on November 29.[20] The mostly positive course of the hearing and the first steps toward legal certainty are generally considered the main reasons for this increase.

---

19. The debt crisis in Cyprus led the European Union and the International Monetary Fund (IMF) to impose a confiscatory special tax on private assets to be deposited with banks.[142]

20. The price of a Bitcoin unit was practically equivalent to the price of an ounce of gold on this day.

A second reason that is often seen as the cause of the enormous price rise is the high demand from Chinese investors. This theory is supported in particular by the timing of the subsequent price slump, which was accompanied by regulatory intervention by the Chinese Central Bank on December 5. Private individuals were subject to greater hurdles, exchanges were subject to stricter regulatory regimes, and financial intermediaries were prohibited from trading in Bitcoin units. [181]

Some analysts assume that neither the increased legal certainty resulting from the closure of Silk Road and the hearing nor the high demand from China were responsible for the record prices. There are indications that the price was driven mainly by fraudulent manipulation on the largest trading platform MtGox. [203]

Despite a significant year-end decline, the Bitcoin price in 2013 closed at around 5,400 percent of the price at the beginning of the year.

2014 On January 9, 2014, the online retailer Overstock announced that it would henceforth accept Bitcoin units as means of payment, [169] making it the first in a number of large companies. This was followed by announcements from the satellite TV operator Dish [80] (May), the online travel agency Expedia [63] (June), and Dell [62] (July) as well as Time Inc. [215] and Microsoft [155] (both December, with Microsoft withdrawing its acceptance at the beginning of 2016). [156]

In the meantime, there have been more and more reports of problems with Bitcoin withdrawals on the MtGox trading platform. [92] At the beginning of February, a general stop on withdrawals was imposed.[21] The measure was justified by the so-called *transaction malleability*, a problem that can lead to difficulties of identifying transactions. When MtGox finally went offline two weeks later and had to file for bankruptcy, many people lost a large part of their Bitcoin units. All in all, Bitcoin units worth half a billion US$ have disappeared on the MtGox exchange. In the following months, numerous indications appeared proving that the theft of the Bitcoin units had nothing to do with the alleged cause. [77,203]

In addition to the direct loss of approximately 850,000 Bitcoin units entrusted to the platform, the events had far-reaching negative effects on the reputation of the entire Bitcoin system, which could not be contained despite a joint press release of the remaining large Bitcoin companies. [86] For many people Bitcoin was MtGox. The Bitcoin unit lost approximately 60 percent of its value in 2014.

2015 On January 4, the bad news regarding centralized exchange platforms continued. The *Bitstamp* platform was hacked and Bitcoin units worth about US$5.1 million

---

21. Owing to the insolvency, the press reports can no longer be seen on the official page. There are, however, alternative secondary sources. [83]

were stolen. This was followed by a further 10 percent drop in prices to US$270, which continued after a brief period of recovery, so the Bitcoin unit was temporarily trading below the US$200 mark in mid-January.

After a weak start to the year, the Bitcoin unit fluctuated between US$200 and US$300 for much of the first three quarters of the year. The year was also characterized by high venture capital investments. The Bitcoin company 21 Inc, which received risk capital of around US$116 million in March, deserves a special mention. Between January and October 2015 alone, the publicly disclosed venture capital investments in Bitcoin and blockchain companies amounted to just under half a billion US$. [64] On the other hand, the final version of the New York BitLicense Regulation [161] from the beginning of June was highly likely to have an inhibitory effect on further investments as well as on the market price of the Bitcoin unit.

In October, a sharp rise in prices finally set in, raising the market price of the Bitcoin unit to over US$400. Among other things, the increase is likely to have been driven by tighter capital controls in China [180] and the October 22 decision by the European Court of Justice [41] on exemption from the value-added tax (VAT). [173] Also, the increased media presence due to new rumors about the identity of Satoshi Nakamoto might at least be partly responsible for the upswing (see box 2.2).

The Bitcoin unit closed 2015 with a price of US$430.

Box 2.6
Increasing Interest in Blockchain Technology

In 2015, many large companies launched their own research projects on blockchain technology, including UBS, [119] IBM, [152] and Nasdaq. [113] Mostly the term *Bitcoin* was avoided, and alternative blockchains such as Ethereum [89] or permissioned ledgers were used.

These were mostly process optimization projects in the area of securities trading and contract execution (smart contracts) as well as possible applications in connection with the highly acclaimed *internet of things* (IoT).

The extent to which interest in blockchain technology has affected the price of Bitcoin units is open to speculation. On the one hand, these applications increase interest in the technology; on the other hand, alternative blockchains might undermine the dominant position of the Bitcoin blockchain.

2016 The year began with a small slump in Bitcoin prices, which was replaced by a slow upward trend. In March and April, a series of hacks from the ShapeShift.io exchange platform attracted media attention. The service was sabotaged by an employee and then robbed several times. In total, almost US$200,000 was stolen in different cryptocurrencies. Customer assets were not affected because of ShapeShift.io's business model. [222] Bitcoin's price development remained relatively stable during these events, and the slow upward trend continued.

At the end of May, the trend culminated in an explosive increase of around 70 percent. This was followed by a correction until the price finally settled between US$600 and 700 in mid-June. Possible triggers of the large price increase are market uncertainties due to a British EU referendum (Brexit), as well as the Bitcoin Reward Halving Event at the beginning of July.

On June 18, shortly before the Brexit decision, Bitcoin achieved the highest price of US$780 in more than two years.

At the beginning of August, Bitfinex, a major Hong Kong based exchange, was successfully attacked, and Bitcoin units amounting to US$60 million were stolen. When the robbery became known, the Bitcoin price was already in decline. It can be assumed that the news of the hack has continued to have a negative impact on the price and has stifled any chance of possible corrections. The price fell significantly below US$600 at times.

When the first major panic had passed and it became clear that the insolvency of Bitfinex could be averted, a steady upward trend began. The rise in prices may have been fueled by the uncertainties surrounding the American presidential election and increased activity in China.

2017 In 2017, Bitcoin has been pushed into the global spotlight to an extent previously unimaginable. The price increased sharply and many other blockchain activities began to form. Everyone was suddenly talking about blockchain and cryptocurrencies. At the beginning of the year, Bitcoin's price was around US$1,000. At the end of the year on December 17, the Bitcoin unit traded at US$19,500.

While Bitcoin remained the dominant cryptoasset at all times, Ethereum, the second largest public blockchain, arguably contributed more to the craze in 2017. Ethereum is a permissionless smart contract platform that is somewhat more flexible than Bitcoin. In particular, it allows anyone to easily create so-called tokens—that is, new cryptoassets that can be traded on the Ethereum blockchain (see section 7.2).

While alternative approaches to create tokens on the Bitcoin base layer (colored coins) or through additional layers (Mastercoin/Omni) have existed for a while, in 2017 token issuance and handling became much easier thanks to smart contract-based tokens. [188] In particular, a smart contract standard, usually referred to as ERC-20, can be used to create these tokens within minutes. Entrepreneurs—and unfortunately also many scammers—started to issue and sell tokens through so-called initial coin offerings

(ICOs), promising that they could be used for a future utility or entitle the owner to a payment stream—that is, a dividend or an interest payment. These tokens became very popular, with many investors being unaware of the risks. In particular, since these tokens include promises, they are subject to counterparty risk. The euphoria lead to obscure episodes. Even projects with no existing product or customer base and teams with little to no prior experience were able to raise millions of dollars.

The high activity with these token sales lead to an increased demand for Bitcoin and Ether.[22] In most cases, people first had to buy Bitcoin or Ether to be able to participate in the token sales. Moreover, when someone wanted to sell a token on an exchange, this person usually sold the tokens for Bitcoin or Ether. The value of Ether grew over 13,000 percent in 2017.

Consequently, the existence of Bitcoin and more generally cryptoassets were increasingly noticed by financial institutions such as commercial banks, central banks, and financial regulators. The fact that the spectacular increase in price was followed by a price crash in 2018 only accelerated the discussion. By now, one can safely say that most individuals and institutions have an opinion about Bitcoin. The word "Bitcoin" has probably become one of the best known "brands" today.

The transaction fees increased throughout 2017 and peaked in high double digit dollar amounts at the end of the year. One explanation certainly is the higher demand for Bitcoin transactions. High fees are simply a result of the fee market in action. The increase fueled the scaling debate that dominated much of the year (see section 6.2). The main proposals were segregated witness (SegWit) to prepare the network for second-layer scaling and various forms of block size increases. Additionally there has been a proposal that tried to reach consensus among the community by combining SegWit with a block size increase. This proposal has been called SegWit2x—SegWit activation plus a block size increase.

On July 21, SegWit has successfully been activated via a soft fork. This happened after much debate and a long period of uncertainty. Shortly thereafter, on August 1, a minority of the community decided to increase the block size (alongside some other changes) and thereby created the Bitcoin Cash or B-Cash forced fork. The SegWit2x proposal had been withdrawn as of November 2017 (see section 2.5.3).

2018 The year 2018 was the year of reckoning. One of the most beautiful price bubbles in the history of money burst. Bitcoin's price reached a low of around US$3,200 on December 15, 2018. The prices of most ICO tokens and other cryptoassets were

---

22. Ether is the native protocol token of the Ethereum blockchain.

slaughtered even more dramatically. The typical low for these assets was around 90 to 95 percent below the all-time high.

This price slump also affected the public discussion. Many pundits emerged, claiming that Bitcoin and the whole space of cryptoassets have no future. For example, in October 2018 Nouriel Roubini stated that "Bitcoin is the 'mother of all scams' and blockchain is most hyped tech ever." [61] The chief executive officer (CEO) of JP Morgan, Jamie Dimon, is also famous for bashing Bitcoin. [236] He is known for having said that "Bitcoin is a fraud" and will eventually "blow up" and that "any trader trading bitcoin" will be "fired for being stupid." It did not help the reputation of the crypto space that many ICOs were outright scams. Weak teams, weak ideas, and weak executions of ideas were rampant. Further, the easy money that could be gained through an ICO attracted many swindlers.

Bitcoin's scaling debate became even more fierce in 2018, and gruesome infights began to emerge. The public accusations and threats between the different camps eliminated any confidence that was left after the steep price decline of the first quarter.

However, behind the scenes there have been many very positive developments on the technical front in 2018. The Lightning Network has been tested on mainnet, and more than 2,000 nodes have been created in the course of 2018.[23] The Lightning Network is one of several scaling proposals that allows for an almost unlimited number of Bitcoin transactions at negligible costs and without burdening the Bitcoin blockchain (see section 6.2). Besides the Lightning Network there have been other improvements. In particular, the general infrastructure built around Bitcoin and other cryptoassets has become more professional.

2019   2019 started relatively quiet, at a price point of US$3,800, with little media attention. It was not until Q2 that the price began to pick up and soon crossed the US$10,000 mark before retreating again to about US$7,000 by the end of the year.

Throughout 2019, news emerged of blockchain projects by established companies. In June, for example, Facebook announced Libra, a blockchain-based stablecoin (see box 6.2). While the Libra project proposal was heavily centralized and arguably had little in common with the Bitcoin blockchain, it brought the topic back to the spotlight. Moreover, the proposal increased the pressure on traditional players, in particular central banks, to issue their own retail Central Bank Digital Currencies (CDBC). The People's Bank of China (PBOC) was one of many central banks publicly stating that they would explore blockchain technology and introduce a CBDC. In section 6.1.5,

---

23. See Bitcoin Visuals, "Lightning Network Statistics," n.d., https://bitcoinvisuals.com/lightning.

we argue that these digital currencies will not be permissionless nor decentralized and therefore undermine the main selling proposition of public blockchains.

As of the end of 2019, several wallets and DAPP browsers have been removed from the Google Play and the Apple app stores. Additionally, YouTube deleted hundreds of crypto-related videos. This action—which ironically turned out to be a mistake—demonstrates both a severe problem with centralized platforms and one of the main advantages of blockchain technology.

Technologically, 2019 was an exciting year. Many companies started to embrace Blockchain as a promising technology by developing infrastructure for cryptocurrencies. Hundreds of projects develop sidechains, scaling solutions, decentralized finance infrastructure, noncustodial storage technologies, asset tokenization, and nonmonetary applications. This acceleration of research and development in the field provides a glance into an exciting future.

Outlook It is quite natural for fundamental innovations to experience boom and bust cycles. The dot-com boom lead to similar ups and downs and also resulted in exaggerated prices and inflated short-run expectations. However, in the long run, the internet became one of the most groundbreaking innovations and the foundation for new technological breakthroughs that would not have been possible otherwise. Consequently, price discussion will not be the focus of this book. We will rather focus on a technological and economic analysis and equip the reader with the tools to understand a technology that may become just as groundbreaking as the internet.

2.6 Exercises

Exercise 2.1: Explain how Bitcoin is classified with regard to monetary control structures and in what way it is primarily different from commercial bank deposits.

Exercise 2.2: Name the subcomponents of the Bitcoin system and explain what transactional requirement each of these elements needs to fulfill.

Exercise 2.3: Explain the Bitcoin system's mode of operation in reference to its three transactional requirements.

Exercise 2.4: Explain the difference between a hard fork and a soft fork. Which of the two software changes is a greater challenge for the Bitcoin network?

Exercise 2.5: Name and describe three important events that shaped the price development of the Bitcoin unit.

II Technical Analysis

3 Transactional Capacity

In this chapter, we will look at the Bitcoin network, differentiate various types of network participants, and show how messages are exchanged in order to achieve consensus. We will also consider the Bitcoin communications protocol and analyze various types of messages.[1]

3.1 Bitcoin Network

The Bitcoin network is the backbone of the Bitcoin system. It connects the individual network participants and allows them to relay transactions and blocks. It is therefore crucial to the system's transactional capacity.

3.1.1 Decentralized Architecture

Bitcoin is a peer-to-peer network (figure 3.1a). In contrast to centralized networks (figure 3.1b), in the Bitcoin network no participant has a privileged role. The participants usually have a large number of connections, and new connections can be established between any two participants. Every participant can hold a local copy of the Bitcoin blockchain, verify the legitimacy of transactions, and send these to other network participants. This permits communication and data storage to work in the absence of a central party.

The decentralized architecture makes peer-to-peer networks particularly resistant to attacks and failures. While in a centralized network the failure of a central node can have fatal consequences and can sometimes lead to data loss or a complete breakdown

---

1. As complements to the technical part of this book (chapters 3–5), we recommend the book by Andreas Antonopoulos,[14] which contains programming examples and is particularly suitable for people with a background in computer science, as well as the book by Arvind Narayanan et al.[159]

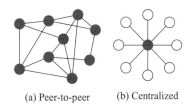

(a) Peer-to-peer   (b) Centralized

Figure 3.1
Different types of networks.

of communication, in a peer-to-peer network every participant can be replaced. Failures are usually easily handled by other network participants, locally lost data is restored, and communication is maintained on alternative connection paths. In this respect, decentralized systems are not dependent on individual nodes. Their structure prevents an individual participant from occupying a system-relevant position and thus makes them more robust.

From a regulatory perspective, decentralization also provides a network with a certain immunity. It is very difficult to regulate the whole network due to the absence of central points of contact. Whenever a node is closed, one can easily create a new one.[2]

In addition, regulation does not have the same degree of urgency in decentralized systems. Centralized networks are based on participants' trust in a central authority. This trust can be abused by manipulating the centrally stored data. Manipulations in their own interest or for the benefit of a client are equally conceivable. Among today's systems, it is assumed that a combination of reputation effects, control mechanisms, and fines provides the appropriate incentives and encourages central authorities to engage in long-term cooperation. In this respect, regulations of centralized systems are indispensable.

In decentralized networks reputational effects are practically nonexistent, owing to the dynamic network topology and the pseudonymity of the participants. The network participants will only comply with the consensus protocol if it is in their own interests. One consequence of this is that every participant has to consider that their peers may be relaying false information. In chapter 4, we will consider the methods that allow network participants to verify the accuracy of the (transaction) messages they receive.

---

2. The existence of illegal file-sharing platforms, which are also based on peer-to-peer networks, accentuate the regulators' powerlessness in confronting decentralized networks. Although big exponents such as torrent websites are regularly closed down, the networks continue to exist.

In the present chapter, we will focus on the network and its structure, participants, and channels of communication.

3.1.2   Network Nodes and Functionality

In part I of this book, we used the term *network participant* as an umbrella term, without distinguishing the various functions these participants may carry out. Specifically, there are three basic functions: the *verification function*, the *wallet function*, and the *mining function*. From now on, we will use the term *network node* for a participant who performs at least one of the three functions.

Verification function.   The verification function covers all the activities that are necessary so that network participants can participate in the network on their own and verify all transactions independently. In particular, participants verify transaction messages, store these messages locally, and forward them to other network participants. The verification function requires a participant to maintain a copy of the Bitcoin blockchain and to verify the validity of all the blocks of the chain. The verification function also facilitates the exchange of blocks. Network nodes who have a verification function are known as *full nodes*.

Wallet function.   A wallet provides safe storage for private keys and monitors and manages a node's personal Bitcoin balance. Wallets are developed for end users and normally provide a graphical user interface that enables Bitcoin units to be received and sent easily. In addition, many wallets offer optional security mechanisms to improve the protection of the private keys.

Mining function.   Nodes that have a mining function participate actively in generating new blocks and contribute to the extension of the Bitcoin blockchain.

A new network node is created when a user installs a Bitcoin client on his computer and begins to exchange information with other network participants. Most clients are open source, and users are free to choose from a range of software packages. Theoretically, a user could also develop his own client and let it communicate with the network. As long as the software packages are compliant with Bitcoin's communication protocol, they can be used to create new nodes and exchange information.

The most popular client is known as *Bitcoin Core*. Bitcoin Core contains the full range of functions. The software creates a full node and can be controlled via a graphical user interface or via the command line.

Bitcoin Core keeps a local copy of the Bitcoin blockchain. The client verifies and relays the transactions and blocks. In addition, Bitcoin Core includes a wallet and a simple mining application. It therefore provides all three functions. Bitcoin Core is a freely downloadable software.[3]

3.1.3 Connection Setup and Topology

After the successful installation of a client, the software will connect to other nodes. The connection is established via the common network protocols (TCP/IP) and by default via port 8333. The node that wants to establish a connection sends an initial message (`version` message) to a known internet protocol (IP) address of another node. The message contains information about the node itself and the local copy of the Bitcoin ledger, enabling the connection to be established. Optionally, the address list of the new peer can be queried (`getaddr` message) so that the node can extend its known network with additional connections.

New nodes face the initial problem of not having any known addresses. To enable the software to establish a connection when the client is started for the first time, an IP list is supplied with the initial download. Alternatively, IP addresses can be entered manually.

Typically, every node attempts to maintain at least eight connections. The actual number can substantially diverge from this value. With regard to standard settings, nodes maintain on average thirty-two active connections.[76] Possible firewall and router settings may limit the number of connections. In general, a broader network connectivity will facilitate the exchange of data.

If an interruption causes a node to have fewer than eight active connections, it will immediately attempt to establish new connections. For this purpose, known IP addresses can be used or new IP addresses requested from other nodes.

To illustrate the connection process, we will use the example shown in figure 2.3 and assume that the network is extended by one node. Let us assume that Tamara downloads and installs the Bitcoin client. After successful installation, the client consults the supplied IP list and establishes a connection with one of the other nodes. In order to do this, the client sends a `version` message to which the other node responds with a `verack` (version acknowledged) message. The process shown in figure 3.2 is automatically executed by the client; the user does not need to do anything manually.

---

3. To download this software, go to Bitcoin Project, Bitcoin Core, https://bitcoin.org/en/download.

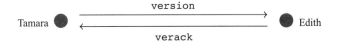

Figure 3.2
Connection setup in the Bitcoin network.

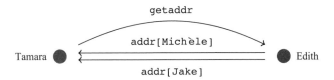

Figure 3.3
Request for new IP adresses.

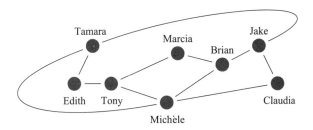

Figure 3.4
Network with a new participant.

Edith can accept the connection by responding with a `version` message and waiting for the `verack` confirmation. Tamara can then request Edith's IP address list. This is achieved using a `getaddr` message. Edith will send a random selection of IP addresses from her large pool of known IP addresses to Tamara using several `addr` messages. The random selection process is termed *bootstrapping*.

In many cases, Edith sends IP addresses that are present in her pool but that she is not currently connected with. This leads to a more robust network topology.

In our example in figure 3.3, Tamara receives the IP addresses of Michèle and Jake. She can use the new IP addresses to send further `version` messages and thus establish new connections. In our example, she uses this opportunity, resulting in the network displayed in figure 3.4.

Admittedly, our example is a simplification. Most of the connections have been kept simple to illustrate how the messages are exchanged. Further, our example consists of a very small number of nodes, with each node having only a small number of connections.

In the real Bitcoin network, bootstrapping creates quasi-random connection paths. These lead to a complex and randomized network topology. Local proximity is irrelevant for the choice of connections. In this respect, the random creation of network partitions is practically impossible. Moreover, if a partition is created, this can be detected by a sudden drop in network computing resources (more precisely regarding the speed at which new blocks are created) and the number of transaction messages. [76]

Partitions generally only become a problem if complete isolation of a certain (geographical) area persists over an extended period of time. This is a manageable risk, considering that any communication between two subnetworks can resolve partitions. Geographical characteristics of the node distribution can therefore be of interest due to geopolitical considerations and to protect against (natural) disasters.

A 2014 study on the geographical distribution of nodes shows that around 40 percent of all nodes are located in China or the United States. Otherwise the nodes are distributed relatively homogeneously over prosperous and densely populated areas.

The more full nodes the Bitcoin network has, the more robust it will be. At the end of 2015, the Bitcoin network consisted of around 5,500 full nodes, compared with almost 15,000 in 2013. [81] At the end of 2019, there were around 9,500 full nodes.[4]

Full nodes are indispensable for the Bitcoin system to function, and a decrease in their number therefore is problematic. The decline in the number of full nodes is mainly attributable to two causes: first, the operation of a full node is costly and there is no compensation for operating a full node (see box 3.1). The direct costs involve the internet connection, electricity, and data storage. Second, Bitcoin can be used without operating a full node. Neither the ownership of Bitcoin units nor the initiation of a transaction requires a user to maintain a full node.

To a certain extent, maintaining a full node is a common good, the provision of which causes individual costs for the operator. It is a common good because the service provided is rivalrous and nonexcludable. From an economic point of view, therefore, the decrease of full nodes is hardly surprising. Box 3.1 deals with possible approaches that could make the operation of a full node more attractive.

---

4. Bitnodes (https://bitnodes.io) runs a service that enables the network to scan for active nodes.

> **Box 3.1**
> **Bitnodes and Other Incentivizing Programs**
>
> In the Bitcoin community it is repeatedly claimed that the incentives to operate a full node are given, among other things, by reciprocal considerations of the participants. Indeed, full node operators often do this out of idealism and/or pure interest in the technology. A motivational basis of this kind is, however, insufficient for a system that is otherwise based on economic incentives. To secure Bitcoin's long-term survival and scalability, it is essential to stop the decline in the number of full nodes and even reverse it.
>
> A program aimed at incentivizing full nodes has been initiated by private stakeholders. The project remunerated operators of full nodes who satisfy certain conditions (availability and reliability). The payments were financed by the program operator's private wealth and by donations. The project had a limited duration that expired at the end of 2015, but its desired outcome was unfortunately not achieved. [234]
>
> A much more sustainable approach would be to establish a systemic reward for services such as the forwarding of transactions [16] or the provision of information for *simplified payment verification* (SPV) clients (see section 3.2.2). Micro transactions could facilitate rewards of this kind. [143]

3.2   Extended Network

The number of full nodes in no way reflects the number of Bitcoin users. The increase in the size of the Bitcoin blockchain and the increase in the number of transactions has led to a growing list of requirements regarding a full node's hardware and internet specifications. This is why many users decide against operating a full node themselves and instead rely on other participants who operate a full node.

An outsourced validation means, for example, that the Bitcoin blockchain does not need to be downloaded and constantly updated. The resource savings can be particularly interesting for clients on mobile devices, where memory is usually scarce and bandwidth limited. Limited network participation offers the possibility for the simple integration of users who could otherwise not participate in the Bitcoin network.

At the same time, however, the abandonment of the verification function generates dependencies. The Bitcoin system offers each network participant the possibility of independently verifying the legitimacy of all transactions included in the Bitcoin blockchain. If a network participant waives this option, he automatically loses part of his independence and must place a certain amount of trust in his information sources.

Figure 3.5
Centralized sub-networks.

The exact structure of these dependencies and the extent of the trust vary greatly. Indirect network participation can take the form of *centralized subnetworks* or *simplified payment verification* (SPV).

3.2.1 Centralized Subnetworks

Centralized subnetworks display the highest form of dependency. The participants are only indirectly connected to the Bitcoin network and rely exclusively on the information and communications channel of a specific node. Figure 3.5 shows two centralized subnetworks.

Clients that are connected to a centralized subnetwork can exercise the wallet function without the need for direct access to the Bitcoin network. The central node is used as a proxy server, which can be consulted periodically to check the Bitcoin balances of the user's addresses. In addition, transaction messages are transmitted to the central node and thus indirectly relayed to the Bitcoin network.

A connection to a centralized subnetwork can be much more convenient for a user since he has only to install a light client or to manage his Bitcoin balances via a web application. The resulting dependencies are hardly noticeable under normal operations. However, it would be possible for a central node to either withhold certain information from the participants or not relay their transactions to the rest of the network and thus block them. This can be done intentionally or can happen as a consequence of technical issues. In this respect, centralized subnetworks lose a large part of the robustness properties of a peer-to-peer network and introduce new vulnerabilities into the system.

In many cases, centralized subnetworks are also accompanied by custody services. In such relationships, the owner transfers complete control of his Bitcoin units to the central node. He does not hold a private key for the corresponding balance but only has a user account on the service provider's platform, with which he can request the delivery of his Bitcoin units. The actual Bitcoin transaction is initiated by the central node. In such a relationship, the user only gets an IOU promising to deliver the Bitcoin units on request. This is comparable to credit money, for which the value of the promise depends on the creditworthiness of the issuer (see section 1.4.2).

> **Box 3.2**
>
> **Connecting to a Client That Uses Its Own Full Node**
>
> In centralized subnetworks, a limited node has to trust the central node. This problem can be circumvented if the user of a limited node additionally operates a full node.
>
> A mobile device which operates a limited node could, for example, access a full node operated on the user's desktop computer and thereby simultaneously profit from all the advantages of lower processing loads and complete verifiability. Some wallets for mobile devices already offer this option.

3.2.2 Simplified Payment Verification Node

SPV clients facilitate the use of the wallet function without it being necessary to store a full copy of the Bitcoin blockchain locally. As opposed to indirect network participants who are tied to a central node, SPV nodes possess direct access to the Bitcoin network. The required data are sourced by various nodes and can be partially verified. The diversity of data sources and the possibility of partially verifying the received data give the SPV node greater security and independence than a connection to a centralized subnetwork.

An SPV node holds only a small part of the blocks—the so-called block header. Among other things, the block header includes the identification number that depends on the transactions included but not the transactions themselves.[5] For this reason, SPV clients require only around a thousandth of the storage capacity of full nodes. An SPV client needs to store only eighty bytes per block. More importantly, this amount remains unchanged regardless of the number of transactions included, resulting in a linear growth path even with a large increase in users and transactions.

Full nodes use the block height to verify a transaction. To ensure that the Bitcoin unit (unspent transaction output) referenced in a transaction has not already been used, the full nodes check the complete Bitcoin blockchain.[6] SPV nodes instead use a heuristic based on the block depth—that is, the number of confirmations that secured a transaction. If the block is referenced by a certain number of additional blocks (usually six), SPV nodes regard the transactions contained in it as valid. Due to the high computational resources required to create these subsequent blocks and the various sources used to obtain the information, the probability of a manipulation attempt is very low.

---

5. The *merkle root* of the transactions is one of the block inputs that influences the identification number.

6. Full nodes have a local database containing unspent transaction outputs (UTXO).

SPVs source information by selectively querying individual transactions. This creates two problems.

First, SPV nodes can verify whether a received transaction actually belongs to a block; however, they do not know whether they are being denied information or whether another, possibly competing transaction exists.

Second, information gathering can lead to privacy problems. If an SPV node asks only for transactions in connection with its own public keys (or Bitcoin addresses), the other nodes will be able to connect these pseudonyms to its IP address and create a distinct user profile. As a countermeasure, the SPV node could request a large amount of additional data. However, the large volume of data would undermine the original purpose for implementing the SPV client.

To counteract the second problem, transactions are usually queried via so-called *bloom filters*. Bloom filters specify a search request using hash functions (see section 4.2). The SPV node sends a request for transactions that match a certain search pattern after applying various hash functions. The precision can vary according to requirements. There is still a trade-off between privacy and data volume. *False positive* results are possible or even desirable because of the probabilistic nature of the system. *False negative* results are not possible. If a transaction is rejected by the filter, it is irrelevant for the SPV client.

Bloom filters serve the purpose of disguising the search queries by SPV nodes. Due to the nature of the hash function, it is much harder to identify the pattern behind the query. The idea originated with an academic essay by Bloom [40] and was formalized by BIP0037 [111] for the Bitcoin system.

3.2.3 Pool Mining

Bitcoin mining is often performed jointly by large groups, referred to as *mining pools*. Classic *solo mining* requires the operation of a full node. *Pool mining*, however, does not. Normally only the pool operator holds a copy of the Bitcoin blockchain and distributes the required information to the pool members in the same way as a centralized subnetwork. Pool mining is therefore a major contributor to the decline in the number of full nodes and fuels concern about centralization encroaching on the Bitcoin system.

3.3 Bitcoin Communication Protocol

The purpose of the Bitcoin network is to allow for the exchange of information. For this information to be processed by various clients, communication must take place in a standardized form. No client can be forced to comply with these standards. The communication protocol merely describes the formatting of the information. If a node wants to communicate with other nodes, it is therefore in its best interest to adhere to this format.

For the Bitcoin network, the exchange of blocks and transactions is primarily relevant. Messages that do not directly serve the exchange of this type of information play a secondary role.

3.3.1 The Exchange of Blocks

When the client software is first started, it spends several hours downloading, verifying, and indexing all the blocks of the Bitcoin blockchain. The first block, the genesis block, is integrated into the client software on delivery. All subsequent blocks have to be procured from the other nodes and verified by the client software. The volume of data contained in the Bitcoin blockchain was approximately 205 gigabytes (GB) at the end of 2019.

Each block needs to be downloaded and verified only once. Long loading times occur only if the client has to catch up on a large number of blocks; that is, during the initial installation of the client software or if the node was not connected to the network for a long time.

The comparison between two copies of the Bitcoin blockchain takes place via the mutual exchange of `getblocks` messages. These messages contain the identification number of the newest block in the local chain. If the two chains are equivalent, no blocks need to be exchanged. However, if one of the two nodes receives a `getblocks` message with an identification number that does not correspond to the last block of the local chain, it will try to locate the block with this identification number within the local chain and send an `inv` (inventory) message with the identification numbers of the successors of this block.[7]

The node that receives the `inv` message, then, has the possibility to request the respective blocks using `getdata` messages. Figure 3.6 shows the messaging history between the two nodes when transmitting blocks.

This principle is used to prevent a node from receiving block data that it already has. Each node can independently decide which data it wants to request from which nodes.

When a node receives a block, he independently examines the validity of the transactions that it contains and verifies that the transactions reference only previously

---

7. An individual `inv` message contains a maximum of 500 block identification numbers.

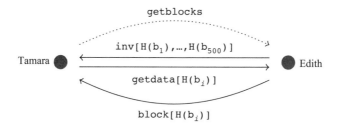

Figure 3.6
The exchange of blocks.

unspent transaction outputs (UTXO) and were initiated by the owner (see section 4.4.1). The node also checks the reference to the old block and examines the current block's identification number to determine whether it meets the threshold value criterion. Each node can thus clearly determine whether a block fulfills the various consensus conditions. If and only if all checks are passed, the node will include the block into his version of the blockchain.

3.3.2   The Exchange of Transactions

Transaction messages are payment orders that nodes can verify, relay, and process. We will look at the structure and the verification of a transaction message in section 4.4.1. In the present section, we focus on how transaction messages are relayed.

The method for exchanging transaction messages is very similar to that used for blocks. The `inv` messages can alternatively include transaction identification numbers. If a node receives an `inv` message that contains an unknown transaction identification number, the node can similarly use a `getdata` message to request the transaction. The actual transmission of the transaction data is subsequently made using a `tx` message. Figure 3.7 shows the messaging history between the two nodes when transmitting transactions.

If a node receives a requested `tx` message, it will first examine it and forward only if the validation is successful. The validation is performed using predefined unlocking conditions and signatures, which we will consider in detail in section 4.5. If validation fails, the transaction will be discarded. This protects the network from certain types of DoS attacks, which cause data transmissions to seize up by flooding the service with a large number of invalid transactions. However, if the validation is successful, the transaction message will be filed in the node's local memory, the so-called *mempool*, and offered to other nodes as part of the `inv` message.

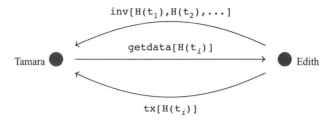

Figure 3.7
The exchange of transactions.

This leads to an exponential increase in the distribution of the transaction message. The more nodes there are that store the message locally, the faster the message will be distributed.[76]

Box 3.3
Incentive Compatibilities Associated with Propagation

Under certain circumstances, nodes may have an incentive not to forward transaction messages. If the transaction fees are a substantial part of the reward, miners can increase their own expected payoff by withholding information.[16] This problem can easily be remedied by the initiator of the transaction by forwarding it to several independent mining nodes.

With regard to the communication of blocks, a similar problem can occur. Sometimes it is advantageous for a miner (*mining pool*) to keep a block with a valid identification number secret and work exclusively on the longest version of the blockchain. Although the miner thereby faces the risk that another miner might compete for his current reward, he can also thereby prevent his competitors from working on the longest version of the chain and thus ensure that they waste a certain proportion of their computational resources. Because the expected payoff for mining is proportional to the total computational resources of all the miners, retaining a valid block can increase the expected payoff of a miner. This phenomenon is known as *selfish mining*.[49,69,91] The retention of blocks poses a far greater problem than the retention of transactions.

There are various approaches that mitigate this problem by ensuring it only becomes beneficial to retain new blocks when the miner has approximately one third of the whole network's computational resources.[91,112]

3.4 Exercises

Exercise 3.1: Discuss the extent to which the decentralized architecture of the Bitcoin network contributes to its robustness.

Exercise 3.2: Explain how a new node can connect with the network and what characteristics of the connection setup ensure that a quasi-random network topology will emerge.

Exercise 3.3: Describe what functions a network node needs to fulfill in order to have the status of full node. Moreover, indicate the extent to which full nodes are important for the state of the Bitcoin network.

Exercise 3.4: Describe how the following restricted network nodes function, and identify the potential advantages and disadvantages of the respective software choices.

    a) Wallet function via a centralized subnetwork

    b) SPV wallet

Exercise 3.5: Describe the purpose of the Bitcoin communication protocol.

Exercise 3.6: Using an example, show how transactions and blocks are relayed over the network. Describe the process intuitively and name the messages involved and their purposes.

4   Transactional Legitimacy

In this chapter, we will look at how Bitcoin units can be assigned to an individual and which principles of mathematics enable a decentralized validation of a transaction's legitimacy. We introduce pseudonyms and expand on the necessary cryptographic foundations. We also present the various transaction types as well as the specific conditions that have to be fulfilled for Bitcoin units to be transmitted.

4.1   Pseudonyms

Owing to the decentralized structure of the Bitcoin network, it is not possible to manage Bitcoin balances and access rights in a traditional manner. There is no central authority that is responsible for opening accounts, recording owners' personal details, and authorizing subsequent access. Therefore, decentralization makes it extremely difficult to examine the legitimacy of ownership claims.

The use of real identities in the form of personal names and personal details is neither feasible nor desirable in the Bitcoin system. It is not desirable because if Bitcoin addresses were registered under personal names, it would be possible to associate all transactions to individuals. Information about salary payments, purchase preferences, and personal wealth would be accessible to everyone. It is not feasible because in a decentralized system it is impossible to provide proof of identity in the same way as in the traditional financial system.

The Bitcoin system uses pseudonyms instead of actual identities to guarantee the legitimacy of transactions. A pseudonym-based solution in a decentralized system requires that the following conditions are met:

1. Participants must be able to create their own pseudonyms without the assistance of a central party.

2. No two pseudonyms may overlap.

3. Ownership claims to the pseudonyms must be publicly verifiable so that access to
   the respective Bitcoin balances can be restricted.

Bitcoin satisfies these conditions by using pairs of cryptographic keys. A pair consists
of a private and a public key. The public key (or the Bitcoin address derived from it) acts
as a pseudonym that represents the identity of the respective participant but cannot
be easily linked to a person (point 1).[1] In practice, the number of pseudonyms is so
large that the probability of two persons choosing the same pseudonym is negligible
(point 2). The private key must always remain in the exclusive possession of the person who generated the pseudonym and thereby provides proof that the owner of the
respective pseudonym is authorized to use it (point 3).

4.1.1 Generating a Key Pair

To create a key pair, a person must select at random an element from an unimaginably
large set of numbers which ranges from 1 to $115, 792, 089, 237, 316, 195, 423, 570, 985,$
$008, 687, 907, 852, 837, 564, 279, 074, 904, 382, 605, 163, 141, 518, 161, 494, 336$; that is,
between 1 and a seventy-eight-digit number.[2] The selected number serves as a private
key and can be subsequently used to provide proof of ownership.

As shown in figure 4.1, the public key is derived from the private key. It is derived
by multiplying a commonly known base point G of the elliptic curve by the previously
selected private key k_{prv} (see section 4.3.4). For this reason, the public key is a point
K_{pub} on an elliptic curve that is represented by an x and a y value. The multiplication
is shown in the formula below:

$$K_{pub} = k_{prv} \circ G.$$

It is crucial that multiplications based on elliptic curves cannot be inverted.[3] Otherwise, every person who knows the pseudonym could then derive the corresponding
right of access in the form of the private key.

Owing to the one-way function, people are able to disclose their public key as a
pseudonym while at the same time retaining exclusive knowledge of their private key.
A person can choose a private key, derive a pseudonym from it, and receive a Bitcoin

---

1. A person can generate any number of pseudonyms in the Bitcoin system.
2. Note that the number of atoms on Earth is estimated to be a fifty-one-digit number and is
therefore approximately one octillion times smaller than the number of elements in this set. The
estimate is based on a publication by Jefferson Labs.[224]
3. Today, the elliptic curve discrete logarithm problem (ECDLP) can be solved only by *brute force*;
that is, a trial and error approach. Due to the large number of computations required, this is
currently impossible. Consequently, with the current state of technology, it is infeasible to derive
the corresponding private key from the public key or to find the private key for a given pseudonym.

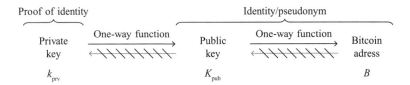

Figure 4.1
Relationship between the pair of keys and the Bitcoin address.

payment on behalf of the pseudonym. Since the person is in exclusive possession of the private key, it can be used to prove ownership of the associated pseudonym and all of its assets.

The most common pseudonyms are Bitcoin addresses. To derive a Bitcoin address from a public key, we need a few additional steps as shown in figure 4.1. The Bitcoin address is nothing more than a hash value (see section 4.2) of the public key. For now, we will consider public keys and Bitcoin addresses as equivalents. We will look at some advantages of Bitcoin addresses later and differentiate them from the public key.

To further describe pseudonyms and access rights, we will follow Tamara, who just joined the Bitcoin network in chapter 3. Tamara now needs a pseudonym, which she will use to receive Bitcoin units. The following steps will be executed by her wallet software.

First, a random number, k_{prv}, is chosen as the private key:

$$k_{prv} = 1006495179124632982185549419637355514199990\ldots$$

$$9193947758089436670762585615234410426.$$

From k_{prv}, the software derives the corresponding public key by means of multiplication on elliptic curves (see section 4.3.2). Tamara obtains the point with the following coordinates as her public key:

$$x_{K_{pub}} = 43086108819063845471784291298828806947352 6\ldots$$

$$45388418363213743744756576526107326,$$

$$y_{K_{pub}} = 74604540087345955209626838334808422259785 4\ldots$$

$$86813648239447613724663528494663884.$$

4.1.2 Representation of the Keys

As we have already seen, all keys and pseudonyms are nothing more than numbers. For the sake of simplicity, we have so far presented these numbers in the classical decimal numeral system. However, the form in which a value is represented can vary.

The keys and pseudonyms are generated and processed by the computer in the binary numeral system; that is, as a long chain of zeros and ones, where each binary digit is termed a "bit." Binary notation is ideal for efficient processing by machines. For humans, binary notation is inconvenient, as it needs more space to represent the information than other numeral systems. For humans it is difficult to read and process information in binary format. This is why computer scientists use a variety of notations, some of which allow people to absorb information more easily.

Common representations include the binary (base 2), the decimal (base 10), and the hexadecimal numeral systems (base 16). Bitcoin also introduced another format: the so-called Base58Check. As the name suggests, this format uses base 58, which consists of the integers 1–9 as well as all uppercase and lowercase alphabetical characters, except for O (uppercase o), l (lowercase l), and I (uppercase i). The large base permits the information to be written very compactly. At the same time, this format avoids alphanumeric symbols that can be confused with others when being transcribed. As a further measure against transmission errors, the format contains a checksum with which some typos can be recognized.

Base58Check is used to display private keys and some pseudonyms, where a prefix identifies the type of data. If the sequence starts with a 1, a 3, or bc, it is a pseudonym. The prefixes 5, K, and L refer to a private key. Private keys in Base58Check are also called *wallet import format* (WIF) keys.

Box 4.1 represents the same private key in various numeral systems. We use the key that Tamara generated in section 4.1.1 for this example.

Box 4.1
Private Key with Different Formats

The same private key can be represented in different formats. All formats represent the same information.

Binary: 11011110100001011001101110111101000010111101110000001111000111 10100100101001001000111000111110011010100100110101101111101010001100 11010111100100011101111010101101001101111100011011111100110000000001011 1110110011011111111010010010011100110110110010111111010

Decimal: 100649517912463298218554941963735551419990919394775808943667076258561523410426

Hexadecimal: de859bbd0bdc0f1e929238f9a935bf519af23bd5a6f9bf300becdfe9279b65fa

Base58Check (*WIF*): 5KWHc3RENTEdyZg1s8WphuWcsPMhivBvCCngWavocfdeDDD7DVS

In addition, so-called quick response (QR) codes can be used to represent keys visually. A QR code is a two-dimensional bar code that can be read by a QR scanner. This is particularly useful if a user wants to import a physical backup of his private key into a wallet software. Below we see Tamara's private (WIF) key in form of a QR code.

Table 4.1

Converter from the binary system to the hexadecimal system.

Binary:	0000	0001	0010	0011	0100	0101	0110	0111
Hexadecimal:	0	1	2	3	4	5	6	7
Binary:	1000	1001	1010	1011	1100	1101	1110	1111
Hexadecimal:	8	9	a	b	c	d	e	f

Public keys are usually presented in hexadecimal. This notation, which employs base 16, uses the integers 0–9 and the characters a–f. In computer science, hexadecimal is widespread as it is very convenient to work with. A single character in hexadecimal represents exactly four bits in binary ($2^4 = 16^1$). The relationship between the two formats is displayed in table 4.1.

When Tamara's public key coordinates from section 4.1.1 are converted into the hexadecimal system, they respectively produce the following two alphanumeric sequences:

$$x_{K_{\mathrm{pub}}} = \texttt{5f41df966899767381592461911e12789393736b29} \ldots$$

$$\texttt{0a5d4beda3ba573d5582be,}$$

$$y_{K_{\mathrm{pub}}} = \texttt{a4f0ac5d9ca56b776db9f10895303efc8450892e0f} \ldots$$

$$\texttt{8bd99db228dbd1206f08cc.}$$

To be presented in a single alphanumeric sequence, the coordinates are concatenated and are supplemented by the prefix 04.[4] This representation is called the uncompressed public key K_{pub}.

$$K_{pub} = 04 \frown x_{K_{pub}} \frown y_{K_{pub}}$$

$$= 045f41df9668997673815 92461911e12789393736b\ldots$$

$$290a5d4beda3ba573d5582bea4f0ac5d9ca56b776d\ldots$$

$$b9f10895303efc8450892e0f8bd99db228dbd1206f\ldots$$

$$08cc$$

Because the public key corresponds to a point on a predefined elliptic curve, the x-coordinate is sufficient to compute the corresponding y-coordinate. More precisely, given any value for x, there are no more than two potential candidates for y. This is due to the symmetry of the elliptic curves (see section 4.3.2). To obtain a unique point, the x value is extended by a prefix. The prefix is 02 if the y value of the public key is even and 03 if the y value is odd. In Tamara's case the prefix 02 is used. This compressed representation of the public key will subsequently be termed $\overline{K}_{pub}$.

$$\overline{K}_{pub} = 025f41df9668997673815 92461911e12789393736b\ldots$$

$$290a5d4beda3ba573d5582be.$$

The compressed public key has the great advantage that it is shorter. For most transactions, public keys have to be included in the transaction at some point (see section 4.5) and therefore become part of the Bitcoin blockchain. A shorter key length reduces the required storage space.

4.1.3   Bitcoin Addresses
The most common pseudonym is the Bitcoin address. It is derived from a public key to which two hash functions are applied one after the other. The double hash is a one-way function; in other words, the public key cannot be derived from the Bitcoin address. Access rights and scripts that are based on Bitcoin addresses are further analyzed in section 4.5.

A Bitcoin address has a length of 160 bits but is generally presented in Base58Check format with the prefix 1. Figure 4.2 shows the necessary steps to derive a Bitcoin address.

---

4. Public keys always have the same bit-length. The hexadecimal number can thus be split between both coordinates at any time.

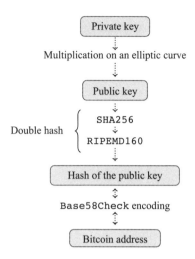

Figure 4.2
From the private key to the Bitcoin address.

SHA256 and RIPEMD160 are the names of the two hash functions (see section 4.2). Bitcoin addresses are also referred to as *public-key-hashes*.

The main advantages of the Bitcoin address over the public key are its convenience, security, and flexibility.

First, a Bitcoin address is significantly shorter than the public key and therefore better suited for daily use. It contains a checksum due to the Base58Check encoding.

Second, the Bitcoin address offers some added security. Even if an attacker were to discover a vulnerability in the elliptic curve, he would only be able to start an attack once he had obtained the public key of the target. The Bitcoin address ensures that the public key has to be disclosed only at the time of a transaction. This makes Bitcoin addresses much more robust against the threat of quantum computers.

Third, Bitcoin addresses can also be constructed as so-called pay-to-script-hash addresses. These addresses are not derived from the hash value of a public key and are therefore not classic Bitcoin addresses. Instead, they are based on the hash value of a whole locking script that binds the access right to a specific condition. This allows unusual pseudonym constructs to be created, which for example require that payments must be signed by several private keys (see section 4.5.4) or can only be spent after a certain amount of time (see box 6.12). These pay-to-script-hash addresses always begin with the number 3.

Box 4.2
Compressed Keys and Bitcoin Addresses

Although the compressed and the uncompressed public keys represent the exact same point on the elliptic curve and derive from the same private key, they lead to different Bitcoin addresses. If Tamara generates her Bitcoin address from the uncompressed public key K_{pub}, she obtains the Bitcoin address B. If she uses the compressed public key $\overline{K}_{\text{pub}}$ instead, she receives the Bitcoin address $\overline{B}$.

$B = $ `1E8jc2eRXmjF2FKebTZwAsxwaRWeDvEwDj`,

$\overline{B} = $ `13HE523Wvpqzjijjb1z3NDUz25AQN2eLw1`.

Tamara can use her private key to access both of these Bitcoin addresses. However, her private key can be represented in two distinct ways. Private keys with the prefix 5 manage Bitcoin addresses generated from the uncompressed public key. Private keys with the prefix K or L are used to manage Bitcoin addresses generated from the compressed public key (see below). The prefix facilitates in particular the import of the keys into a wallet software. The information in the prefix instructs the software which pseudonyms it needs to check for balances and therefore significantly increases efficiency.

The "compressed" WIF version of Tamara's private key $\overline{k}_{\text{prv}}$ corresponds to the following string:

$\overline{k}_{\text{prv}} = $ `L4gGHffx1goCCfDCpGAdZYmjKPgNk1mBnT2dPakUkRWjEec7ArQY`.

Strictly speaking, however, the term "compressed" private key is incorrect. It is not a compressed version of the information but merely a signal that indicates which pseudonyms to use. In fact, the "compressed" private key is even 8 bits or 2 hexadecimal characters longer than the uncompressed format. The length of the private key is not very crucial because it is never transmitted with transactions and therefore will not burden the blockchain.

4.1.4 Disposable Pseudonyms

All pseudonyms in the Bitcoin system are designed to be used only once. This may not seem intuitive (compared with bank account numbers), but it is based on the fact that the Bitcoin blockchain is public. If a person always uses the same pseudonym, it will be easier for others to identify patterns in transactions and to track down the corresponding identity to the pseudonym. If the identification succeeds, all past and future transactions of the person concerned could be queried and monitored.

To make such analyses more difficult, most wallets create a new key pair for each transaction and always use different Bitcoin addresses. When a payment is made, the wallet sends the invoiced amount to the invoice issuer's address and additionally generates new addresses to which the remaining balance is transferred. Observers cannot

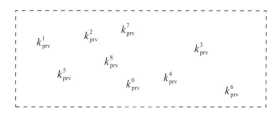

Figure 4.3
Structure of a nondeterministic wallet.

distinguish between the invoice amount and the change and are equally unable to discover which pseudonym is retained by the owner.

The constant need for new addresses poses questions regarding the selection process and the organization of the access data. New pseudonyms can either be generated from random, independent private keys or be based on an initial value, a so-called *seed*. Section 4.1.5 discusses the various possibilities for organizing private keys.

4.1.5 Deterministic and Nondeterministic Wallets

To implement pseudonyms that are only used once, a wallet must generate and store a large number of keys and pseudonyms. There are various approaches to this which differ in the selection procedure as well as in the organization and administration.

Nondeterministic implementations (figure 4.3) rely on a large number of randomly selected private keys when creating pseudonyms. A new random number is selected for each private key. An example of such a nondeterministic approach is the original implementation of the Bitcoin Core wallet. The wallet generated hundred key pairs and associated Bitcoin addresses during the setup process. Whenever there has been a need for additional pseudonyms, the wallet subsequently generated new addresses.

The problem with the nondeterministic method is that backups of each new private key must be made. To reduce the need for frequent backups, a much larger number of key pairs could be created at the beginning. However, once the initial key pool is exhausted, a backup must be created for each additional key. In addition, a process that creates and stores a large number of key pairs is not efficient.

Deterministic wallets are an alternative (figure 4.4). These use a very large random number s, which serves as the seed for selecting all private keys. This method can be implemented in simple ways; for example, by employing a cryptographic hash function $H(i, s)$ that computes the hash value of the seed s concatenated with index i that then uses the hash value as the private key as shown below:

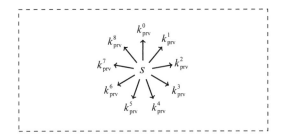

Figure 4.4
Structure of a simple deterministic wallet.

$$k^i_{\mathrm{prv}} = H(i, s).$$

The procedure allows an unlimited number of new private keys k^i_{prv} to be selected, which can all be restored by means of the initially backed up seed value. [149] It is important to emphasize that no key in this sequence (thanks to the hash function) permits any inferences to be made about the seed or any of the other keys. It is also important to mention that it is impossible to distinguish the pseudonyms that were derived from the seed from pseudonyms that were generated by a nondeterministic wallet.

Hierarchical deterministic (HD) wallets (figure 4.5) have all the advantages of simple deterministic wallets but extend their functional scope by a strict hierarchy of generated keys and pseudonyms, which opens up interesting applications. They are also based on an initial seed s from which a master key k^m_{prv} is generated. Later keys are derived in a tree structure. New branches can branch off from each key, which in turn lead to new subkeys. An extended key (key and chain code)[5] allows the derivation of all subkeys of the same type (private or public). Conversely, subkeys cannot be used to infer their predecessors.

The strict hierarchy has two major advantages. First, it is possible to share certain branches of the tree with other people. For example, a company could generate separate branches for each business unit. The headquarters holds the master key k^m_{prv} and thus remains in control of all pseudonyms. At the same time, the various business units can generate their own subkeys and thus work independently.

The principle of derivation applies to both the extended private key (*xprv*) and the extended public key (*xpub*). It can therefore be used to generate public subkeys from the extended public key. What is particularly interesting about this option is that additional

---

5. Not to be confused with the term chain code that describes smart contracts in some alternative Blockchain implementations.

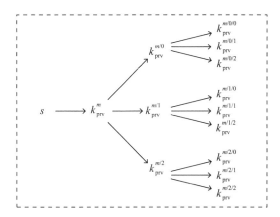

Figure 4.5
Structure of a hierarchical-deterministic wallet.

pseudonyms can be generated without the respective private keys. This means that a potentially unsecure device can be used to create pseudonyms for incoming payments without ever having to have access to a private key.

These extended public keys can also be used for accounting applications and auditing. They allow all transactions made with any of the pseudonyms of a branch to be tracked without having to transfer control of the Bitcoin balances to the observer.

The standard for HD wallets was stipulated by the two Bitcoin Improvement Proposals, BIP0032 [229] and BIP0044. [170] BIP0039 [171] specifies the standard regarding the simplified representation and intercompatibility of seeds (see box 4.3).

Box 4.3
Mnemonic Seeds

Seeds for hierarchical-deterministic wallets are long binary sequences and therefore hard to remember. In addition, there is a risk of transmission errors with handwritten backup copies. To counteract these problems, a combination of *mnemonic words* and a cryptographically secure key derivation function are used.

The key derivation function PBKDF2 (Password Based Key Derivation Function) enables the seed to be generated from a smaller binary sequence. It is usually sufficient to use 128 to 256 random bits for this.

Mnemonic seed (Greek mnēmonikós = possessing a good memory) re-encode the random binary sequence into several words and thereby simplify the user's management of his seed.[a] The standard BIP0039 [171] also allows seeds to be easily imported into and exported from different wallets and allows the simultaneous use of a deterministic wallet on several devices.

Box 4.3 (continued)

In principle, mnemonic words can be regarded as an encoding format with base 2,048; that is, there are 2,048 different "characters" for each position. Words from a predefined English dictionary are used to represent the characters. Each word replaces exactly 11 bits ($2^{11} = 2,048$). Depending on the bit-length of the random numbers, between twelve and twenty-four words are used. The format also includes a checksum that depends on the length of the random data and ensures that the binary sequence can be divided by eleven. The checksum consists of the first few bits of the SHA256 hash value and is appended after the random bits.

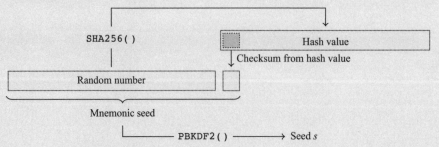

The following example shows a *mnemonic word sequence* of length 128 bits (checksum = 4 bits):

```
question panther horror middle faith skill
wheat style junk boost settle suffer.
```

_____
a. Or the data that are needed in order to derive the seeds.

4.1.6 Public Key Security Considerations

Because the private keys are numbers selected from a closed (although very large) set, all possible values are known. Every user can select one or several such numbers as his private key and then derive the corresponding pseudonym.

Theoretically, this might lead to a collision. If Edith and Tamara were to choose the same number and thereby the same private key, they would both have unrestricted access to a jointly owned pseudonym. A particularly disruptive scenario would be a situation where Edith managed her savings via a pseudonym and Tamara subsequently selected the same private key—Tamara would then be in the position to steal Edith's savings.

A second possibility of a collision is that Edith and Tamara choose different private keys, but their public keys have the same hash value and thus the same Bitcoin address.

This scenario would result in a single Bitcoin address being controlled by several private keys.

The theoretical existence of such collisions becomes apparent when one considers that the number of possible Bitcoin addresses (approximately 2^{160} possible values) is well below that of private keys (approximately 2^{256} possible values).

In the following we consider the probability of success of three possible attacks.

Attack 1: Finding a key for a specific address. Tamara discovers a Bitcoin address on the blockchain that holds a large number of Bitcoin units. In order to steal these Bitcoin units she must find the associated private key. Since the elliptic curve point multiplication method (which uses a private key to generate a public key) and the dual hash functions method (which use a public key to generate the Bitcoin address) are unidirectional functions, Tamara can find the private key only by means of a brute-force attack. There are 2^{160} candidates.

The probability of finding a private key to the given address in a single attempt corresponds to the ratio $\frac{1}{2^{160}}$. If we assume that Tamara owns a modern computer with a specialized graphics card and if we further assume that she would be able to generate sixty billion key/address pairs per second, then Tamara would need over seven octillion years (octillion = one with twenty-seven zeros in the decimal system) to find a corresponding private key with a 1 percent probability. The age of the universe is estimated at 13.82 billion years—about 506 quadrillion times less than the time Tamara would need to find a suitable key with a relatively low probability. One can therefore assume that this type of a brute-force attack is infeasible.

Attack 2: Finding a key for any address with a positive balance. Instead of targeting a specific address, Tamara could attempt to find a private key that would give her control over any Bitcoin address that has a positive Bitcoin balance.

To estimate the probability of such an attack being successful, we make an extreme assumption. We assume that twenty-one million Bitcoin units are divided into 2.1 quadrillion satoshi (smallest possible fractions of a Bitcoin) and that each satoshi has its own Bitcoin address. This results in 2.1 quadrillion potential target addresses.

The probability that Tamara would find an address with a satoshi balance in a single attempt is $\frac{2.1 \cdot 10^{15}}{2^{160}}$. Even under these assumptions, Tamara would need almost 3.7 trillion years to obtain control over one of these 2.1 quadrillion addresses with a 1 percent probability.

What we have not yet considered in our analysis is the fact that the computational resources can be used in mining. Even if Tamara were to get lucky and succeed in amassing the required computational resources, she would earn a reward of 1 satoshi or 0.00000001 Bitcoin. Alternatively, she could use the same computational resources for other much more profitable tasks, such as mining.

Attack 3: Bitcoin birthday. Finally, we consider the probability of an arbitrary address collision—that is, the probability of finding at least two private keys within the whole Bitcoin network that will provide access to the same Bitcoin address.

This question corresponds to a well-known problem in mathematics usually referred to as the birthday paradox. The paradox shows that in a group of fifty people there is a surprisingly high probability that at least two people will have birthdays on the same day. In fact, there is approximately a 97 percent probability that this will be the case. A similar surprise might also exist with Bitcoin addresses. So it is worthwhile analyzing the risk of a collision in the entire network.

An analysis[13] shows that if the total number of Bitcoin addresses equals $5.4 \cdot 10^{22}$, the probability of a collision occurring is still estimated to be only 0.01 percent. To arrive at a probability of 99.9999 percent, the minimum number of Bitcoin addresses would have to be $6.35 \cdot 10^{24}$. With this number of Bitcoin addresses, it would be necessary to have approximately 300 trillion terabytes (TB) of storage space to securely store the addresses and the corresponding private keys.

Assuming that every person on earth possessed an average desktop computer and would generate Bitcoin addresses nonstop, it would still take more than 300 years before the total world population would be able to exceed the critical number of generated keys. Moreover, approximately 50,000 TB of storage space would have to be available for each person.

In summary, a system based on keys and pseudonyms is cryptographically secure. It should, however, be mentioned that we have assumed that the private keys were randomly selected. Private keys that display a specific pattern or that correspond to the hash value of words or sentences which can be guessed through dictionary attacks are unsafe. It is therefore absolutely imperative that a private key is selected using a truly random process.

For this purpose, a cryptographically secure pseudo-random number generator (CSPRNG) is used. Some wallet implementations are also based on external random data, such as mouse cursor movements or keyboard strokes. If implemented correctly, these procedures are safe.

Alternatively, private keys can also be selected manually. Physical phenomena can lead to real random numbers and are therefore the safest method of creating private keys. Two examples of such a process are given in box 4.4.

Box 4.4

Creating Private Keys with Coins and Dice

A private key is nothing more than a number selected from an extremely large set of potential candidates. It is important that the selection is random.

A simple (albeit very time-consuming) option is the use of a coin. The coin c can be thrown 256 times, and the respective result can be recorded with ones and zeros.[a]

The private key is created as the binary sequence ($b = 2$) of the coin flips. Alternatively, the same private key can be written in decimal format ($b = 10$). This is achieved by multiplying the result of flip i with 2^{256-i} for $i = 1, \ldots, 256$ and subsequently sum up all the products.

$$k_{\text{prv}} = c_1 \frown c_2 \frown (\ldots) \frown c_{255} \frown c_{256},$$
$$_{b=2}$$

$$k_{\text{prv}} = \sum_{i=1}^{256} c_i \cdot 2^{256-i}.$$
$$_{b=10}$$

By rolling a dice d, private keys can be represented as a so-called heximal number. The heximal number system has base 6 and must not be confused with the hexadecimal system that has base 16. A person rolls the dice—the face with six dots is recorded as a zero—ninety-nine times and records the outcome (the number of dots) each time. A private key is then generated by concatenating the results of the throws. The number can then be converted from heximal to the decimal numeral system or any other representation for that matter.

$$k_{\text{prv}} = d_1 \frown d_2 \frown (\ldots) \frown d_{98} \frown d_{99},$$
$$_{b=6}$$

$$k_{\text{prv}} = \sum_{i=1}^{99} d_i \cdot 6^{99-i}.$$
$$_{b=10}$$

The two methods shown here have the great advantage of leading to truly random results and thus providing the highest possible security when creating private keys.

---

a. Some numbers that could theoretically be obtained by using the coin method are not possible, owing to the characteristics of the Elliptic Curve Digital Signature Algorithm (ECDSA) (see section 4.3.4). In particular, a zero must appear at least once among the first 128 coin flips so that the number falls within the specified range. Otherwise, the number will be too large and the process will have to be repeated. There is also a minimum value, which means that at least one one must appear among the 256 coin flips.

4.2   Hash Functions

Many parts of Bitcoin's functionality are based on hash functions. For example, the block identification number from section 2.4.3 is nothing more than the hash value of the block header. The Bitcoin address from section 4.1.3 is a hash value of the associated public key, and even individual transactions can be identified by their hash values. In this respect, a short digression to explain hash functions is indispensable.

Consider hash function H, which assigns a hash value h to an input m so that $H(m) = h$. The input is not subject to any form requirements and can be a character string of any length.[6] The hash value h, however, has a limited set of values and is displayed as a binary string of a certain length. The mapping is deterministic. A given input m will therefore always lead to the same hash value for a given hash function. Hash functions are not injective, so it is possible that different inputs may produce the same hash value. Such overlaps are called "collisions."[46,194]

A simple application of hash values are checksums. In the case of the International Bank Account Number (IBAN) in the traditional banking system, the first two characters after the country code, for instance, form a hash value that is computed on the basis of the rest of the account number.[118] If a person makes a typing error when entering the IBAN, this checksum usually no longer matches the account number entered. The entry can therefore be immediately identified as invalid, and the person is notified of the mistake before the payment order gets transmitted.

For the hash function to serve its purpose, it must have the following two properties:

1. When trying different inputs, all hash values should occur with the same probability.
2. Even small changes to the input should cause a change in the hash value.

A hash function with the described characteristics will only protect against accidental discrepancies such as typing mistakes. As soon as the areas of application are more complex and deliberate manipulation may lead to problems, it is crucial to use *cryptographic hash functions*. With these functions it is impossible to deliberately generate hash values with specific characteristics or induce collisions (collision resistance).

Cryptographic hash functions open up new applications. Two of these applications that are of particular importance for Bitcoin are explained below.

---

6. There is a technical limit. However, for any practical use, this limit is nonbinding.

4.2.1   Integrity Through Hash Values

Cryptographic hash functions can ensure the integrity of the original input. This protection works for texts of any length. For this purpose, the hash value of the input that needs to be protected is computed and stored. Since any adjustments to the original input inevitably lead to a different hash value, a modification of the original input will be recognized immediately. Due to the properties of the cryptographic hash functions, it will also not be possible for a person to deliberately generate a collision; that is, to find an alternative input, which results in the same hash value.

The hash value will react to the smallest change in a text. Even simply changing a single letter or punctuation mark will cause the hash value to be completely different. This can best be illustrated by using two examples of texts whose hash values were computed using the hash function SHA256.[7] It is striking how similar the example texts are, while their hash values are clearly very different.[8]

$m_1 = $ "The transactions A and C are valid."

$h_1 = $ 89ab2d7d31d072477c5416916cb9d358e8cd5451601ad909b7a183a136f50571

$m_2 = $ "The transactions A and B are valid."

$h_2 = $ 08914363734543c80e7983ca7c85e921effecc017688daa59813221d05a8e72d

4.2.2   Hash Values as Proof of Work

Since it is not possible to deliberately generate hash values with specific characteristics, cryptographic hash functions can also serve as proof that on average, a certain amount of computational resources were used to generate a hash value with predefined characteristics. For example, if someone has to present the inputs to a hash value that has a 0 at the first hexadecimal position, this person will have to invest some computational resources and try various inputs. On average only every sixteenth input will lead to a hash value that meets this criterion.[9] If the first two positions both have to assume the value 0, the probability drops to $(\frac{1}{16})^2$. By tightening or loosening this requirement, any level of difficulty can be achieved. To prevent hash values from being created in reserves and used as proof for multiple applications, the input usually contains an application specific part. To get the variation, the input also contains a variable part with arbitrary

---

7. The hash values each consist of 256 bits and are displayed here in a hexadecimal format.
8. Ken Shirriff published a video in his blog [202] in which he manually computes one round (of 64 rounds) of the hash function SHA256. It shows the different computation steps of SHA256.
9. Hexadecimal formats can assume sixteen different values for each position.

data that can be chosen freely. This source of variation allows different hash values to be computed from otherwise equal data.

Cryptographic hash functions form the foundation of Bitcoin's consensus protocol. In section 2.4.3 we have already used it to compute the blocks' identification numbers. A comprehensive discussion follows in section 5.2.2.

4.3 Signatures

We will now turn to signatures. We will show how the public and private keys are mathematically linked together and how private keys can be used to prove ownership of a particular pseudonym or as proof of the authenticity and integrity of a transaction message.[10]

Since we have to delve into the basics of cryptography, this section will inevitably be more complex and mathematical than the rest of the book. However, the focus continues to be on comprehensibility, which can at times conflict with mathematical precision. Hence, the mathematician may encounter deliberate simplifications in these discussions.

4.3.1 Applications of Asymmetric Cryptography

Classical applications of cryptography are based on symmetric encryption methods. Two parties want to encrypt their communication and agree on a secret key that can be used to encrypt and decrypt the messages. The same key can therefore be used for reciprocal communication.

Symmetric encryption methods have a crucial restriction. For two parties to agree on a key k without a third party being able to intercept this information and thus learn about the key, they must initially have a secure communication channel through which they can exchange the key.

Asymmetric encryption methods remove the need to use a secure communication channel. They enable an initial key exchange via channels that are potentially compromised and can be tapped. Instead of a common key k, each party creates its personal key pair consisting of a private key k_{prv} and a public key K_{pub}.

The public key can be disclosed. However, the private key must be kept strictly confidential at all times.

Key pairs have the mathematical property that the public key is derived from the associated private key but cannot itself be used to derive the private key (see figure 4.1). Another interesting characteristic of these key pairs is that the messages which are

---

10. Section 4.3 is based on the following cryptographic literature.[46,67,123,187,194]

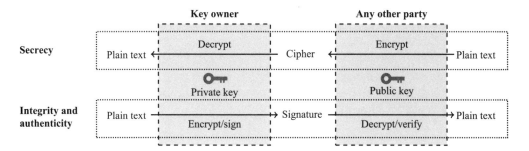

Figure 4.6
Two areas of application for asymmetric cryptography.

encrypted with one key can be decrypted with the other key. This feature facilitates two possible applications, as illustrated in figure 4.6.

Secrecy. Any party can use the public key of another party to encrypt a message. Since the associated private key is required for decryption, the owner of the key pair is the only party able to decrypt this message. For example, if a person's credit card information is encrypted with an online merchant's public key, then only that merchant can view the data.

Authenticity and integrity. If one party encrypts a message with its own private key, the information can be decrypted by any other party. Only the corresponding public key is required for this. This feature can be used to ensure the authenticity and integrity of a message. Decryption with a public key is only possible if the message has been encrypted with the corresponding private key and the encrypted text has not been changed. This feature guarantees that the message was indeed generated by the owner of the key pair (authenticity) and was not subsequently altered (integrity). This cryptographic principle is also known as a digital signature.

Bitcoin uses digital signatures to verify the authenticity and integrity of transaction messages.

4.3.2 The Foundations of Elliptic Curves

Bitcoin technology uses an asymmetric encryption that is based on elliptic curves. In contrast to other asymmetric encryption methods, signatures based on elliptic curves require significantly shorter key lengths to achieve a certain degree of security.[11] In addition, the encryption process itself is much more efficient.

---

11. Compare, for example, the cryptosystem RSA (Rivest–Shamir–Adleman).[182]

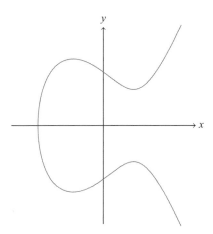

Figure 4.7
Elliptic curve.

Elliptic curves, in their general form, are defined by the Weierstrass equation and consist of all the points in the field that are solutions to this equation. In addition, there is a point in infinity zero that approximately assumes the role of zero (a neutral element) as shown below:

$$\{y^2 = x^3 + ax + b\} \cup \{0\}.$$

Depending on the parameterization, elliptic curves can assume extremely diverse forms.[12] If an elliptic curve is defined over the field of real numbers, $\mathbb{R}$, the plot will be reminiscent of a form that is traditionally associated with an elliptic curve. The curve in figure 4.7 was generated, for example, by the parameters $a = -2$ and $b = 2$. As we will show later, elliptic curves can also be defined by Galois fields (finite fields) over $\mathbb{F}_n$. Such curves play a crucial role because they are the basis of cryptographic applications.

The Addition of Two Points   To understand the cryptographic procedures based on elliptic curves, we first have to deal with some basic algebraic operations. We start with the addition on elliptic curves:

$$P_3 = P_1 + P_2.$$

The addition of two points P_1 and P_2 is accomplished geometrically with a straight line connecting the two points. The line will intersect the elliptic curve in exactly one

---

12. For the parameterization, the following restriction holds: $4a^3 + 27b^2 \neq 0$.

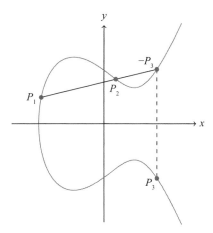

Figure 4.8
Geometric addition $P_1 + P_2 = P_3$.

additional point. This point corresponds to $-P_3$. By mirroring on the x-axis, we finally obtain the required point P_3 (the inverse of $-P_3$). The geometric addition is shown in figure 4.8.

The geometric representation provides a good intuition of the procedure. For the implementation, however, an algebraic method of adding two points is required. To do this, first compute the slope s of the straight line connecting P_1, P_2, and $-P_3$. This can be done by calculating the slope as the ratio of the change in the vertical axis (y-axis) to the change in the horizontal axis (x-axis).

$$s = \frac{y_{P_1} - y_{P_2}}{x_{P_1} - x_{P_2}}.$$

Given the slope, the x- and y-coordinates of P_3 can then be computed as follows:

$$x_{P_3} = s^2 - (x_{P_1} + x_{P_2}),$$

$$y_{-P_3} = y_{P_1} + s(x_{P_3} - x_{P_1}).$$

By transforming the equation, we obtain the y-value of the inverse P_3.

$$y_{P_3} = s(x_{P_1} - x_{P_3}) - y_{P_1}.$$

Precisely two exceptions exist, which oblige us to slightly adapt our description of the geometric addition:

1. A vertical line leads to the addition of point P and its inverse $-P$. Therefore, the third intercept is the point in infinity.

    $$P + (-P) = 0.$$

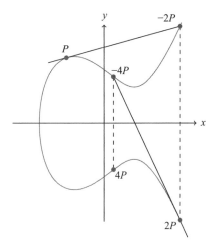

Figure 4.9
Point doubling.

2. The point of tangency P counts as two intercepts because it represents the addition of P with itself (see the section on Point Doubling).

    $P+P=2P.$

Point Doubling   Point doubling is a special case of addition. If one adds point P to itself, one obtains Point $2P$.

    $P+P=2P$

This relationship can be illustrated geometrically by the tangent of P. This tangent will intersect the elliptic curve at precisely one further point $-2P$, the inverse of which is the solution to the equation above. Figure 4.9 visualizes the geometric procedure.

    For the algebraic computation, we will once again need the slope s. Because the equation used so far is based on the horizontal and vertical differences between two points, its result in the present case will be zero. Therefore, we instead compute the slope using the first derivative of the tangential point P, where a corresponds to the parameter of the Weierstrass equation.

$$s = \frac{3x_P{}^2 + a}{2y_P}.$$

 The computation of the coordinates is achieved in the same way as for "normal" addition, with the difference in the specific case being that $P_1 = P_2 = P$. In this way, the two equations for calculating the coordinates of $2P$ can be simplified as follows:

$$x_{2P} = s^2 - (2 \cdot x_P),$$

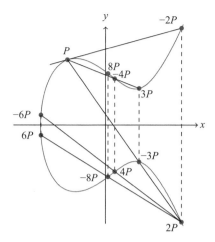

Figure 4.10
Point doubling and addition.

$$y_{2P} = s(x_P - x_{2P}) - y_P.$$

Addition and point doubling can be combined as desired. In fact, point doubling is only a special case of addition, which has to be handled somewhat differently algebraically but basically follows the same rules. For example, the following holds:

$$\underbrace{P + 3P}_{\text{Addition}} = 4P = \underbrace{2P + 2P}_{\text{Doubling}}.$$

Figure 4.10 shows the geometric relationships between the two methods of addition and point doubling.

4.3.3 Elliptic Curves over Finite Fields

Bitcoin uses the standard `secp256k1`, which defines the elliptic curve over a finite field $\mathbb{F}_p$, where p represents an unimaginably large prime number. The parameters $a = 0$ and $b = 7$ are used to describe the curve. The specification results in the following equation:

$$\{(x, y) \in \mathbb{F}_p \mid y^2 = x^3 + 7\} \cup \{0\}, \text{ with } p = 2^{256} - 2^{32} - 2^9 - 2^6 - 2^4 - 1,$$

where $(x, y) \in \mathbb{F}_p$ simply means that x and y can only assume the integer values between 0 and $p - 1$.

Because the number p that Bitcoin uses is far beyond human comprehension and cannot be represented graphically, we will discuss the basic principles by using an elliptic curve over the field $\mathbb{F}_{37}$. In our examples, we exclusively allow integer values between 0 and 36 for x and y.

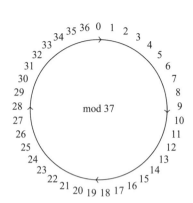

Figure 4.11
Modular arithmetic for the finite field mod $\mathbb{F}_{37}$.

The modular arithmetic for this is visualized using the turntable in figure 4.11. If an operation causes the result to exceed the maximum value of 36, then the count continues clockwise. A similar rule applies to negative numbers. If a value falls below zero, the turntable can be followed counterclockwise. In principle, every (positive) number mod 37 can be divided by 37, whole number quotients can be discarded, and the rest can be retained as the result.

To illustrate this, we include the following examples:

$$(5 + 13) \bmod 37 = 18,$$

$$(13 + 32) \bmod 37 = 8,$$

$$(3 - 7) \bmod 37 = 33,$$

$$(5 \cdot 8) \bmod 37 = 3.$$

The examples cover three of the four basic operations: addition, subtraction, and multiplication. Because division is merely the multiplication of the numerator A by the inverse of the denominator B—that is, $A \cdot B^{-1}$—a division requires to find the inverse of $B \bmod p$. This procedure, however, requires that the inverse of B exists.

The existence of the inverse of B is guaranteed if a prime number is selected for p; that is, if $\mathbb{F}_p$ represents a so-called field of prime numbers. Since the cryptographic application is dependent on the existence of inverses, prime numbers are the obvious choice for these applications.

To compute the inverse of a number B, the latter has to be multiplied by B^{-1} in the same field in order to result in the value 1.

$$(B \cdot B^{-1}) \bmod p = 1$$

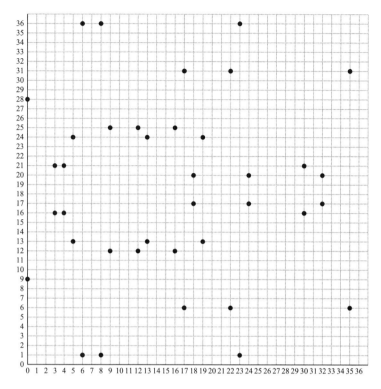

Figure 4.12
Elliptic curve $y^2 = x^3 + 7$ in $\mathbb{F}_{37}$.

The problem can be solved either by trying out various values for B^{-1} or by using the *Euclidean algorithm*.[127] For the simplified examples, a trial-and-error approach is sufficient.

The discrete prime field will inevitably have a considerable effect on the graphic representation of the elliptic curve. Instead of continuous curves, we obtain a collection of dispersed points. The elliptic curve in the finite field $\mathbb{F}_{37}$ in figure 4.12 contains precisely thirty-nine such points (thirty-eight points are visible in the figure plus the point in infinity). The number of points is also termed the order of the cyclic group. The curve in our example therefore has the cyclic order 39.

Now the question is how to transfer the addition and the point doubling from the real numbers $\mathbb{R}$ to finite prime fields. The answer is relatively simple: the calculation is analogous to the calculation for $\mathbb{R}$. To make this procedure more comprehensible, we will consider the following examples.

Example 1: Addition   Let $P_1 = (24, 17)$ and $P_2 = (35, 6)$ for $y^2 = x^3 + 7$ in $\mathbb{F}_{37}$. We want to find $P_3 = P_1 + P_2$.

The computation of slope s is performed using the same equation that is used for elliptic curves over the real numbers $\mathbb{R}$. The only difference is that the formation of the inverse values—essential for performing division—is slightly more complicated.

$$s = \left[\frac{y_{P_1} - y_{P_2}}{x_{P_1} - x_{P_2}}\right] \bmod p$$

$$= \left[(y_{P_1} - y_{P_2})(x_{P_1} - x_{P_2})^{-1}\right] \bmod p$$

$$= \left[(17 - 6)(24 - 35)^{-1}\right] \bmod 37$$

$$= \left[(11)(-11)^{-1}\right] \bmod 37$$

When computing the slope, we come to a point where we have to determine the inverse of -11. This corresponds to 10 because $[(-11) \cdot 10] \bmod 37 = 1$. We can now insert this value in the above equation. The resulting equation can then be directly solved for s. The value represents the slope of the straight line that connects the three points P_1, P_2 and P_3.

$$s = (11 \cdot 10) \bmod 37$$

$$= 36$$

The value $s = 36$ can subsequently be used to compute the coordinates of P_3. For this, we use an equation that we used earlier.

$$x_{P_3} = \left[s^2 - (x_{P_1} + x_{P_2})\right] \bmod p$$

$$= \left[(36)^2 - (24 + 35)\right] \bmod 37$$

$$= 1237 \bmod 37$$

$$= 16$$

By inserting the value of s into the equation and solving it, we obtain the result 1237, which in $\bmod 37$ corresponds to the value 16. The x-value of P_3 is then used to compute the corresponding y-value.

$$y_{P_3} = \left[s(x_{P_1} - x_{P_3}) - y_{P_1}\right] \bmod p$$

$$= [(36)(24 - 16) - 17] \bmod 37$$

$$= 271 \bmod 37$$

$$= 12$$

We have thus established that the new point P_3 has the coordinates $(16, 12)$.

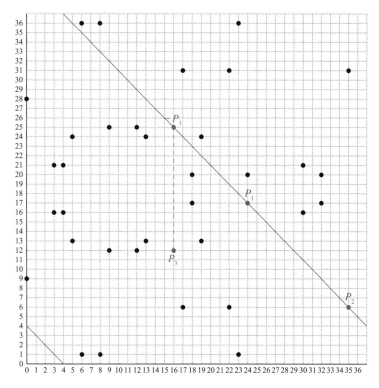

Figure 4.13
Graphic representation of the addition $P_1 + P_2 = P_3$ with $P_1 = (24, 17)$ and $P_2 = (35, 6)$ on $y^2 = x^3 + 7$ in $\mathbb{F}_{37}$.

In analogy to the algebraic solution, the result of the addition can also be presented geometrically (see figure 4.13). The diagonals are only used for illustrative purposes; as we are looking at a discrete space, straight lines (which equate to a continuous set of points) do not exist.

This also explains why the three points P_1, P_2, and $-P_3$ in figure 4.13 can be connected either by a line with the slope $s = 36$ or by a second line with the slope $s = -1$. Because $36 = -1 \mod 37$, the two slopes are equivalent in $\mathbb{F}_{37}$.[13] We decided to use the graphic representation of $s = -1$, as this slope value provides a clearer illustration.

Example 2: Addition   Let $P_1 = (30, 16)$ and $P_2 = (13, 13)$ for $y^2 = x^3 + 7$ in $\mathbb{F}_{37}$. We want to find $P_3 = P_1 + P_2$.

---

13. Both slopes lead to the same results for all values that are relevant to the finite field $\mathbb{F}_{37}$.

Once again, we first have to compute the slope s.

$$
\begin{aligned}
s &= \left[\frac{y_{P_1} - y_{P_2}}{x_{P_1} - x_{P_2}} \right] \bmod p \\
&= \left[(y_{P_1} - y_{P_2})(x_{P_1} - x_{P_2})^{-1} \right] \bmod p \\
&= \left[(16 - 13)(30 - 13)^{-1} \right] \bmod 37 \\
&= \left[(3)(17)^{-1} \right] \bmod 37
\end{aligned}
$$

In order to proceed, we have to subsequently form the inverse value of 17. This can be achieved by solving the equation $17 \cdot (17)^{-1} \bmod 37 = 1$. Because $[(17) \cdot 24] \bmod 37 = 1$, we obtain $(17)^{-1} = 24$. By inserting this value in the equation and solving it, we obtain the result 35.

$$
\begin{aligned}
s &= [(3)(24)] \bmod 37 \\
&= 72 \bmod 37 \\
&= 35
\end{aligned}
$$

The slope can be represented graphically with this example computation as well. Because $35 = -2 \bmod 37$, the line can be shown with the line $s = 35$ or $s = -2$. In figure 4.14, we have chosen the graphic representation using $s = -2$. Both of these values can be used to compute the two coordinates x_{P_3} and y_{P_3}. We will use $s = -2$.

$$
\begin{aligned}
x_{P_3} &= \left[s^2 - (x_{P_1} + x_{P_2}) \right] \bmod p \\
&= \left[(-2)^2 - (30 + 13) \right] \bmod 37 \\
&= -39 \bmod 37 \\
&= 35
\end{aligned}
$$

In analogy to the other computation, the x-value of P_3 is used to compute the corresponding y-value.

$$
\begin{aligned}
y_{P_3} &= \left[s(x_{P_1} - x_{P_3}) - y_{P_1} \right] \bmod p \\
&= [(-2)(30 - 35) - 16] \bmod 37 \\
&= -6 \bmod 37 \\
&= 31
\end{aligned}
$$

We thus obtain the coordinates $(35, 31)$ for P_3.

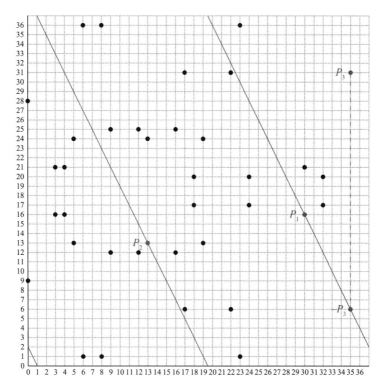

Figure 4.14

Graphic representation of the addition $P_1 + P_2 = P_3$ with $P_1 = (30, 16)$ and $P_2 = (13, 13)$ on $y^2 = x^3 + 7$ in $\mathbb{F}_{37}$.

Example 3: Point Doubling Let $P = (8, 1)$ on $y^2 = x^3 + 7$ in $\mathbb{F}_{37}$. We want to find $2P = P + P$.

Point doubling can also be used in the context of elliptic curves in finite prime fields.

$$
s = \left(\frac{3x_P^2 + a}{2y_P} \right) \bmod 37
$$
$$
= \left[(3x_P^2 + a)(2y_P)^{-1} \right] \bmod 37
$$
$$
= \left[(3 \cdot 8^2 + 0)(2 \cdot 1)^{-1} \right] \bmod 37
$$
$$
= \left[3(8^2)(2)^{-1} \right] \bmod 37
$$

The inverse of 2 is 19, since $(2 \cdot 19) \bmod 37 = 1$. By inserting this value in the equation and solving it, we obtain the value of the slope s.

$s = (3 \cdot 64 \cdot 19) \bmod 37$

$= 3648 \bmod 37$

$= 22$

To compute the two coordinates of $2P$, we can use the same equation as before, where $P_1 = P_2 = P$.

$x_{2P} = \left[s^2 - (2 \cdot x_P)\right] \bmod 37$

$= \left[22^2 - (2 \cdot 8)\right] \bmod 37$

$= 468 \bmod 37$

$= 24$

$y_{2P} = [s(x_P - x_{2P}) - y_P] \bmod 37$

$= s(8 - 2.24) - 1 \bmod 37$

$= -353 \bmod 37$

$= 17$

We thus obtain the coordinates $(24, 17)$ for $2P$.

4.3.4 Elliptic Curves, Cyclic Groups, and Signatures

In order to establish the *Elliptic Curve Digital Signature Algorithm* (ECDSA), we need a cyclic (sub)group, based on our elliptic curve. A cyclic subgroup is a group of points that originates from a base point G. It contains the elements $\{0, G, 2G, \ldots, (n-1)G\}$, where n is termed the order and represents the number of points in the subgroup. For factors larger than $n-1$, the cycle starts from the beginning; that is, $(n-1)G + G = nG = 0$.

An elliptic curve of the order N can produce subgroups of the order n, where n must necessarily be a factor of N. In this section, we will examine an example of a cyclic subgroup with $n = 13$.[14] Figure 4.15 visualizes this subgroup and the individual steps of the cycle.

Generating a Pair of Keys The cyclic subgroup constitutes the set of integers from which the key pairs can be drawn. To do this, we first generate a private key k_{prv} by choosing a random element from the set $\{1, \ldots, n-1\}$. Since the cyclic subgroup in our simplified example has the order $n = 13$, we need to choose a value between 1 and 12. Our example thus comprises only twelve possible values for the private key (see box 4.5).

---

14. Our elliptic curve has the order 39, and 13 is a factor of 39.

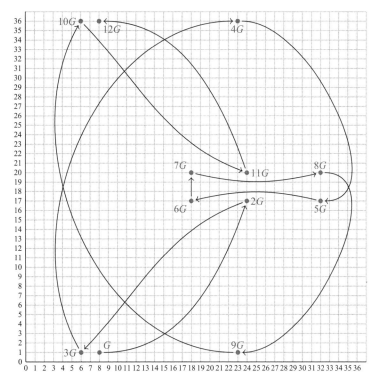

Figure 4.15

Cyclic subgroup of the order $n = 13$ generated by using the base point $G = (8, 1)$ on $y^2 = x^3 + 7$ in $\mathbb{F}_{37}$. The subgroup consists of 12 visible points and the point in infinity ($0G$). An arrowed line leads from $12G$ to the nonvisible point $0 = 0G$ that is connected with G by a further path. The two nonvisible connections close the cycle.

Box 4.5
Small Key Space

Obviously, such a small set of potential private keys is not safe. As we saw in section 4.1.6, the security principle of a system of keys and pseudonyms is based on an extremely large set of possible values. An attacker would have no problem in trying out the twelve possible values in our example. The present example is purely used to illustrate the basic principle.

The cyclic subgroup that is used with Bitcoin has the order 115,792,089,237,316,195, 423,570,985,008,687,907,852,837,564,279,074,904,382,605,163,141,518,161,494,337 and therefore has a large set of possible numbers (see section 4.1.6).

Let us suppose that our simplified Bitcoin model uses the cyclic subgroup from figure 4.15 (order $n = 13$) and that the private key is $k_{prv} = 9$. From this, we can use point doubling and addition to derive the public key K_{pub}. In order to do so, we take the base point $G = (8, 1)$ and multiply it with the private key $k_{prv} = 9$, which gives us the point $(23, 1)$. This point represents her public key.

$$K_{pub} = k_{prv} \circ G$$
$$= 9 \circ (8, 1)$$
$$= (23, 1)$$

Box 4.6
Compressed Public Keys

In section 4.1.2, we introduced compressed public keys $\overline{K}_{pub}$, which only require the x-coordinate of the point and an added prefix. When considering figure 4.15, it becomes evident why the x-value is not sufficient on its own; it contains no information regarding whether the public key corresponds to the point $(23, 1)$ or to the point $(23, 36)$.

The mentioned prefix gives information as to which of the two points with a given x-value should be used as the public key.

Thanks to the combination of point doubling and addition, the public key K_{pub} can be derived very quickly from the private key k_{prv}. One could first double the base point three times and then add an additional G to it. This procedure allows the computation of the public key in only four steps. The larger the private key is, the more time saving the *double and add* algorithm will be. In information technology we speak of an algorithm that runs in polynomial time.

For the inverse step, on the other hand, no such shortcut is known. If a person possesses only the public key K_{pub} and the base point of the curve G, he will be able to discover the private key by trial and error only. This phenomenon is known as the *elliptic curve discrete logarithm problem.*

Signing the Message   For a computer, messages are nothing other than numbers. Consequently, a message can contain any kind of text. In the context of Bitcoin, this will primarily be transaction messages. With her signature Tamara is able to prove that she is in possession of the private key belonging to the pseudonym and therefore may dispose of the Bitcoin balance.

In what follows we assume that the number $t = 4$ represents a transaction message with which Tamara transmits a Bitcoin unit to Edith. Just as with the key space, this also corresponds to a simplified example. Usually the numbers that represent the text are much larger.

The signature of the message is then created in five steps:

1. Tamara once again selects a random number i between 1 and $n-1$. This number will be used only a single time.[15]
2. Tamara computes the point $P = i \cdot G$.
3. Tamara computes the first part of the signature $r = x_P \bmod n$; that is, the x value of the computed point $\bmod n$.
4. Tamara computes the second part of the signature $s = [i^{-1}(t + r \cdot k_{\mathrm{prv}})] \bmod n$.
5. Tamara publishes the message t together with the public key K_{pub} and the signature (r, s).

In step 1, Tamara chooses the number $i = 7$. She can use this number in step 2 to compute the point $P = i \cdot G$. The computation steps follow the process detailed in section 4.3.3 and lead to the coordinates $(18, 20)$.

In step 3, Tamara computes the value r, which represents the first part of the signature. For this, she uses the x-coordinate of the point $P = (18, 20) \bmod 13$ and obtains the result $r = 5$.

$$r = x_P \bmod 13$$

$$= 18 \bmod 13$$

$$= 5$$

In step 4, Tamara computes the second part of the signature.

$$s = \left[i^{-1}(t + r \cdot k_{\mathrm{prv}})\right] \bmod n$$

$$= \left[7^{-1}(4 + 5 \cdot 9)\right] \bmod 13$$

To solve the equation, Tamara needs the multiplicative inverse of the number $i = 7$. Because $(2 \cdot 7) \bmod 13 = 1$, the inverse of $7 \bmod 13$ is 2.

By inserting the values above, she obtains the following equation:

$$s = [2(4 + 5 \cdot 9)] \bmod 13$$

$$= [2(49)] \bmod 13$$

---

15. If the same number is used in combination with the same private key more than once, it then becomes possible to derive the private key from the publicly available information.

$$= 98 \bmod 13$$

$$= 7$$

The signature of the message $t = 4$ is thus $(r, s) = (5, 7)$.

In step 5, Tamara can now send the signature $(r, s) = (5, 7)$, the message $t = 4$, and her public key $K_{pub} = (23, 1)$ to the other network nodes to prove the authenticity and integrity of the message.

Verifying the Signature of a Message   One of the network nodes receives Tamara's transaction message and now wishes to verify the signature. The verification process consists of four steps:

1. The receiver of the message computes $\left[u_1 = (s^{-1}t)\right] \bmod n$.
2. He computes $\left[u_2 = (s^{-1}r)\right] \bmod n$.
3. He computes the point $P = u_1 \circ G + u_2 \circ K_{pub}$.
4. He knows that the signature is valid if $r = x_p \bmod n$.

In steps 1 and 2, the message receiver needs the multiplicative inverse of $s = 7$. Since $(2 \cdot 7) \bmod 13 = 1$, the inverse of $7 \bmod 13$ corresponds to the value 2. For the first step, this value is inserted in the following equation.

$$u_1 = \left(s^{-1}t\right) \bmod n$$

$$= (2 \cdot 4) \bmod 13$$

$$= 8 \bmod 13$$

$$= 8$$

This results in $u_1 = 8$. For the second step, he again takes the computed inverse of 7 and multiplies it by $r = 5$, by which he obtains the result $u_2 = 10$.

$$u_2 = (s^{-1}r) \bmod n$$

$$= (2 \cdot 5) \bmod 13$$

$$= 10$$

In step 3, the message recipient inserts the two values for u_1 and u_2 in the following equation. He can then solve the resulting equation by means of point doubling and addition and thereby obtain the result $P = (18, 20)$.

$$P = u_1 \circ G + u_2 \circ K_{pub}$$

$$= 8 \circ (8, 1) + 10 \circ (23, 1)$$

$$= (32, 20) + (8, 36)$$

$$= (18, 20)$$

In step 4, the authenticity of the signature can be verified using the x-coordinate of P. Because $x_P \bmod 13 = r = 5$, the message recipient knows that the signature is valid and that the transaction message has been composed by a person who holds the private key and is thereby authorized to use the balance of the pseudonym $K_{pub} = (23, 1)$. Moreover, the message recipient can rule out that the transaction message has been modified during transmission because any alteration of the message would cause the value of t to change and thus make the accompanying signature invalid.

4.4 Transactions

In previous chapters, we have already discussed transactions and transaction messages without describing their precise structures. We will now provide a more detailed analysis.

Transactions are messages that are relayed over the Bitcoin network and usually assume the function of a payment order. They are the basis for every change that is made to the Bitcoin ledger and the only method possible for transferring Bitcoin units. If Edith wishes, for example, to transfer Bitcoin units to Daniel, she has to generate a payment order in the form of a transaction message, sign it cryptographically, and send it to other network participants.

When a network node receives the transaction message, the node will verify its legitimacy—that is, in most cases, verify Edith's cryptographic signature—and subsequently forward it to other nodes. The new recipients will themselves do the same so that in due time, the whole network will have learned of the transaction. The speed with which a transaction message spreads throughout the network depends primarily on the network topology (see section 3.1.3).

Owing to the continuous process of message forwarding, published transactions develop a certain momentum of their own and cannot be canceled under normal circumstances.[16] As soon as Edith has published her payment order, it will spread over the network and with a high probability be added to the Bitcoin blockchain as a confirmed transaction. In chapter 5, we will look at exactly how the Bitcoin blockchain functions and how transactions are recorded. First, however, we will focus exclusively on transaction messages and assume that transactions that are sufficiently widely propagated over the network will find their way into the Bitcoin blockchain.

---

16. Under certain circumstances, it is possible to initiate a competing transaction that references the same output. *Double spending* attempts of this kind are discussed in section 5.3.5

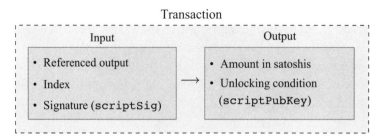

Figure 4.16
Components of a transaction.

Confirmed transactions form the basis of the Bitcoin blockchain. Instead of keeping track of account balances, all past transactions are recorded in the Bitcoin blockchain and are publicly visible. Consequently, refering to account balances of Bitcoin addresses is in fact a simplification. The Bitcoin system uses the so-called UTXO model, and this will be explained in the course of the next few sections.

4.4.1 Structure of a Transaction

For a transaction to be valid, it has to fulfill several criteria and be issued according to a standardized format. Figure 4.16 shows a transaction that includes the required components. In particular, transactions consist of at least one input and one output. An input assigns a certain quantity of Bitcoin units to the transaction. This quantity is distributed to any number of newly generated outputs. For each transaction, it is imperative that the sum of the Bitcoin units of all inputs at least equals the sum of all outputs.

Outputs also contain a specific unlocking condition[17] that determines the control rights over the balance and under what circumstances the Bitcoin units may be transferred again. Usually outputs are created in favor of a Bitcoin address. The address is derived from the corresponding public key so that the unlocking condition can be fulfilled using a signature of the underlying private key (see sections 4.1 and 4.3).

In principle, however, there is a certain flexibility in determining the unlocking condition. In section 4.5 we look at alternative conditions for spending the output and possible use cases. Regardless of the exact form, the aim of such conditions is always to restrict access and to ensure that only a predefined group of people have control over a specific output.

---

17. The unlocking condition is implemented using the locking script scriptPubKey (see section 4.5)

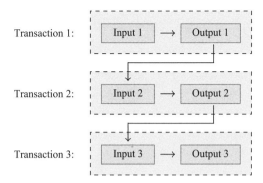

Figure 4.17
Transaction chain.

Each output can be used exactly once as an input for a new transaction. If a network node receives a transaction message that references an already used output as input, it will ignore the second transaction. In figure 4.17, only the output of transaction 3 has not yet been used as an input and is therefore available for new transactions. In this context, we also speak of unspent transaction outputs (UTXO)—that is, outputs that have not yet been used. The UTXO are stored as part of the Bitcoin blockchain and can be referenced in a new transaction at any time. For efficiency reasons, all unspent transaction outputs are also stored in the random access memory (RAM) of all full nodes.

Bitcoin units can exist only in this form. When we talk about Bitcoin units, we therefore refer to unspent transaction outputs.

Inputs reference the outputs of previous transactions. To do this, it is mandatory that the corresponding transaction contains a verifiable solution for the condition for spending the referenced output. If the unlocking condition is met, the Bitcoin units can be used by the new transaction. The transactional sequence of inputs and outputs creates a transaction chain similar to figure 4.17.

4.4.2   Types of Transactions
If an output (UTXO) is referenced in an input, it must always be used completely. It is not possible to reference partial outputs. This leads to the need for a variety of transaction types. There are transactions that combine several inputs into one large output or split a large input into several smaller outputs. Some outputs take on the role of "change" when, for example, someone has to reference a large output for a low value transaction.

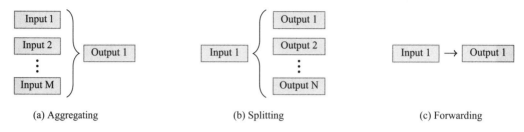

(a) Aggregating   (b) Splitting   (c) Forwarding

Figure 4.18
Various types of transactions.

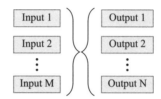

Figure 4.19
Combined (M to N) transaction.

A transaction must satisfy the minimum requirement of having one or more inputs and one or more outputs. This leads to the four types of transactions illustrated in figures 4.18 and 4.19.

Figure 4.18a shows the transaction type, which combines any number of inputs into a single output. This transaction type allows you to link multiple small amounts to a single unlocking condition.

Figure 4.18b visualizes a transaction in which a single input is divided into many outputs. This splitting transaction is the most common transaction form. If an input to be used exceeds the invoice amount, the initiator of the transaction will often choose a splitting transaction and generate a second output with the "change" in his favor. Ideally, he uses a new address for this purpose so that an observer cannot distinguish between the payment and the change (see section 4.1.4).

Figure 4.18c displays a so-called forwarding transaction. It takes a single input and generates a new output. The transaction is used for a change of ownership. Except for any transaction fees, the new output will hold the same Bitcoin value as the old one.

In addition to these three basic transaction types, a fourth type exists which is called a combined transaction. Transactions of this type have $M > 1$ inputs and $N > 1$ outputs and, therefore, are a mix of the splitting and aggregating transactions. Figure 4.19 illustrates a combined transaction. Since each output can be linked to a different unlocking condition, transactions with multiple outputs can transfer Bitcoin units to different recipients or add individual restrictions to the different outputs.

Regardless of the number of inputs and outputs, the sum of all inputs must be at least as large as the sum of all outputs. If the value of the outputs exceeds that of the inputs, the entire transaction becomes invalid.[18] However, if the sum of the inputs exceeds that of the outputs, a difference is automatically recorded as a transaction fee and is claimable by the miner, who includes the transaction in the blockchain. As explained later, transactions with higher fees are usually added faster to the Bitcoin blockchain. In this respect, an initiator of time-critical transactions may have an incentive to voluntarily set a relatively high transaction fee.

4.4.3 Traceability and Fungibility

As a result of the linking of transactions, as shown in figure 4.17, a clear transaction trail is created in which each output has a clearly differentiated and traceable origin. In our simplified example, it is evident that the output of transaction 3 resulted from transactions 1 and 2. However, even in the real Bitcoin blockchain it is still possible to trace back all transactions to their respective *coinbase transaction*.

The linking of transactions makes it possible to precisely identify and locate every transaction output. When Tamara propagates a transaction message, the transaction inputs refer back to previous transaction outputs and thus to a specific traceable origin. If the same transaction is received by a node more than once, it will be able to immediately recognize the duplicate transaction message and reject it. This also applies to transactions that reference the same output and would therefore compete with the first transaction. In contrast to systems with classic account balances, it becomes clear for each transaction whether the corresponding transaction output has already been used and whether the new transaction is therefore in conflict with a different transaction.

Bitcoin units differ in their transaction histories and are not fungible in a strict sense. Fungibility requires that any two units of a monetary instrument are indistinguishable. The traceability of Bitcoin transaction outputs is in most cases not important. In some cases, however, the traceability of transaction outputs may significantly impair the real value of the amounts involved.

For example, if information on the source of a transaction output exists, it may allow conclusions to be drawn about the identity of other persons who reference

---

18. The *coinbase transaction* that is used to create new Bitcoin units is an exception to this rule.

the corresponding transaction chain. This can undermine their pseudonymity, theoretically leading to a certain impairment of the corresponding transaction output.

Another problem concerns outputs that are proven to originate from questionable or even illegal sources. If, for instance, it is known that a certain output stems from a robbery or a hacker attack, the legitimacy of this output can be questioned. Differentiability allows the so-called *blacklisting* of transaction outputs. Blacklisting is a term used to describe the creation of lists that declare various transaction outputs invalid or no longer tradable (and thus valueless). Although blacklisting may seem sensible in certain cases, it leads to enormous transaction costs since every payment must be preceded by a consultation of the blacklist. The less fungible a medium of exchange is, the less suitable it is as a payment instrument. We would like to stress that blacklisting in a decentralized system cannot be accomplished easily. There is no single blacklist, nor is there a centralized party to maintain it. What we see instead is that some financial intermediaries use their own blacklist to decide whether or not they accept a specific Bitcoin unit. [71,148]

4.5   Script Conditions

The conditions under which a UTXO can be referenced are written and verified in Script. As the name suggests, Script is a scripting language that has a predefined list of commands: so-called *OP codes*. The language itself is very simple and has been deliberately restricted.[19] In particular, Script does not support loops, as these would potentially facilitate attack vectors. Nevertheless, the commands can be flexibly employed, permitting surprisingly complex unlocking conditions.

Script is a stack-based language. When a function is evaluated, it places the corresponding value on top of the stack. If a function requires arguments, these in turn are taken from the topmost positions of the stack (*cellar principle* or *last in, first out*). Only if all commands are executed without errors and the end result of the batch is 1 (TRUE) the transaction is considered valid. The success of the unlocking condition depends on two sub-scripts, the scriptPubKey (or locking script) and the scriptSig (or redeem script). Figure 4.20 shows the two scripts in the context of a transaction chain.

- scriptPubKey is the locking script of the output. It contains precise specifications about the referenced output's unlocking conditions and about the associated verification process. A script of this kind forms part of every transaction output.

---

19. Script is not Turing-complete.

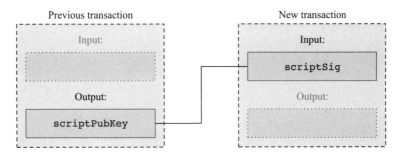

Figure 4.20
scriptPubKey and scriptSig in transactions.

- scriptSig is a component of the transaction input and can be seen as a solution (redeem script) to the referenced output's unlocking conditions. It consists of the signature and other possible components that are relevant to the solution.

In the following, we analyze the most important transactions, their scripts, and the stack.

4.5.1 Pay-to-Public Key

```
scriptSig: <sig>
scriptPubKey: <pubKey> OP_CHECKSIG
```

The pay-to-public key unlocking condition links the output directly to a public key so that only a signature through the associated private key can release the balance. This unlocking condition is considered outdated and has been largely replaced by pay-to-address.

The redeem script (scriptSig) includes only one signature (<sig>). The public key (<pubKey>) is part of the locking script (script PubKey). Only if the signature can be decrypted with the given public key can the output be successfully referenced as input in a new transaction. The signature is verified using the command OP_CHECKSIG, which is also an integral part of the unlocking condition.

The technical process and stacking procedure are illustrated in figure 4.21. In a first step, the public key of the unlocking condition (figure 4.21b) is added on top of the provided signature from figure 4.21a. Next, using OP_CHECKSIG, the two stack items are checked to ensure that they belong together and are then either accepted (1) or rejected (0).

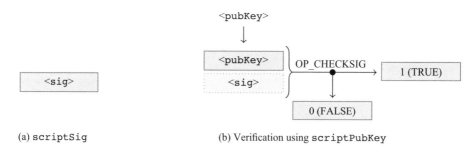

(a) `scriptSig`   (b) Verification using `scriptPubKey`

Figure 4.21
Stacking procedure for pay-to-public key.

4.5.2 Pay-to-Address / Pay-to-Public-Key-Hash

```
scriptSig: <sig> <pubKey>
scriptPubKey: OP_DUP OP_HASH160 <pubKeyHash> OP_EQUALVERIFY
OP_CHECKSIG
```

With pay-to-address, the output is linked to a Bitcoin address instead of the public key. The Bitcoin address is derived from the public key (see section 4.1.3). It offers a higher security against certain attacks. Should a vulnerability be discovered in the ECDSA, Bitcoin balances with pay-to-address unlocking conditions would still be protected as the public key is not disclosed until the transaction takes place and the conversion from public key to Bitcoin address is a one-way function.

The reference of an output with this unlocking condition is valid only if the `scriptSig` contains the corresponding public key (`<pubKey>`) as well as an appropriate signature (`<sig>`).

Figure 4.22 shows the redeem script and the locking script and how the stack changes with the script execution. First, the signature and the public key are placed on the stack as part of the `scriptSig`. The script then uses it for checking. The locking script `scriptPubKey` duplicates the public key using `OP_DUP` and converts the top item into the corresponding Bitcoin address using `OP_HASH160`. Then the Bitcoin address specified in the locking script is placed on top of the stack, and `OP_EQUALVERIFY` is used to check whether the Bitcoin address derived from the public key is actually the address specified by the unlocking condition. If the two addresses are equivalent, only the signature must be checked for validity. This step is equivalent to the procedure in figure 4.21b.

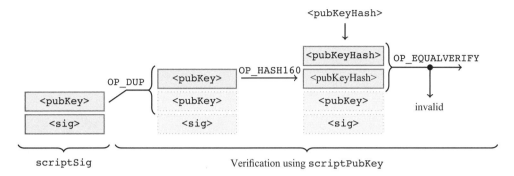

Figure 4.22
Stacking procedure for pay-to-address.

4.5.3 Multisig (M of N)

```
scriptSig: OP_0 <sig1> <sig2>
scriptPubKey: M <pubKey1>...<pubKeyN> N OP_CHECKMULTISIG
```

Multisig enables unlocking conditions that require *M*-of-*N* signatures to reference the corresponding transaction output. The `scriptPubKey` locking script contains *N* public keys. At least *M* of the associated private keys must provide a valid signature in the `scriptSig`. Only then can the output be referenced and used in a new transaction. The unlocking condition was defined in the Bitcoin Improvement Proposal BIP0011[6] and subsequently included in the standard protocol.

Multisig has numerous applications. On the one hand, it can be used to increase the security of an individual person's Bitcoin balance. For example, if a *2-of-3* script is generated, the owner can keep one key at his home, a second with a trusted person, and a third one in a bank deposit box. To fulfill the unlocking conditions and thus be able to use the Bitcoin units in this setup, it is necessary to have at least two of these three keys. This approach may protect the owner from theft and misuse as well as from loss of their private key through domestic fire or other unforeseeable events.

In addition to the advantages for an individual, multisig can be used to emulate certain restrictions regarding bank accounts; for example, the shared account (1 of 2 signatures) or corporate accounts where partners have only joint access to the assets (e.g., 2 of 2 signatures).

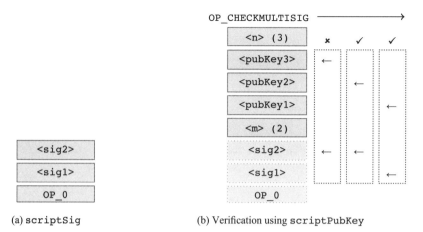

(a) `scriptSig`   (b) Verification using `scriptPubKey`

Figure 4.23
Stacking procedure with multisig (2 of 3 script).

The stack is illustrated in figure 4.23. The example shows a script that requires 2-of-3 signatures. Figure 4.23a shows `scriptSig` with the two necessary signatures and a dummy.[20] Figure 4.23b shows the locking and redeem scripts.

The command `OP_CHECKMULTISIG` draws N public keys and M signatures. It iteratively checks the different key and signature combinations and is successful only if all signatures are valid and can be assigned to another public key of the script.

The pairwise validation procedure is performed in the same way as the previously applied command `OP_CHECKSIG`. The validation starts with the public key and the signature that are on the top of the stack. After each validation step, the next public key in the script is used. If the validation of a pair fails, the same signature is then compared with the subsequent public key on the stack. If the validation attempt is successful, the procedure will then validate the next signature on the stack.

In our example in figure 4.23b, `<pubKey3>` and `<sig2>` are matched first. The validation fails because signature 2 cannot be verified with public key 3. In step 2, `<pubKey2>` and `<sig2>` are matched and successfully validated. Step 3 successfully matches `<pubKey1>` and `<sig1>`. With the minimum required number of M valid signatures, the unlocking condition is fulfilled and the reference for the transaction output is valid.

---

20. The dummy `OP_0` is needed as a placeholder because the command `OP_CHECKMULTISIG` takes away one element too many from the stack. `OP_0` has no relevance beyond this.[6]

4.5.4 Pay-to-Script-Hash (Flexible Scripts)

```
scriptSig: Any valid script
scriptPubKey: OP_HASH160 <scriptHash> OP_EQUALVERIFY
```

Pay-to-script-hash is a flexible unlocking condition. The locking script (`script-PubKey`) contains only the hash value of the unlocking condition. To reference the transaction output, a person has to provide a `scriptSig` with a script whose hash value corresponds exactly to the hash value stipulated in the `scriptPubKey`. If this first verification is successful, then the whole script is processed in a second step. The reference of the transaction output will be valid only when the provided script can be executed successfully.

The hash value[21] is used to ensure that the unlocking condition can be satisfied only by disclosing a previously defined script. The full script is revealed as part of the `scriptSig` and executed only if it corresponds to the hash value in the unlocking condition. As such, the script is not part of a pay-to-script-hash UTXO. This is important since UTXO are stored in every full node's RAM and may not be used for a long time. Adding large scripts to a UTXO would therefore place a significant burden on full nodes. A further advantage of the pay-to-script-hash is that it can be represented with a special type of Bitcoin address with the prefix 3.

Naturally, the pay-to-script-hash unlocking condition also has disadvantages. One risk is that Bitcoin units may be locked if someone uses an invalid locking script. Since the hash value does not allow any conclusions to be drawn about the script, it is possible to transfer Bitcoin units in favor of a script that is invalid and therefore cannot be fulfilled. Additionally, the owner must always keep the script. It is not part of the blockchain. The owner losing the locking script is similar to losing the private key. In other words, there is no way to validly reference the pay-to-script-hash transaction output without the corresponding script.[22]

In sum, it must be emphasized that pay-to-script-hash unlocking conditions offer a wide spectrum of interesting applications, particularly for more advanced users. However, these opportunities impose a greater degree of responsibility on the user and

---

21. The hash functions `SHA256` and `RIPEMD160` are used in succession, similar to the way in which Bitcoin addresses are generated.
22. Standardized scripts are an exception. An example of one of these proposals is found in `BIP0067`.[126]

substantially increase the risk of mistakes, which could result in the total loss of the user's Bitcoin holdings.

> **Box 4.7**
> **Multisig with Pay-to-Script-Hash**
>
> The flexibility of pay-to-script-hash enables alternative implementation of multisig transactions. In contrast to classic multisig condition for spending the output from section 4.5.3, pay-to-script-hash uses addresses that facilitate payments. Moreover, the `scriptPubKey` does not have to contain public keys for all the authorized parties and is therefore much more compact. The smaller data volumes also entail lower transaction fees.
>
> Pay-to-script-hash is the standard used today for *M-of-N* unlocking conditions and has widely replaced native multisig.

4.5.5 Null Data (`OP_RETURN`)

```
scriptSig: Non-existent.
scriptPubKey: OP_RETURN <0 to 40 bytes of data>
```

Null data unlocking conditions are not transactions in a strict sense of the term. They are used only to write data with a maximum length of 40 bytes (320 bits) into the Bitcoin blockchain. Just like other transactions, these data cannot be changed once they are embedded in the Bitcoin blockchain.

One possible application of this transaction type is to irreversibly record a *proof of existence*—a record proving that a certain data file existed at a certain point in time. For this, the hash value of the data is stored in the blockchain using a null data transaction. The stored data allow the author of the data to provide unequivocal evidence in the future that the data existed in precisely this form at the time the hash value was recorded in the blockchain. This is only one of a large range of applications. Also, many *colored coin* implementations employ the additional data for the purpose of defining the attached promise of payment.

Originally, data were stored in other ways; for example, via 1-of-3 multisig transactions where the data were entered instead of the two additional keys in `scriptPubKey` or via alleged Bitcoin addresses, which in reality corresponded to the data. These workarounds have resulted in non-referenceable transaction outputs that remained in the RAM of the full nodes and thus placed a heavy load on the Bitcoin network.

Table 4.2
The table shows the six signature hash types and describes what is signed for each one of them.

	All Inputs	Only Your Input
All outputs	SIGHASH_ALL	SIGHASH_ALL|SIGHASH_ANYONECANPAY
Single output	SIGHASH_SINGLE	SIGHASH_SINGLE|SIGHASH_ANYONECANPAY
No outputs	SIGHASH_NONE	SIGHASH_NONE|SIGHASH_ANYONECANPAY

As a countermeasure, the null data unlocking condition with the operation code OP_RETURN was created. The operation code indicates that a transaction output cannot be used as a new input and aborts the script. The transaction output is thereby visibly marked as being non-referenceable and therefore must not be retained in the full nodes' RAM but nevertheless is stored in the blockchain's permanent memory.

The heterogeneity of people's interests lead time and again to political debates about regulating the levels of permitted data volume. Thus, there have been calls to raise the limit of maximum data stored to 80 bytes and for some forks this value has been increased. [54]

4.6   Signature Hash Type

We have discussed ECDSA and various transaction scripts in great detail, but we have not yet discussed which parts of a transaction are signed. By default, signatures are applied to the entire transaction except the scriptSig (see transaction malleability in section 4.7.1). In some cases, this might be undesirable. A signer might only want to protect certain inputs and outputs of the transaction so that other people can modify selected parts of the transaction. To allow such an option, there are 3 base SIGHASH types plus a modifier that can be applied to any one of the base types. The name of the base type indicates how many of the outputs are signed. The ANYONECANPAY modifier changes how many of the inputs are signed. This leads to a total of six possibilities of how a transaction is signed. These possibilities are shown in table 4.2 and discussed below.

SIGHASH_ALL signs all inputs and all outputs. If any of the inputs or outputs are modified, the signature will become invalid. SIGHASH_ALL is the default value. If not explicitly stated otherwise, this signature hash type will be used.

SIGHASH_SINGLE signs all inputs and one output only. If any of the inputs or this particular output are modified, the signature will become invalid. Other people can, however, change any of the unsigned outputs.

`SIGHASH_NONE` signs all inputs but none of the outputs. Consequently, anyone can freely modify the unlocking conditions and choose to which address the Bitcoin units are assigned without invalidating the signature. Changes to any of the inputs make the signature invalid.[23]

`SIGHASH_ALL|SIGHASH_ANYONECANPAY` signs only the signer's inputs and all outputs. This signature hash type allows anyone to freely add or remove other inputs but prevents them from changing any of the outputs. As an example, think of a crowdfunding campaign where you are willing to contribute to a specific project as long as a minimum threshold amount is reached.

`SIGHASH_SINGLE|SIGHASH_ANYONECANPAY` signs only the signer's inputs and one output. Other people are free to add or remove additional inputs and outputs. Any change to the signer's part of the transaction will invalidate the signature.

`SIGHASH_NONE|SIGHASH_ANYONECANPAY` signs only the signer's inputs and no outputs. Anyone can add or remove other inputs and outputs and use the signed input in any way.

Transactions can contain multiple signatures that use different signature hash types. If this is the case, the most restrictive one is binding. Failing to comply with the restrictions will render the signature invalid and prevent the corresponding input from being spent.

4.7 Segregated Witness (SegWit)

Segregated Witness (or SegWit) is a network upgrade with the main intent to fix transaction malleability. Transaction malleability refers to a known issue in the original Bitcoin protocol that allowed people to slightly modify the `scriptSig` of an unconfirmed transaction and thereby change the transaction's hash value (transaction ID). Before SegWit, these changes to the transactions' hash values did not invalidate the transaction or alter its meaning.

Transaction malleability made it difficult to identify a transaction based on its transaction ID. For example, if a propagated but unconfirmed transaction is subsequently modified and the modified version included in the blockchain, the transaction is confirmed and indexed under a different transaction ID. If the sender is looking for the

---

23. This signature hash type is similar to a transaction fee, where a miner can freely change the outputs' unlocking conditions through the coinbase in order to claim the Bitcoin units.

original transaction ID, he cannot find it and may falsely assume that it is still pending or has failed to confirm.

Some early exchanges used transaction hash values to check if a withdrawal request has been processed. Accordingly, some customers of the exchange were able to mislead the exchange in issuing another transaction on their behalf. The corresponding losses are certainly the result of a somewhat naïve implementation on the part of the exchange. In particular, exchanges could have easily circumvented any trouble by not using the transaction's hash value as an identifier. However, a reliable transaction identifier is crucial for many second-layer scaling solutions like the Lightning Network (see section 6.2). For this reason, fixing the transaction malleability problem was an important factor for the success of Bitcoin.

The basic problem that leads to transaction malleability is that the `scriptSig` cannot be signed since the signature itself is part of it. Trying to sign the signature would create an infinite loop where the process of signing would change the underlying data and therefore lead to the requirement of a new signature. The `scriptSig` therefore has to be excluded when the transaction is signed. Yet, the `scriptSig` is part of the transaction data that is used to compute the transaction's hash value or transaction ID. Consequently, there are certain modifications that can be applied to the `scriptSig` and thereby change the transaction ID without invalidating the signature.

To address the malleability problem, SegWit *segregates* the redeem script from the transaction's `scriptSig` and moves it into a separate data field called *witness*. The empty `scriptSig` field is still relevant for the computation of the transaction's hash value but does not allow for variation since it has to be empty. Any potential changes to the witness field have no effect on the transaction's hash value, making the transaction identifier unambiguous.

As an additional side benefit, SegWit increases the number of transactions that can be included in a one megabyte (MB) block (see section 4.7.5). [68] Of course, the witness data still has to be propagated through the network and stored for nodes to be able to verify the legitimacy of the transaction, so it is very similar to a block-size increase in terms of the actual data that has to be stored. The crucial difference is that it allowed something that is essentially a block-size increase to be implemented through a soft fork (see section 4.7.2). SegWit was activated on July 21, 2017. [146]

4.7.1 Malleability Sources
There are several ways in which the input script can be modified and therefore several sources for transaction malleability.

Signature-Based Malleability Sources   The first signature-based malleability source is the result of an encoding ambiguity. In particular, the software library OpenSSL allows values for r and s to be encoded in a variety of ways without invalidating the signature. Depending on encoding, the transaction may assume various transaction IDs.

Another signature-based malleability source can be found in ECDSA signatures themselves. Using the negative of the number s (modulo the curve order) does not invalidate the signature. This can be best shown using our example from section 4.3.4 under "Signing the Message."

Let us assume that the attacker changes the value for s from 7 to -7. Since $(11 \cdot -7) \bmod 13 = 1$, the inverse of 7 mod 13 corresponds to the value 11. For the first step, this value is inserted in the following equation.

$$u_1 = (-s^{-1}t) \bmod n$$

$$= (11 \cdot 4) \bmod 13$$

$$= 5$$

This results in $u_1 = 5$. For the second step, he again takes the computed inverse of -7 and multiplies it by $r = 5$, by which he obtains the result $u_2 = 3$.

$$u_2 = (-s^{-1}r) \bmod n$$

$$= (11 \cdot 5) \bmod 13$$

$$= 3$$

In the third step, the message recipient inserts the two values for u_1 and u_2 in the following equation. He can then solve the resulting equation by means of point doubling and addition and thereby obtain the result $P = (18, 17)$.

$$P = u_1 \circ G + u_2 \circ K_{\text{pub}}$$

$$= 5 \circ (8, 1) + 3 \circ (23, 1)$$

$$= (32, 17) + (8, 1)$$

$$= (18, 17)$$

As shown previously, we use the x-coordinate of $P \bmod 13$ and compare the result to r. Since $18 \bmod 13 = 5 = r$ holds true, the signature is valid despite our modification to s. As a result, the transaction is still valid but will have a new transaction ID.

Please note that both of the signature-related issues have been mostly mitigated with the strict Distinguished Encoding Rules (DER) encoding requirements proposed in BIP0066.[231]

Operation Code–Based Malleability Sources Operation code–based malleability sources cannot be easily resolved. In particular, even after the `BIP0066` related changes, it still has been possible to modify the `scriptSig` without affecting the transaction. One common example is the addition of the `DATAPUSH` operator followed by a `DROP` operator. This modification affects neither the stack state nor the execution of the `scriptPubKey` since the addition is immediately discarded. Yet, when computing the hash value, the change leads to an entirely different transaction ID. SegWit resolves this issue by moving the actual script into a data structure that does not influence the transaction ID.

4.7.2 Soft Fork Implementation

SegWit has been implemented through a soft fork (see section 2.5.3). This means that nodes that missed or decided against the network upgrade are still able to process transactions with SegWit outputs. To them, these outputs look as if they could be spent by anyone. Consequently, old nodes will accept the transaction despite the missing signature. New nodes interpret the empty input script differently. In particular, they look for the witness data and expect to find a valid signature there. They will accept the transaction only if valid witness data are provided.

Considering the above-mentioned implementation, it should become clear why the SegWit network upgrade is a soft fork. As long as the majority of computing resources is allocated to the new consensus rules, there will be only one version of the chain. This version is accepted by old and new nodes. If, however, the majority of computing resources is allocated to non-SegWit nodes (old consensus rules), we would end up in a situation with two competing blockchain versions. The longest chain (old version) would allow anyone to spend the SegWit outputs without the need for a valid signature. New version nodes would look for the witness data and potentially reject blocks created by the old nodes. They would therefore not accept the longest version of the blockchain as it is not in accordance with their consensus rules.

Accordingly, it has been of the utmost importance to ensure that the vast majority of miners accept these changes before activating them. Only after it became clear that most miners supported SegWit were the changes activated. While this design choice certainly has its drawbacks, it outweighs the potential disadvantages of a hard fork. The soft fork implementation mitigated the risk of splitting the network and ensured that the existing infrastructure could still be used.

4.7.3 SegWit Transaction Types

Transactions look slightly different with SegWit. In this section, we discuss two transaction types that are similar to the pay-to-public-key-hash and the pay-to-script-hash transactions discussed in section 4.5. Moreover, we will look at how these transactions can be embedded in pay-to-script-hash transactions for compatibility reasons.

Pay-to-Witness-Public-Key-Hash

```
scriptSig:
scriptPubKey: 0 <pubKeyHash>
witness: <sig> <pubKey>
```

Pay-to-witness-public-key-hash (P2WPKH) is the SegWit equivalent to pay-to-public-key-hash. Despite the similarities, the locking script (`scriptPubKey`) of the SegWit version is much simpler. It only consists of two values: a version number (usually zero) followed by the 160-bit hash of the compressed public key. Interpreted by a non-SegWit node, the output can be spent without the need for a signature because the `scriptSig` field is empty. In contrast, new clients will interpret the locking script as "look for and verify the signature in the witness data." For this reason, the new witness field includes the same information as in the `scriptSig` field of a corresponding pay-to-public-key-hash transaction.

Pay-to-Witness-Script-Hash

```
scriptSig:
scriptPubKey: 0 <scriptHash256>
witness: Any valid script
```

Pay-to-witness-script-hash (P2WSH) is the SegWit equivalent to pay-to-script-hash. The simplified locking script of the SegWit version contains the version number (usually zero) followed by the 256-bit hash of the script.[24] The interpretation is similar to pay-to-script-hash (P2SH); however, the script has to be provided in the witness field.

P2SH Embedded SegWit Transactions   To use P2WPKH and P2WSH, both the sender and the receiver need wallets that recognize native SegWit transactions. Considering

---

24. The differences in bit-length are a deliberate choice to distinguish between P2WPKH and P2WSH. While P2WPKH uses SHA256 followed by RIPEMD160, P2WSH only employs SHA256.

that SegWit has been implemented through a soft fork, we cannot presume that all clients use the SegWit consensus rules. Fortunately, there is a trick that allows clients who are unaware of SegWit to issue (P2SH-embedded) SegWit transactions.

Let us assume that Emanuel runs an upgraded wallet with SegWit support. Tamara on the other hand is unaware of SegWit and uses a non-SegWit wallet. Let us further assume that Emanuel is selling a book to Tamara and wants to receive the payment in the form of a SegWit-compatible output. Obviously, Tamara cannot create P2WPKH or P2WSH outputs as the creation of these outputs would require her wallet to support SegWit. Instead, Emanuel can create a P2SH Bitcoin address by embedding the hash of the SegWit script in the P2SH locking condition:

```
OP_HASH160 <scriptHash> OP_EQUALVERIFY
```

In the case of P2SH(P2WPKH), the `<scriptHash>` corresponds to the 160-bit hash value of the P2WPKH locking script:

```
<scriptHash> = 0 <pubKeyHash>
```

The compressed public key used throughout this chapter as an example leads to the following P2SH(P2WPKH) address: 3MZBEmWc3xLrEmkw2WqcqDN1CM2heYfuzr.

In the case of P2SH(P2WSH), the `<scriptHash>` corresponds to the 160-bit hash value of the P2WSH locking script:

```
<scriptHash> = 0 <scriptHash256>
```

Both create regular P2SH Bitcoin addresses that start with a 3, as described in section 4.5.4. Tamara can then use this address to send Bitcoin units to Emanuel, even if she is completely unaware of SegWit.

4.7.4   Native SegWit Address (Bech32)

Bech32 is the native SegWit address format that has been proposed and specified in BIP0173.[232] These addresses can be used as an alternative to the standard Bitcoin address format. Bech32 addresses are easily recognizable, as they always start with bc1.

The new address format is needed to encode native SegWit outputs in an efficient and secure way. Recall that this is not possible with P2SH addresses. Moreover, Bech32 introduces case insensitivity, making addresses more readable and less prone to typos while only being 17 percent larger than Base58. Additionally, base 32 values are less expensive to convert, may use more compact QR codes, and provide stronger checksums.[233] In particular, the Bose–Chaudhuri–Hocquenghem (BCH) checksum implementation guarantees to detect any error in which at most four characters have been changed. If more characters are involved in the mixup, the error will still be detected with a very high probability.[232]

The first two characters bc indicate that the following data is a Bitcoin address.[25] The number 1 separates the human readable part from the data part. The data part consists of a version number (q, which represents zero in the Bech32 character set), the witness script, and a six-character checksum. The data part may use any alphanumeric value excluding "1", "b", "i" and "o".

Bech32 addresses have length 42 when used for P2WPKH and 62 for P2WSH respectively. The addresses below are based on the compressed public key used as an example throughout this chapter (P2WPKH) and an example script from the original proposal (P2WSH).

$\bar{BC}_{pkh}=$ bc1qryqazre3l42dvj8jrg8ed9s6t56aql6puy8wk8

$BC_{sh}=$ bc1qrp33g0q5c5txsp9arysrx4k6zdkfs4nce4xj0gdcccefvpysxf3qccfmv3

4.7.5 Confirmation Capacity Increase

SegWit increases the number of transactions that can be included in a block by moving a large part of the transaction data from the scriptSig to the witness field. Old clients are unaware of the witness field and do not count this data toward the block size limit of 1 MB. New clients, however, introduce a new metric, the so-called block weight W. The block weight limit is 4 MB; that is, only blocks with $W \leq 4$ are accepted by the new consensus rules.

Block weight W is computed using the following equation, where $bs(\mathtt{all\text{-}wit})$ is the bytesum of all transactions in this block excluding the witness field and $bs(\mathtt{all})$ is the bytesum of the same transactions including the witness field.

$$W := 3 \cdot bs(\mathtt{all\text{-}wit}) + bs(\mathtt{all}).$$

Now let $\beta \in (0,1)$ denote the fraction of the data that is stored in the witness field. This allows us to rewrite the equation as follows.

$$W = 3 \cdot (1 - \beta) \cdot bs(\mathtt{all}) + bs(\mathtt{all})$$
$$= bs(\mathtt{all}) \cdot [3 \cdot (1 - \beta) + 1]$$

The block weight limit $W \leq 4$ implies that

$$bs(\mathtt{all}) \leq \frac{4}{3 \cdot (1 - \beta) + 1}.$$

---

25. For testnet addresses, this part is changed to tb.

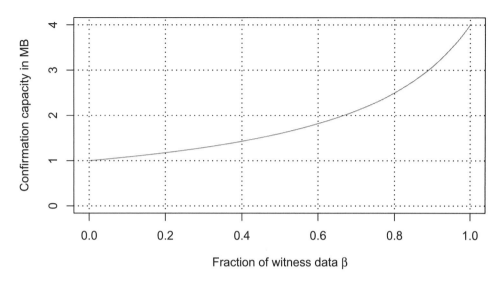

Figure 4.24
Confirmation capacity C in MB as a function of weight limit $W = 4$ MB and the fraction of witness data.

The term $C := \frac{4}{3 \cdot (1-\beta)+1}$ is the confirmation capacity. It is the maximum quantity of transaction data that can be included in a block. It depends on the fraction of witness data β and the weight limit 4 MB. Obviously, an increase in the weight limit or an increase of β increases C. In particular, there are the following three situations:

No SegWit transactions ($\beta = 0$) : When there is no witness data, we get $bs(\texttt{all}) = 1$. In this case, $bs(\texttt{all})$ has the exact same size as $bs(\texttt{all-wit})$ and the old 1 MB block size limit.

Only SegWit transactions ($\beta = 1$) : This is a theoretical case, as there will always be some non-witness data (e.g., coinbase transaction). However, in theory, β could get really close to one which would imply that $bs(\texttt{all})$ approaches four. In this case, the block size is well below 1 MB, despite the almost 4 MB confirmation capacity.

Some SegWit transactions ($\beta \in (0, 1)$) : In this case the confirmation capacity is in between 1 MB and 4 MB. Figure 4.24 shows the confirmation capacity as a function of β.

As shown in figure 4.24, the capacity C increases with the proportion of SegWit transactions in the block. In fact, the increase is nonlinear. For low values of β, an increase in β allows for only a few additional transactions since the derivative of C with respect to β is less than 1 at $\beta = 0$. In contrast, for high values of β, an increase in β allows many additional transactions since the derivative is larger than one at $\beta = 1$.

Overall, it is in the best interest of the network to switch to SegWit transactions. The same is true for individuals who pay transaction fees in proportion to the bytesum—the transaction contributes toward the block size limit. As such, there are strong incentives, which should encourage the network toward SegWit-only blocks in the long run.

4.8 Exercises

Exercise 4.1: Explain why the Bitcoin system uses pseudonyms and name the most common forms of pseudonyms.

Exercise 4.2: Explain why a person is not able to derive a private key from a given pseudonym.

Exercise 4.3: Name at least three common formats that are used to encode private keys.

Exercise 4.4: What are the risks if a user repeatedly employs the same pseudonym?

Exercise 4.5: Explain the procedure used to deterministically derive multiple private keys from a single random seed.

Exercise 4.6: Use the signature from the solution of the previous problem and show how the signature can still be verified if you change s to $-s$.

Exercise 4.7: Outline three examples of transactions and identify what type of transaction they are with regard to the number of inputs and outputs that they have.

Exercise 4.8: Describe an example of each of the following unlocking conditions and identify the corresponding `scriptPubKey` and `scriptSig`.

  a) Pay-to-public-key
  b) Pay-to-public-key-hash
  c) Multisig
  d) Pay-to-script-hash
  e) Null data
  f) Pay-to-witness-public-key-hash
  g) Pay-to-witness-script-hash

5   Transactional Consensus

In this chapter, we explain how transactions find their way into the Bitcoin blockchain and show how the network is able to reach consensus on the current state of the ledger. We study the data structure of blocks, discuss how these blocks are linked together, and analyze the basics of Bitcoin mining, the underlying game theory, and the proof-of-work consensus mechanism.

5.1   Blocks and the Blockchain

In the previous chapters, we have explained how network participants generate and relay transaction messages, and we have shown how they can verify the authenticity and integrity of other participants' transaction messages. Each full node maintains its own set of verified transactions (the so-called mempools) that have not yet been confirmed, waiting for inclusion into the Bitcoin blockchain. These mempools are likely to differ. The Bitcoin system must therefore provide a procedure that allows the network to agree on which transactions should be included in the Bitcoin blockchain.

5.1.1   The Bitcoin Blockchain

The Bitcoin blockchain is the public ledger of the Bitcoin system that contains all the transactions that have been processed since the genesis block. It is a continuously expanding database, which allows users to query the allocation of Bitcoin units for any point in time. To obtain relevant information from it, all the data have to be parsed—that is, suitably formatted.

At the end of 2019, the Bitcoin blockchain held a data volume of approximately 205 GB. Figure 5.1 shows the development of the data volume over time. This growth and the fact that the Bitcoin blockchain has to be stored and processed by every full

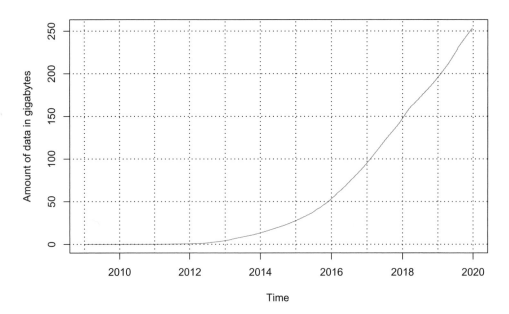

Figure 5.1
Growth of the blockchain.
Source: Data from Blockchain Explorer, n.d., https://www.blockchain.com/explorer.

node in the system raises concerns about the scalability of the Bitcoin system. We will deal with some of these issues in section 6.2.

Every network participant can download a copy of the Bitcoin blockchain and independently verify every transaction. It is also possible to modify the downloaded copy. Owing to the consensus protocol (see section 5.2.2), a modified copy of the blockchain will be accepted by the other network participants only if it fulfills a well-defined set of rules. If a node does not comply with these rules, then the locally held copy of the Bitcoin blockchain will be ignored by everyone else.

5.1.2 Components of a Block

The Bitcoin blockchain is composed of so-called blocks. Each block contains at least one transaction. Figure 5.2 shows an example of a block and lists its contents. Every block must include these contents and be formatted in the correct way. In addition to the transaction data, a block must include a so-called *block header*, which consists of 640 bits (80 bytes) of descriptive data that allow the block to be identified and located within the blockchain. We discuss the individual components of the block header in depth below.

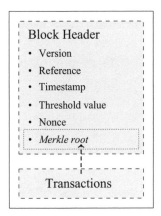

Figure 5.2
Structure and components of a block.

Version. The version field identifies the version of the protocol that was used to generate the block. It is a 32-bit number that provides information about the underlying set of rules operating when the block was generated and thus references the rules that must be applied to validate the respective block. The version input is essential for the modifiability of the rules. If all the blocks in the blockchain had to be validated using the same rules, it would not be possible to change any rules, even if the whole network agreed that it was necessary to do so.

Reference. The reference field links the block to a previous block, usually referred to as *parent block*.

Timestamp. The timestamp field contains information relating to the time at which the block was generated. The timestamp must lie within a time interval. The lower bound is the median value of the timestamps of the previous eleven blocks, and the upper bound is two hours after the time at which the block was accepted into the blockchain.

Threshold value. The threshold value field contains the maximum value that a block's hash value can have for it to be considered valid by the network. The threshold value plays an important role in the consensus protocol and is discussed in section 5.2.3.

Nonce. The *nonce* field allows for the inclusion of arbitrary data. Modifying the nonce field ensures that blocks with otherwise equivalent contents may nevertheless have

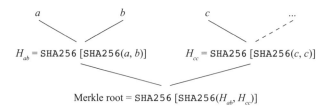

Figure 5.3
Hash tree with the three transactions *a*, *b*, and *c*.

different hash values. This entry plays a crucial role for the consensus protocol, and we will therefore return to it in section 5.2.2.

Merkle Root. The *merkle root* field contains the root of the merkle tree that is constructed from all transactions included in the block. The transactions themselves are not incorporated in the block header. The merkle root's purpose is to guarantee the integrity of the transactions included in the block.

In a *merkle tree* the transactions are arranged in pairs and the hash values of each pair are calculated.[1] The hash values of the pairs are continuously arranged into new pairs until only one hash value remains. This value is the merkle root; in other words, the cryptographically secure root of the merkle tree. If only a single transaction in the tree is altered, the merkle root will assume a totally different value.

Any modification to the transactions will have the effect that the original merkle root is no longer consistent with the modified transactions. The original block will thereby become invalid. The merkle root is the link between the block header and the transactions in the block and guarantees that the transactions cannot be altered without the changes being noticed.

Figure 5.3 presents an illustration of a small merkle tree that includes only three transactions: *a*, *b*, and *c*. Whenever a merkle tree has an odd number of elements, the last element is duplicated and the hash value of the two identical elements computed. In our example, we see that this procedure is applied to the value *c*.

The advantage of the merkle tree is that it allows efficient verification of specific transactions. With N transactions, a maximum of $2\log_2(N)$ computational steps are needed to verify whether a transaction is an element of the merkle tree and, therefore, an element of the respective block.

---

1. The double hash function SHA256d is used here as well.

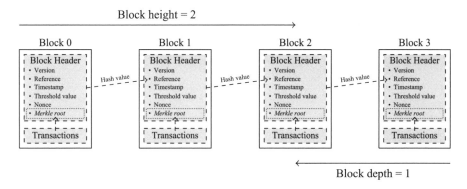

Figure 5.4
Example of a blockchain.

5.1.3 Chain Structure

A block references precisely one parent block.[2] These references generate a sequence of blocks that is analogous to a chain, from which it derives its name, blockchain.

Every valid block has a specific position within this chain, which is defined by two terms: *block height* and *block depth*. The term block height identifies the position of a given block within the chain, where the first block (the so-called genesis block) is assigned the number zero. The term block depth refers to a block's distance from the most recent block. For this reason, a block's block depth increases with each block that is added to the Bitcoin blockchain. The block depth is important for security analyses. Moreover, it also offers SPV nodes a heuristic for evaluating the validity of transactions (see section 3.2.2).

Figure 5.4 shows an example of such a chain and the respective terms used to identify a block's position within the blockchain. In this example, the third block from the left has the block height 2. As this block has only one successor block, it currently has a block depth of 1.

A third possibility for identifying a block is the block's identification number; that is, the block header's hash value. To calculate it, the block header is fed into the SHA256d hash function where the individual bits are deterministically rearranged and modified by means of a process involving sixty-four rounds of various nonlinear processes. The resulting hash value is then fed into the hash function for a second run of another

---

2. The first block (genesis block) forms an exception. It is the first element in the Bitcoin blockchain and therefore has no parent block.

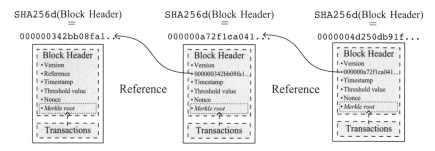

Figure 5.5
References based on the hash values of the antecedent block header form a chain structure.

sixty-four rounds. The hash function's resistance against collisions (see section 4.2) ensures that no two blocks in the chain have the same identification number.

SHA256 hash values have a length of 256 bits. For the sake of simplicity, these values are most often formatted as a sixty-four-digit hexadecimal number. An example of such a hash value is `000000342bb08fa10ea042f4a6ce3b140c390f997816b7f353ddd80` `6ac5db1ec`. This hash value corresponds to the identification number of the first block in the example of the chain presented in figure 5.5.

Let us now have a look at the chain structure. Every new block references the last block in the chain as its predecessor (so-called parent block). To link a block to its parent block, the reference field in the block header of a block includes the hash value of its parent block. Figure 5.5 presents two examples. The second block in the chain references the first block's hash value. The third block of the chain references the second block's hash value.

Since the reference field is part of the block header, it affects the hash value of the respective block. Consequently, if someone modifies the reference filed or any of the other inputs of a block, the hash value of the block will change.[3]

In figure 5.6 a transaction was added to block 1. This addition changed the block's merkle root and, thereby, the hash value of the block header. The new value is `ae2` `1f25523ae1d4e3864583d2b99d27bfc4cf00dbf6281951aff01fe809e9534`. The second block's reference field still contains the old value `000000342bb08fa10ea04` `2f4a6ce3b140c390f997816b7f353ddd806ac5db1ec`. Since the new hash value of block 1 is not referenced in block 2's reference field, the link between the two blocks is broken.

---

3. In section 4.2, we illustrated this by using two inputs that contained only minimal differences but led to totally different hash values. Analogous to this example, a modification to the block header will also cause the block header's hash value to change.

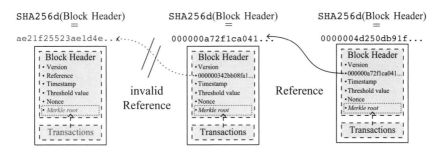

Figure 5.6
The modification (gray) to block 1's contents changes its hash value and makes block 2's reference invalid.

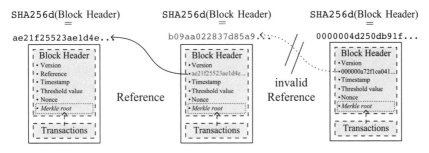

Figure 5.7
The modification (gray) of block 2's reference field changes its hash value and breaks the link between block 3 and block 2.

To restore the link between block 1 and block 2, the reference field in block 2's header must include block 1's new identification number. This modification, however, will immediately break the link between block 2 and block 3 because it invalidates block 3's reference of block 2. Figure 5.7 shows how the modification to block 2's reference affects its hash value and how this causes block 3's reference to become invalid.

This example displays the chain reaction that is at the foundation of the blockchain's security model. If one block is modified, the chain is broken, and all subsequent blocks will become invalid. Modifications therefore have the effect of shortening the chain. For a chain to retain its original length with the modified information, the modified block and all subsequent blocks have to be recomputed.

5.1.4   Extending the Chain

To extend the blockchain, nodes create new candidate blocks. They may use any subset of transactions from their mempool, compute the merkle root, and assemble new

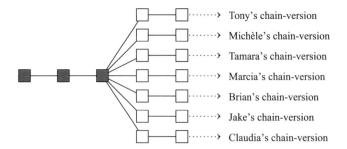

Figure 5.8
Various versions of the blockchain that are identical up until the third block and then diverge. This causes seven competing versions of the chain to develop.

candidate blocks. As reference value they take the identification number of the last block of the chain.

Tony is a network participant who carries out this function and tries to generate new blocks. He chooses some transactions from his mempool for inclusion in his candidate block. Tony already verified the legitimacy of these transactions when he received them. He therefore knows that each transaction is accompanied by valid redeem scripts for the unlocking conditions of all the referenced outputs. In addition, he verifies that the transactions use only unspent transaction outputs. Tony also references the last block in the consensus version of the Bitcoin blockchain.

He then computes the hash value of his new candidate block and subsequently sends it to other nodes. This step is problematic, however. Tony is not the only network participant who has generated a new candidate block. Other nodes have also formed new candidate blocks. All these candidate blocks reference the same parent block. The simultaneous production of new blocks has the potential for new competing and mutually incompatible versions of the Bitcoin blockchain to emerge. An example of such a situation is shown in figure 5.8.

The present example highlights that the chain structure does not itself guarantee that the different nodes can agree on a single valid version. Only if we add additional rules will it be possible to reach a network-wide consensus.

5.2 Consensus Protocol

In the Bitcoin network anyone can adjust his personal copy of the Bitcoin blockchain. There is no centralized party that determines which blockchain version corresponds to the true state. Accordingly, there may be situations where the network participants do not agree on the true state of the blockchain. To counteract this problem, the Bitcoin system is based on a predefined set of consensus rules that enables one version of the Bitcoin ledger to be identified as the true version.

The most commonly used Bitcoin software client follows all consensus rules by default. The default settings, however, do not offer any protection against deviant behavior. Network participants could write their own software client or adapt existing software clients with a different set of rules. In economics, rational choice theory assumes that a rational person will disobey the rules if it is profitable to do so. The consensus protocol therefore has to be constructed in such a way that individuals adhere to the existing rules through pure self-interest.

The respective incentives are achieved through various mechanisms. The basic principle is that fraudulent behavior is expensive and that all network participants are able to uncover it immediately. Honest behavior, however, is rewarded by the system's incentive scheme. In the following, we discuss each of the fundamental components of the consensus protocol and show how they influence the network participants' behavior.

5.2.1 Only Legitimate Transactions

The most basic consensus rule is that the Bitcoin blockchain may contain only legitimate transactions. The legitimacy of transactions can be validated independently by every full node as described in chapter 4. In addition, there is a whole series of other tests, all of which determine the validity of a transaction and the blocks who include them. Many of these tests only serve as protection against a forced overload of the network (DoS attacks).[4]

Performing these verification steps is computationally inexpensive. Thus, candidate blocks that have invalid transactions are immediately exposed and are ignored by the rest of the network. Consequently, if someone adds fraudulent transactions to a candidate block, it causes the candidate block to be rejected by all other network participants. This ruins any chances of being rewarded for producing the candidate block. It is, therefore, rational to include only valid transactions.

5.2.2 Proof of Work

In our example in figure 5.8, seven competing versions of the blockchain have emerged because far too many valid blocks have been generated simultaneously. The computing power needed to generate a candidate block is so small that the process can be

---

4. A complete list of all the sub-steps of the verification procedure can be found at Bitcoin Wiki, "Protocol rules," August 25, 2017, https://en.bitcoin.it/wiki/Protocol_rules.

accomplished in a fraction of a second, even with a mobile device. This has the consequence that new candidate blocks can be produced much faster than the time it takes to exchange them over the network. We therefore need an artificial restriction that makes it harder to create a valid candidate block and therefore gives the network the time it needs to exchange data and to reach consensus. This is achieved through the so-called proof-of-work consensus mechanism.

Proof-of-work was originally developed to counteract spam email messages and DoS attacks (see section 5.3.5). The fundamental idea is that if an activity can be executed too quickly, it should be slowed down. This is achieved by requiring the activity to present the solution to a time-consuming mathematical problem. The mathematical problem involved can be only solved by using a trial-and-error method. On average, only every xth attempt will produce the desired result.

This principle imposes artificial costs on the activity. These costs provide protection by hindering excessive activity in the context of spam emails and DoS attacks. At the same time, the costs accrued through normal use are insignificant. In the context of Bitcoin, this process has several effects, which are listed as follows:

- It solves the problem that blocks are generated too quickly.
- It ensures that the chain cannot be altered and recreated without incurring costs. It is therefore safeguarded by the hashing power spent to build it.
- It induces the nodes to behave honestly, as the costly hashing power that they invest would otherwise be wasted.

Proof of work is implemented in the Bitcoin network by using the candidate block's block header. Its *hash value* must possess an extremely rare feature: it must be below a certain threshold value; that is, it must display several zeros at the beginning of the *identification number*. Only then will the candidate block be considered valid by the rest of the network.

Let us assume that the current threshold is 1000000000000000000000000000000000 0000000000000000000000000000000000. In this case, all the identification numbers that had a zero in the initial position in hexadecimal notation would be valid.[5] The threshold would have the effect that, on average, only every sixteenth candidate block would be within this range.[6] With this threshold the whole network would have to generate sixteen candidate blocks on average to produce one valid block.

---

5. The criterion is satisfied by all values between 000000000000000000000000000000000000 000000000000000000000000000 and 0FFFFFFFFFFFFFFFFFFFFFFFFFFFFFFFFFFFFFFFF FFFFFFFFFFFFFFFFFFF.
6. Hexadecimal notation uses sixteen possible characters (0–9 and A–F).

Miner   Peers of this miner

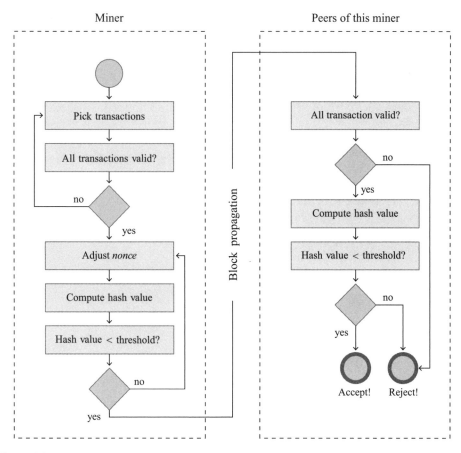

Figure 5.9
Simple mining process model.

If the block header's hash value is above the threshold, the block is rejected. The mining node will then make minimal changes to the block content and compute a new hash value. This iterative process is called mining.

The source of the variation is primarily the nonce. A nonce is a field with arbitrary data that, given otherwise identical block contents, will cause the hash value to change.[7]

Figure 5.9 summarizes the mining process. The miner starts by picking transactions from his mempool and verifies that the transactions are valid; that is, that they include

---

7. If the variation space in the nonce is not sufficient, then the timestamp and the redeem script of the *coinbase transaction* (*extra-nonce*) can be adapted. The timestamp is itself an element of the block header and changes in the *coinbase* will cause the block's merkle root to change.

a valid redeem script and only reference unspent transaction outputs. He then picks a nonce value and computes the hash value of the block's header. If the hash value is above the current threshold, he chooses another nonce value and recomputes the hash value. Only if the candidate block's hash value happens to be below the current threshold, he will relay this block to the network (see Block propagation in figure 5.9). The right-hand side of figure 5.9 shows what the other full nodes do once they receive the block. They verify all transactions and, if everything is fine, compute the hash value of the block's header to assure that the threshold condition is met. If it is met, they add the block to their copy of the Bitcoin blockchain.

"Mining" is the relentless adjustment of the nonce in search of a valid candidate block. One cycle begins with the adjustment of the nonce and ends with the comparison of the hash value to the current threshold. This cycle is repeated until a valid hash value is found.

Figure 5.10 shows a simplified example of this cycle. We have generated a short message that represents the block header and aim to demonstrate the effect of the nonce adaptation. Candidate blocks are generated one after another with equivalent contents, apart from the nonce. Only the nonce 0000000D generates a hash value with a zero at the first position.

5.2.3   Dynamic Threshold and Difficulty

In the Bitcoin system the mining difficulty is dynamically adjusted to ensure that the total network, on average, generates one valid block every ten minutes. The difficulty is calibrated every 2,016 blocks. Assuming a ten-minute average for block creation, the expected time between adjustments is $E(t) = 20{,}160$ minutes (about fourteen days). Due to the probabilistic mining process and changes in the hashing power, the realized time t for the network to generate 2,016 blocks will vary.

The difficulty is adjusted via a change of the threshold value δ. Any full node is able to compute the threshold value independently by using the following equation:

$$\delta_{new} = \delta_{old} \frac{t}{E(t)}.$$

If $t < E(t)$, then $\delta_{new} < \delta_{old}$. A lower δ threshold makes it more difficult to find valid blocks, which has the effect that the rate of block generation will drop back closer to the ten-minute average. If $t > E(t)$, then $\delta_{new} > \delta_{old}$. This makes it less difficult to find valid blocks and, hence, increases the rate of block generation.

Another way to show how the threshold changes over time is through the difficulty parameter D. The current difficulty level D_i can be computed by dividing the initial

m_1 = My candidate block with nonce 00000000

h_1 = a67b08e5d7b65533125014d399ae6c9ab5830830fbdf46974b4c34d719ba0642

m_2 = My candidate block with nonce 00000001

h_2 = dd03867b713d3985d7a624b40fc1f902560d930c7e473dc1d7738b6a7650026b

m_3 = My candidate block with nonce 00000002

h_3 = 5dc1f3b165a0f1e6b65f3c8e9376e4adce1c6d3a19288196b71ebf394f96f833

m_4 = My candidate block with nonce 00000003

h_4 = 20f2e43a6d1c0da9d7b864f45ca5352d869ae00df3feb14f9507f0da031020ca

m_5 = My candidate block with nonce 00000004

h_5 = b7fc5158ba18d1c986ba5fc6640db1937280e0b2b01666d16139f94618a13b76

m_6 = My candidate block with nonce 00000005

h_6 = 97d6c9f2c931d2a94927cebe9fbb68b0ba448a101f048e22070d82cbc5918d06

m_7 = My candidate block with nonce 00000006

h_7 = db141411f817695fa52e3ed16d3f7be6c66dc3a21b3f15c47a09e4692e0ce98a

m_8 = My candidate block with nonce 00000007

h_8 = 282399238370ca95129718f1157a757ed7d60a31c9c07fd9d0e1660d36defd74

m_9 = My candidate block with nonce 00000008

h_9 = 285da6c7b152c438facd0daafa826588b7a723f6bf75bc88882287901ddfd6e3

m_{10} = My candidate block with nonce 00000009

h_{10} = c3eaf0ba56e2b1cf715031088c69cbceb29449cbf111a446f890d3b82dc3f238

m_{11} = My candidate block with nonce 0000000A

h_{11} = d2ae6dc2eee6facc2ad45e39a268977a20397bc085efe0d8877421c42d0526a8

m_{12} = My candidate block with nonce 0000000B

h_{12} = fe09d1f958bee9cb9c75727ddc28115c5212ff83200ed26e0b534ab6451e2dfd

m_{13} = My candidate block with nonce 0000000C

h_{13} = 34e0bd54ea7faded52059d4e11deb76abc649fa8efc2eb9ed225a68db18f9716

m_{14} = My candidate block with nonce 0000000D

h_{14} = 0dc551f942fb38b407bfdadd2145fef1bbf97c31af7b99c38bbfa02e5a289627

m_{15} = My candidate block with nonce 0000000E

h_{15} = 299c86f0cc85ff43d5f621498c298396ec529133fc65e1c1069f7ebea3ca91a2

m_{16} = My candidate block with nonce 0000000F

h_{16} = 5e9002cd6d0a6b2a1874dc4df5f12295ff135295c441cff5088d0e8d8386f0ee

Figure 5.10
Iterative changes of the nonce when generating candidate blocks. The valid nonce is `0000000D`.

threshold value $\delta(B_0)$[8] by the current threshold value $\delta(B_i)$.

$$D_i := \frac{\delta(B_0)}{\delta(B_i)}.$$

The *difficulty* develops in precisely the opposite direction to the *threshold value*. If the threshold value decreases, it becomes more difficult to find a valid block, and the difficulty therefore increases. Figure 5.11 shows that the hashing power involved in Bitcoin mining has increased dramatically over time. It also shows the sharp increase in the difficulty in 2017 and 2018.

Box 5.1
Hashing Power

The relevant unit used to measure mining is the number of hashes per second; that is, how many hash values can be computed per second. In the Bitcoin network, total hashing power is currently measured in exa-hashes (quintillion or 10^{18}) per second.

The increase in hashing power derives from higher prices for Bitcoins and a sharp increase in the efficiency of *mining hardware* (see box 5.3). In section 6.4.1 we will analyze the energy consumption of the network.

5.2.4 Mining Reward and Bitcoin Creation

Proof of work imposes costs on the nodes when generating blocks. This is a deliberate design decision that is absolutely indispensable for the system to function. In particular, the mining process secures the Bitcoin network. By securing the Bitcoin network, the miners provide a public good because the benefits are nonexcludable and nonrivalrous.

The costs of mining are carried individually by the miners while the benefits of mining are provided to the whole network. This begs the question as to why a rational individual would wish to assume a *mining* function. Every node should prefer others to invest the necessary resources and enjoy the utility without making any contributions themselves. The answer to this question lies in the Bitcoin system's native reward mechanism.

Full nodes that generate valid blocks receive new Bitcoin units. They will be rewarded in proportion to the amount of hashing power that they have allocated to this activity. The compensation is paid out to the miners using a *coinbase transaction*. This type of

---

8. That is, the threshold at the time of the genesis block.

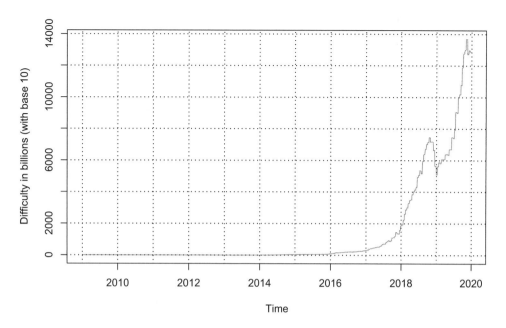

Figure 5.11
Increase in the difficulty ratio over time.
Source: Data from Blockchain Explorer, n.d., https://www.blockchain.com/explorer.

transaction does not have to reference an UTXO. It creates new Bitcoin units with an unlocking condition of the miner's choice.

Each candidate block contains a coinbase transaction. However, just like any transaction, the coinbase transaction is relevant only if the candidate block is included into the consensus version of the blockchain; if not, it is worthless. Further, the size of the reward is predefined, and if a miner does not follow the consensus rules, the block will be ignored by the other nodes.

For approximately the first four years the reward amounted to 50 Bitcoin units per block. This amount has subsequently been halved every 210,000 blocks. From block 0 to block 209,999, each coinbase transaction therefore carried 50 Bitcoin units plus transaction fees. Between blocks 210,000 and 419,999, coinbase transactions carried 25 Bitcoin units plus transaction fees. At the time of writing, the coinbase reward amounts to 12.5 Bitcoin units. There is, however, another reward halving scheduled shortly before the release of this book (mid-2020). With block 630,000, the coinbase reward will drop to 6.25 Bitcoin units per block.

The value of the coinbase transaction will continue to be halved and converge to zero. Then no further new Bitcoin units will be created. This is expected to happen in the year 2140, when the maximum number of Bitcoin units of twenty-one million will be reached.[9]

> **Box 5.2**
> **Transaction Fees**
>
> Miners also earn income from transaction fees associated with the block. These fees consist of the sum of all transaction inputs minus the sum of all transaction outputs. They are thus a kind of residual amount that has not been used and can be claimed by the respective miner.
>
> A transaction initiator adds a transaction fee to incentivize miners to include their transactions into a candidate block. Generally, miners prefer transactions that will pay them a higher fee per byte.
>
> As the amount of the coinbase reward declines, transaction fees will become increasingly important. Section 6.3.2 deals in depth with this topic.

5.2.5   The Consensus Version

One important rule to ensure consensus still remains to be discussed. If two or more versions of the blockchain are in circulation, there must be a mechanism in place that allows the nodes to decide which of these versions corresponds to the true state of the Bitcoin blockchain. For consensus to be achieved, all nodes—or at least the majority of nodes—must agree on the same outcome.

Since we have already become acquainted with the proof-of-work algorithm and the difficulty ratio, this principle can now be explained concisely. The consensus chain is the one that has the largest accumulated difficulty. In section 2.4.3, we presented this criterion in a simplified form by referring to the "longest chain." This was a simplification that normally leads to the same result.

5.2.6   Connecting the Dots

The combination of these consensus rules will lead to a dominant version of the Bitcoin blockchain. In the following section we would like to revisit some of these concepts with an emphasis on the interaction between the individual rules.

Legitimacy. Legitimacy prevents inconsistent and invalid transactions from entering into the consensus version of the blockchain.

---

9. The predefined growth of the total amount of Bitcoin units is illustrated in figures 2.11 and 6.1.

Linking. Linking connects the blocks and ensures that blocks have to be recomputed after a modification of the chain. This applies to modified and all subsequent blocks.

Proof of work. Proof of work makes it difficult to create valid blocks. If a chain is modified, it can be rebuilt only by employing substantial resources. This makes modifications resource-intensive.

Threshold value. The variable threshold value ensures that the rate of block generation remains constant at a ten-minute average, irrespective of the amount of hashing power employed.

Rewards. Rewards incentivize nodes to make hashing power available and to utilize it to maintain the consensus version of the blockchain.

Aggregated difficulty. This criterion serves to ensure that, when there are conflicting versions of the blockchain, the version that has received the most work will be considered the consensus version.

5.3 Bitcoin Mining: Incentives and Examples

In this section we look at the allocation of hashing power and examine the incentive compatibility of certain parts of the consensus rules. In particular, we evaluate whether a deviation from the consensus rules can lead to a higher payoff, and we consider various attack vectors.

5.3.1 The Economics of Allocating Hashing Power

The amount of hashing power that a node will provide depends on its cost structure and the current value of the expected reward. The costs are mainly determined by the efficiency of the available hardware and the operating cost such as maintenance, electricity, and cooling. These components determine the marginal cost for the calculation of a certain number of hash values.

The reward is paid out in Bitcoin units. The incentives to mine are therefore directly dependent on Bitcoin's market value. The probability of receiving a reward depends on the miner's hashing power in relation to the total hashing power of the network.

The mining market is extremely competitive. The barriers to entry are very low. If the costs are homogeneous,[10] additional hashing power will flow into the market until the

---

10. A mathematic model of the mining market under the assumption of heterogeneity can be found in Schär (2020).[200]

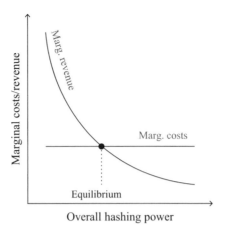

Figure 5.12
Equilibrium of hashing power.

expected marginal revenue from further hashing power corresponds to the marginal costs of providing it.

In the following we assume, for the sake of simplicity, that the marginal cost of computing one hash value is equal and constant for all miners. Declining marginal costs owing to better technology or increasing returns to scale are important elements in practice but do not significantly change the short-run dynamics of the mining market.

The expected marginal revenue of computing one hash value is decreasing in the total hashing power of the network. The reason is that an increase in the total network hashing power also increases the difficulty and therefore lowers the probability of finding a valid block, given the same amount of hashing power. The decreasing marginal revenue of computing one hash value is shown in figure 5.12. It also shows the intersection of the marginal cost and the expected marginal revenue.

Fixed costs, such as the costs of procuring hardware, play a role for market entry and exit and the long-run behavior of the mining market. However, once a miner is in possession of the hardware, these costs can be ignored. In the short run, therefore, the only variable that is relevant for the allocation of hashing power is the ratio of the expected marginal revenue from computing hash values to the marginal cost of doing so.

If this ratio is larger than one, additional hashing power will be made available, until this ratio is back to one. New hashing power is typically diverted from mining other blockchains. As shown in figure 5.13a, the network's hashing power will converge to the equilibrium level. If this ratio is smaller than one, the miners will make losses. Computational power will exit and used elsewhere until this ratio is back to one. This case is illustrated in figure 5.13b.

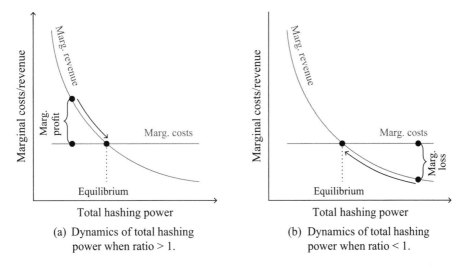

(a) Dynamics of total hashing power when ratio > 1.

(b) Dynamics of total hashing power when ratio < 1.

Figure 5.13
Adaption of the network's overall hashing power.

Box 5.3
Efficient Mining Hardware

The efficiency of mining hardware has increased enormously over the years. In the beginning, mining was conducted exclusively by using a computer's central processing unit (CPU). Because graphics processing units (GPUs) are much more suitable for computing hash values, many people started to employ GPUs for mining. The step to so-called *field programmable gate arrays* (FPGAs) enabled circuit boards to be configured for the mining process, which led to a new leap in efficiency.

Since 2013, *application specific integrated circuits* (ASICs) have been used. ASICs are highly specialized hardware modules that are customized for a particular task. In the case of Bitcoin ASICs, they are optimized to compute SHA256 hash values.

The improvement of the hardware's efficiency does not reduce the cost of maintaining the network. It only increases the network's amount of hashing power. The reason is that a higher difficulty ratio will offset the higher level of hashing power. [206]

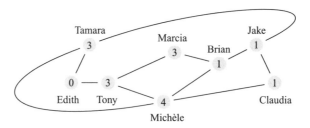

Figure 5.14
Allocation of mining hashing power.

5.3.2 Allocation of Hashing Power and Mining Pools

In this section we consider the allocation of hashing power and pool mining through the means of an example. In this example we assume that the allocation of hashing power is given and constant and that the participants provide a total of sixteen units of hashing power. The hashing power of the nodes is represented by the number in the respective circle in figure 5.14. The probability that a node can create the next block corresponds exactly to this number divided by the total hashing power of sixteen units.

Edith operates a full node but does not want to mine. She therefore has a zero probability of finding a valid block but is nevertheless in the position to verify the legitimacy of all transactions and blocks in the chain. All other nodes participate in the creation of new candidate blocks. Michèle has a hashing power of four and therefore a 25 percent chance of creating the next valid block. The remaining twelve units of hashing power are split among the other network participants.

A miner never knows in advance whether and when he will receive a block reward. The payment pattern is equivalent to a lottery and the hashing power to the number of lottery tickets that a miner holds. The more hashing power he has, the greater will be his chance of success.

In order to counteract the problems of payment volatility and to smooth their earnings, miners have the ability to form so-called *mining pools*. These pools consolidate the hashing power of the participants and act as a single group. The combined hashing power leads to more regular rewards, which can be distributed pro rata to all members of the pool. The expected payout remains unchanged,[11] but the volatility of the rewards decreases significantly.

---

11. In reality, mining pool operators often charge a percentage fee. In this case, the expected payment to the pool members decreases.

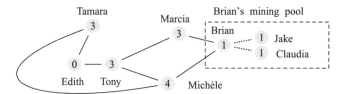

Figure 5.15
Brian's mining pool.

In our example in figure 5.14, Brian, Jake, and Claudia act as individual miners. Each one of them controls $\frac{1}{16}$ of the overall network hashing power and, given a reward of 12.5 Bitcoin units per block, can consequently expect to receive a payment of $\frac{12.5}{16}$ Bitcoin units per ten minutes of mining activity. The possible payouts are 15×0 and 1×12.5 Bitcoin units, resulting in a high standard deviation of the pay of 3.125.

In figure 5.15, the three individuals decide to form a mining pool. The standard deviation of the reward thereby significantly decreases to 1.63 because the pool members each receive a proportional reward of $\frac{12.5}{3}$ Bitcoin units in three out of ten possible cases. The expected value of the reward is not affected by their alliance. This can be illustrated using a very simple equality, which equates the payment for *solo mining* with that of *pool mining*:

$$12.5 \cdot \frac{1}{16} = 12.5 \cdot \frac{3}{16} \cdot \frac{1}{3}$$

If the hashing power of the respective miner is h, the overall hashing power of the network is H, and the current reward per block is R, then the individual expected value of the reward will not be affected by the aggregate amount of hashing power of the *mining pool P*.[12]

$$R \cdot \frac{h}{H} = R \cdot \frac{P}{H} \cdot \frac{h}{P}$$

In reality, a *solo miner* would have to wait months or even years to create a single valid block and be paid for it. This is the reason why mining pools are very popular and why they play an important role within the Bitcoin network.

---

12. The premise is based on the assumption that a change in P, owing to the dynamic of the equilibrium amount, will not have an effect on the overall hashing power H.

Mining pools are one of the factors that lead to creeping centralization in the Bitcoin system. If a large part of the network's hashing power is concentrated, the bookkeeping is somewhat centralized. This makes the Bitcoin network more vulnerable. In addition, miners connected to a pool often do not operate a full node (see also section 3.2.3). They are connected to the operator of the mining pool via a centralized subnetwork and receive all the information that is relevant for mining exclusively through this channel. Often, such miners are termed *hashers*, characterizing the fact that they only compute hash values on behalf of another party and do not assemble the candidate blocks themselves.

In our example in figure 5.15, this applies to Jake and Claudia. As a result of their decision to join Brian's mining pool, they have given up their full node status and from now on will compute hash values at Brian's request. The network has suddenly lost two full nodes and now has a large pool operator that controls almost 20 percent of the network's hashing power.

5.3.3   Acceptance of Other Participants' Blocks

After a while, Michèle is able to successfully generate a candidate block, which has a hash value that is below the current threshold. The block also complies with all the other requirements of the consensus rules and will therefore be accepted by other nodes and added to their locally stored versions of the blockchain.

However, Brian still hesitates a little. He would have preferred to have already secured the reward for his pool and is therefore playing with the idea of violating the consensus rules and not accepting Michèle's valid block. Should his pool succeed in creating a block that is based on the previous block, the pool would have a chance to dispute Michele's reward.

The situation is presented in figure 5.16. Michèle has successfully generated a block that is based on block 3 and has thereby extended the consensus version of the blockchain. Brian, Jake, and Claudia now try with their mining pool to generate a block based on block 3 and thus attempt to steal Michèle's reward.

In order for the pool to overtake the consensus version of the chain with Michèle's block, they will have to generate the next two valid blocks. At the same time, the rest of the network will be working on the current consensus version; that is, Michèle's version of the blockchain.

The different paths represent the possible versions of the blockchain. Blocks of Brian's pool are shown in gray. All other blocks are shown in white. The dotted blocks can be generated only with a certain probability and are situated on one of the possible paths.

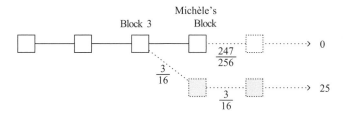

Figure 5.16
Probabilities and payouts for Brian's pool, given deviant behavior.

Let's first look at the lower path. Since Brian's pool controls three units of hashing power, the probability that the pool can create the next block corresponds to $\frac{3}{16}$. The probability that this will happen twice in a row corresponds to $\frac{3}{16} \cdot \frac{3}{16}$ or $\frac{9}{256}$. If these three pool participants succeed, their version with two blocks would overtake Michèle's version with one block and would therefore be accepted as the new consensus version of the blockchain. In this case, the pool would receive two reward payments of 12.5 Bitcoin units.

In all other cases, competing miners will be able to add at least one block to the consensus version. This would put us on the upper branch of the chain (the version based on Michèle's block) so that any blocks of the lower chain would be irrelevant.[13] The probability that the consensus version wins corresponds to the complementary probability of $\frac{9}{256}$, which is $\frac{247}{256}$. The deviating pool's expected value is:

$$25 \cdot \frac{9}{256} + 0 \cdot \frac{247}{256} \approx 0.88.$$

For comparison, we consider the situation where Brian's pool follows the consensus rules and accepts Michèle's block. The pool will therefore generate its own candidate block on the basis of Michèle's block and work together with the rest of the network on the consensus version of the blockchain. The possible paths along which the chain might develop are shown in figure 5.17.

---

13. Brian's pool could decide to continue the attempt to overtake the consensus chain. An attack would therefore also be conceivable if the consensus version is ahead with more than one block. However, this would not change the basic intuition, nor would it make Brian better off. The hashing power would only have to be allocated over an even longer period of time to a version of the chain that has an increased risk of failure, whereby the expected value of the payout would generally be even lower.

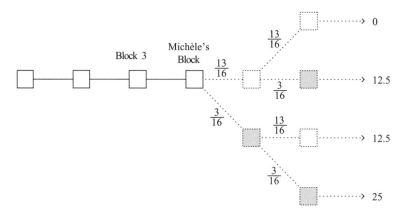

Figure 5.17
Probabilities and payouts for Brian's pool, given behavior that complies with the consensus protocol.

As all miners work according to the respective consensus version, no rewards will be lost. If Brian's pool succeeds in generating a valid block and adding it to the blockchain, his pool will be certain to obtain the reward.

Again, we consider the period over which the next two blocks will be created; that is, an average of about twenty minutes. During this time, the pool has two chances, each with probability $\frac{3}{16}$ to generate the next block. The four paths show the different states in which the pool contributes none, one (two possible paths), or both blocks. By following the consensus rules, the pool receives the following expected payout:

$$0 \cdot \frac{169}{256} + 12.5 \cdot \frac{39}{256} + 12.5 \cdot \frac{39}{256} + 25 \cdot \frac{9}{256} \approx 4.69.$$

The example illustrates the strong incentive that motivates the miners to cooperate. The expected value of the payment is substantially higher if the miners decide to adhere to the consensus rules than if they deviate from them. It is therefore in the miners' best interest to accept valid blocks of other participants and always keep their own version of the blockchain up to date.

From a closer perspective, we see that the expected value resulting from deviating is exactly equivalent to the expected value resulting from one of the honest-behavior paths. However, honest behavior offers additional chances that can also lead to the payment of a reward and is therefore strictly better.

This advantage derives from the fact that for Brian's expected payout, it is immaterial whether Michèle receives a reward or not. The mathematical properties of the Poisson process ensure that the payouts do not compete. In other words, if Michèle

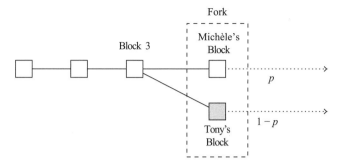

Figure 5.18
Block race after the simultaneous generation of two competing blocks.

is able to generate a valid block, this will not influence all the other miners' expected payouts—unless they ignore Michèle's block and try to create a competing version of the chain.

In addition to the lower expected value, the miners who do not base their candidate blocks on the current consensus version of the Bitcoin blockchain also accept a higher volatility in their payments.

5.3.4   Block Race

Since mining is a probabilistic process, it is possible that two competing blocks could be found at the same time. Both blocks reference the same parent and thus form two different versions of the chain.

Let us assume, for example, that block 3 corresponds to the last block of the current consensus version and that both Michèle and Tony find a block that references block 3 and has an identification number that is below the threshold value. This leads to the situation visualized in figure 5.18.

The consensus rule concerning the longest chain (or the highest accumulated difficulty) will not resolve the issue decisively in a case like this. Both chains are equivalent and will coexist over some time. Only if one of the two chains is extended by an additional valid block will that chain take the position of the consensus version rendering the other version of the chain irrelevant. This scenario is referred to as a *block race*.

The allocation of hashing power influences the outcome of the race. Whichever of the two versions of the chain receives the larger share of hashing power will be the one that is more likely to be extended by an additional block.

The hashing power of Michèle and Tony will be used to extend their respective versions. By default, all other miners will prefer the block they received first. So if either Michèle or Tony succeeds in propagating their respective block more effectively, they can win more nodes and thus more hashing power for their version of the chain. We call the share of hashing power allocated to Michèle's version p. Accordingly, the share of Tony's hashing power is $1 - p$.

Efficiency in propagating blocks depends primarily on the network connections of the respective miners. The more numerous, the more varied, and the faster a node's connections are, the more efficiently the block will be propagated. The speed of the propagation is inversely related to the size of the block. If a given block contains substantially more transactions, this additional data may slow it down significantly. For this reason, miners may have an incentive to include fewer transactions in blocks than are possible to include. [114]

As soon as a new block is found, all miners have an incentive to work on the consensus version of the blockchain, which ensures that the network automatically regains its state of consensus. To the network it is irrelevant which version of the chain is able to prevail. It is important only that the network agrees unequivocally on a single state of the blockchain.

For Michèle and Tony, however, it matters. The reward is part of their respective version. If their version loses the race, the reward it contains will also be lost. In this respect, the losing miner might have an incentive to allocate his own hashing power to his version even if the competing consensus version is further advanced. If the losing miner succeeds in creating the next two blocks, he could overtake the other version and save the original reward.

Consider a situation where Michèle succeeds in creating another valid block. Tony therefore faces a decision. If he complies with the rules and switches to the consensus version, he would lose his reward. But by mining on the consensus chain he would subsequently have two chances to generate a new valid block with a probability of $\frac{3}{16}$ and thus receive a new reward of 12.5 Bitcoin units for each block. The expected value of his reward would be approximately 4.69 Bitcoin units.

If, however, Tony were to decide to continue to work on his own version of the chain, he will succeed only if he can create the next two blocks. This would allow him to secure the two rewards from the new blocks as well as the reward from the block already created, which would correspond to an expected reward of $\frac{3}{16} \cdot \frac{3}{16} \cdot 3 \cdot 12.5 \approx 1.32$. The payouts in the case of deviating behavior are shown in figure 5.19.

In spite of the additional incentive from the reward embedded in the inferior version of the chain, Tony would be worse off if he chose to deviate. A deviation would be profitable for Tony only if his share in the overall hashing power is above a specific level. We can calculate the critical value that he needs by replacing the $\frac{3}{16}$ ratio with a variable that reflects Tony's relative hashing power $\frac{h}{H}$.

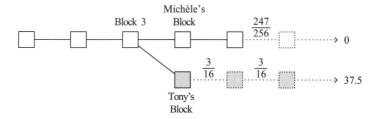

Figure 5.19
Incentive for giving preference to an inferior version of the chain to capture an orphan block's payout.

On the left side of the following equation, we see the expected value of Tony's reward if he were to work on his own version of the chain. The right side of the equation shows the expected value of Tony's reward if he were to follow the consensus version. R represents the size of the reward, which is eliminated in the following calculations:

$$3\left[\frac{h}{H}\right]^2 R = 2\frac{h}{H}R$$

$$\frac{h}{H} = \frac{2}{3}$$

Tony will therefore be indifferent between these options if he controls exactly two thirds of the total hashing power. For a smaller fraction of hashing power, a deviation from the consensus rule will make him strictly worse off. If, however, he controls more than two thirds of the overall hashing power, it will be profitable for him to exclusively work on his own chain.

If Tony has a longer time horizon and is willing to continue working on his own chain even if the rest of the network continues to move away, things become much more complex. In simple terms, though, miners who control more than 50 percent of the network's total hashing power could theoretically always work on their own chains since they can let their chains grow faster on average than any competing versions.[14]

Further, a dominant miner would have the possibility to launch certain attacks on the network, which we will discuss in the next section. The dominance of a miner (or of a colluding group of miners) thus presents a possible threat to the Bitcoin network.

---

14. See note 3.3 for the cases in which a hashing power of less than 50 percent is sufficient.

> **Box 5.4**
> **Goldfinger Attacks**
>
> If a miner wants to maximize his payout from the system's native rewards, they will normally not deviate from the protocol. There may, however, be other reasons for a miner to deviate from the protocol. For example, it is conceivable that a node is primarily motivated by exogenous incentives.
>
> Scenarios in which exogenous motivations lead a miner to inflict damage on the Bitcoin system are known as *Goldfinger attacks*. [135] They are based on the assumption that a resource-rich entity would profit from a loss of confidence in the Bitcoin system. The benefits might be of a political nature or might be directly linked to the falling price of the Bitcoin unit.
>
> Depending on the benefits, it would be possible for an entity to incur costs to deliberately damage the system. This danger was particularly great in the early days. Increasing adoption, higher hash rates, and sharply rising market capitalization, however, make attacks of this type more expensive and thus less likely.

5.3.5 Attacks on the System

Miners who possess a high share of the network's total hashing power are able to substantially shape the consensus chain's development. If, for example, a miner refuses to include a specific transaction in any of his candidate blocks, this will delay the average time it takes to process that transaction. The greater this miner's hashing power, the less likely it is that the transaction will be included in a block in the near future.

If this dominant miner wants to prevent the transaction from being confirmed, he must have a large amount of hashing power. If another miner creates a valid block that contains this transaction, the dominant miner can attack this block by continuing to create candidate blocks based on the parent of the block, which contains the transaction. If the dominant miner is able to do this, he will be able to create an alternative version of the chain in which the transaction was not processed.

Figure 5.20 shows an example of such a situation. Block 4 of the consensus chain includes a transaction from Raphael to Lucas. If a miner wants to undo this transaction, he can try to start an alternative chain on the basis of block 3. The more confirmations a block has already received—that is, the further down that a block is in the chain—the more difficult it is to carry out such an attack. For most transactions, two to three confirmations make a block sufficiently secure. A block that has more than six confirmations is considered irreversible, as are all the transactions that are contained within it.

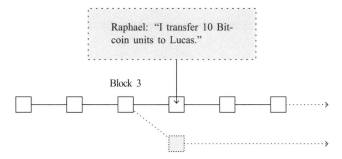

Figure 5.20
The miner working on the alternative chain wishes to cancel the transaction sent by Raphael to Lucas.

We would like to stress that blocking transactions is very costly and usually cannot be sustained over a long period of time. Even if the rogue miner succeeds in undoing the transaction, Lucas (or anyone else for that matter) could simply broadcast the same transaction again, and eventually it will be included into a block by another miner. It is therefore almost impossible to prevent a transaction from being added to the blockchain—especially once we consider the fee market that incentivizes miners to include transactions.

If, however, Raphael himself is trying to cheat, things are a little more complicated. In certain situations, he may have an incentive to undo his own transactions. For example, if Raphael buys a gold bar from Lucas, he might try to reverse the Bitcoin transaction after receiving the gold bar. Even if Raphael does not possess any hashing power himself, he could hire a miner to execute the attack. If this attack succeeds, he would be in possession of the gold bar and Bitcoin units. An attack of this kind is known as a *double spend.*

To prevent Lucas from rebroadcasting the transaction message already signed by Raphael at a later date, Raphael will have to create a competing transaction that references the same transaction output. This is shown in figure 5.21. Raphael can specify any receiver (including himself) for the new transaction. If the version of the chain that contains the new transaction were to prevail, the transaction message crediting Lucas would reference an output that has already been used elsewhere. The transaction would therefore be invalid and no longer be considered for inclusion into later candidate block.

The attacks described above are generally called *51 percent attacks*. The name derives from the condition that the attacker controls a substantial share of the overall hashing power. Contrary to what its name implies, 51 percent attacks can also be carried out

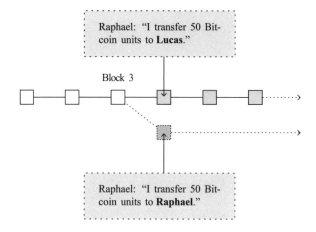

Figure 5.21
The miner who is working on the alternative chain wishes to cancel the transaction from Raphael to Lucas. He therefore include a competing transaction to prevent the first communication from being sent again.

with a relative share of hashing power below 50 percent. The amount of the hashing power only affects the attack's probability of success.

> **Box 5.5**
> **Limited Opportunities for 51 Percent Attacks**
>
> Even if a 51 percent attack succeeds, the attacker's capabilities are very limited. For example, an attacker is never able to issue new transactions on behalf of another person or confiscate a Bitcoin unit over which he has no control. Regardless of the allocation of the hashing power, the transaction outputs are always secured by the respective locking scripts.
>
> A 51 percent attack might, at worst, reverse a transaction or prevent a transaction from being added to the Bitcoin blockchain. By taking the respective precautions (waiting for confirmations), attacks of this kind are manageable problems.
>
> Moreover, miners who have such a large share of the systems' overall hashing power would generally not be interested in undermining confidence in the Bitcoin system as this would in turn erode the basis of their income.

There is also a form of double spend attack that does not require any hashing power. Raphael can therefore try to carry out this attack without the help of a miner.

We show this attack again in an example. This time Raphael buys a coffee at Daniel's Takeout and pays with Bitcoin units. Given Daniel's business, it is not possible for him to wait ten minutes for a confirmation before handing over the coffee to his customers.

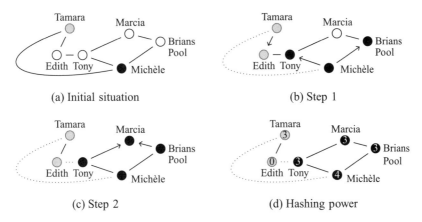

(a) Initial situation   (b) Step 1

(c) Step 2   (d) Hashing power

Figure 5.22
Dissemination of the transaction message through several steps.

Consequently, he also accepts unconfirmed transactions on the assumption that they will indeed be included in the next block.

Raphael tries to take advantage of this situation and creates a second transaction when buying the coffee, which references the same unspent transaction output but uses a locking condition in the favor of himself. He sends the first transaction in favor of Daniel to one node and the second transaction to another node. Both transactions are shared over the network, with the nodes usually preferring the transaction message they first receive.

Raphael hopes that Daniel's client will learn only of the existence of the first transaction message. At the same time, he wants the second transaction message to spread as widely as possible over the rest of the network. The more miners who keep the second transaction in their mempool, the higher Raphael's chance of getting his Bitcoin units back—in addition to the coffee, that is. Unconfirmed transactions can therefore always become the target of a double spend attack and must be considered unsecure. Consequently, when accepting Bitcoin payments, one should always wait for at least one confirmation of the transaction.

Figure 5.22 shows the schematic spread of two competing and simultaneously propagated transactions in the Bitcoin network. We assume that all connections have the same speed; that is, one step per unit of time. Whenever a node has a transaction in its mempool, we assume that the transaction gets relayed to its peers. If a node already holds an alternative transaction that references the same unspent transaction output, it will ignore the second one.

In our simple example, Raphael sends the transaction in favor of Daniel to Tamara. He simultaneously sends the competing transaction benefiting his own account to Michèle. Now a race begins between the two transaction messages. The network topology, the allocation of the hashing power, and chance will determine which of the two transactions will prevail.

The likelihood that Raphael's double spending attempt will succeed depends on which of the transactions has a competitive advantage regarding the number of miners or units of hashing power employed in processing it. In our example in figure 5.22, the double spend will succeed with a relatively high probability of $\frac{13}{16}$. This means that thirteen of sixteen units of hashing power will work on block candidates, which include Raphael's second transaction. Daniel therefore will receive his Bitcoin units only if Tamara can generate the next block, which will happen with a probability ratio of only $\frac{3}{16}$.

At this point, we again highlight the fact that this type of double spend can be carried out only with nonconfirmed transactions and that Daniel could have prevented it by applying the respective precautionary measures. Moreover, this potential attack has to be seen in the relevant context. Every medium of exchange carries certain risks: counterfeit cash, the possibility of *chargebacks* with credit cards, or double spend attempts with Bitcoin. In contrast to counterfeiting and chargebacks, it is possible to eliminate the danger of Bitcoin double spends by applying technical measures.

5.4 Exercises

Exercise 5.1: Sketch a block showing its most important components. Add a second block to your sketch and explain how a chain can develop from these blocks.

Exercise 5.2: Describe the Bitcoin referencing principle with regard to the block header hash values (identification numbers). How can blocks be secured by this principle?

Exercise 5.3: List the most important components of the Bitcoin consensus protocol and how they interact to ensure consensus.

Exercise 5.4: Explain the concept of threshold in the context of proof of work. Why does the Bitcoin system use a dynamic threshold, and how is the threshold established?

Exercise 5.5: Assume that one unit of hashing power costs 0.6 monetary units per hour. Also assume that the blockchain is secured by 2,000 units of processing power in the competitive market equilibrium and that the current pay corresponds to 12.5 Bitcoin units. What price in monetary units should a Bitcoin unit have under these assumptions?

Exercise 5.6: Discuss what would change in Exercise 5.5 if mining hardware with a 500 percent increase in efficiency could suddenly be purchased. Justify your explanations.

Exercise 5.7: Explain the role that block depth plays in guaranteeing the security of the transactions contained within the block.

Exercise 5.8: Identify the two types of double spend attacks with which you are familiar, and show their differences in the attacker's prerequisites and capabilities.

Exercise 5.9: Consider the example in figure 5.22. How likely is it that Raphael would successfully complete a double spend if he had communicated the second transaction to Marcia instead of Michèle?

III Further Remarks

6   Bitcoin's Challenges

Satoshi Nakamoto's paper "Bitcoin: A Peer-to-Peer Electronic Cash System"[158] is one of the most influential contributions in monetary economics of the past fifty years. Interestingly and perhaps tellingly, the article was published in 2008 via a mailing list for cryptography and not in a peer-reviewed scientific journal. The paper combines several technologies to create a virtual asset that is substantially different from any other asset. For the first time, ownership of virtual property is possible without the need for a central authority—a novelty with the potential to fundamentally change the current financial system and many other sectors.[32]

Bitcoin technology is fascinating, but there are many challenges. For some observers, these challenges are unsurmountable. For example, Stephen Williamson argues that "Bitcoin's future seems dismal. It represents a poor payments system, the ability to replicate it means that it cannot survive as a safe store of value like gold, and it may even provide poor services for criminals." He concludes that "Most likely, the value of Bitcoin is going to zero."[228]

We are more optimistic about the future of Bitcoin. That being said, we do not want to neglect the fact that Bitcoin faces some severe challenges. In this chapter we take a closer look at some of those challenges and discuss potential solutions. The issues include high price volatility, scalability, energy consumption, regulatory uncertainty, and low levels of adoption.

6.1   Price Volatility

First we look at Bitcoin's predetermined supply path and the claims that Bitcoin is a deflationary currency. This section will help us to understand the origin of Bitcoin's price volatility.

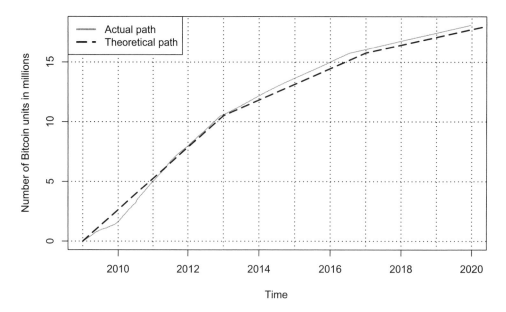

Figure 6.1
Number of Bitcoin units in circulation.
Sources: Data from Blockchain Explorer, n.d., https://www.blockchain.com/explorer; Coin MarketCap, website, n.d., https://coinmarketcap.com.

6.1.1 Bitcoin's Supply Path

The supply of Bitcoin is predetermined and converges to twenty-one million units, after which no additional Bitcoin units will be created. Bitcoin's supply path is displayed in figure 6.1. The gray solid curve shows the actual path while the dashed curve shows the theoretical path. The differences arise because the difficulty threshold value is adjusted only every 2,016 blocks. The changes in slope on the theoretical path correspond to the points in time at which the block reward is halved.

Figure 6.2 compares the growth rate of Bitcoin with the growth rate of the US dollar monetary base. The chart highlights the high initial Bitcoin growth rate. The decline of the growth rate has two causes. First, a temporarily constant block reward meets an increasing monetary base which results in lower growth rates over time. Second, the periodic halving of the block rewards further decreases the growth rate. An example of such a sudden decrease can be observed at the end of 2012.[1]

---

1. An interesting question to study is how the predetermined supply path for Bitcoin units affects monetary policy in a currency competition model. [95,193]

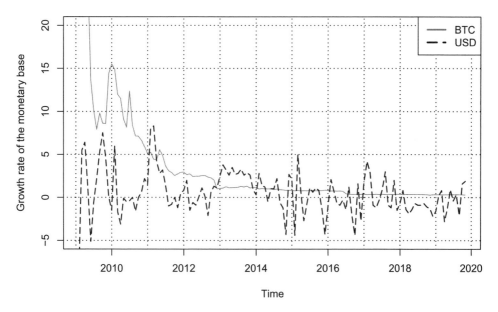

Figure 6.2
Growth of the monetary bases of Bitcoin and the USD. Monetary growth rate as a percentage change compared with the previous month. The data are not seasonally adjusted.
Sources: Data from Blockchain Explorer, n.d., https://www.blockchain.com/explorer; FRED Economic Data, Federal Reserve Bank of St. Louis, n.d., https://fred.stlouisfed.org.

The high volatility in the growth rate of the US dollar monetary base is striking. In contrast, Bitcoin's money supply has a relatively smooth growth rate in the second half of the chart. Nevertheless, Bitcoin's price volatility is substantially larger than the price volatility of the US dollar (see section 6.1.3).

6.1.2   Is Bitcoin Deflationary?
The limit on Bitcoin's quantity makes it a scarce resource and a potentially interesting store of value. It could lead to a situation where an ever-increasing aggregate demand for Bitcoin units will meet a constant supply.[2] This could in theory cause a substantial increase in the value of Bitcoin and is the reason why Bitcoin could be deflationary in the long run.

Consequently, many users are convinced that Bitcoin's value will increase forever. This belief needs to be challenged. Bitcoin has no intrinsic value. It cannot be consumed

---

2. The loss of private keys can even lead to a decrease of the supply.

or used in production, nor does it generate a cash flow. The price of an asset without intrinsic value is determined solely by expectations about its future price. A buyer is willing to buy a Bitcoin unit only if he or she assumes that the unit will sell for at least the same price later on.[3]

A key insight from modern monetary theory is that currencies with no intrinsic value have many equilibrium prices.[102] One of them is always zero. If all market participants expect that Bitcoin will have no value in the future, then no one will be willing to pay for it today and the resulting market price will be zero. A positive price can also be an equilibrium price. For example, if agents believe that Bitcoin will be priced at US$1 million tomorrow, they will be willing to pay US$1 million today (assuming no discounting), and so today's equilibrium price will be US$1 million.

Box 6.1
Is Bitcoin Digital Gold?

One potential use case for Bitcoin is as a safe-haven asset. In this context Bitcoin is often referred to as "digital gold." Many economists oppose this view and argue that Bitcoin is not scarce because it is straightforward to create a new cryptoasset. If anyone can easily create copies, then how would Bitcoin be able to serve as a store of value? This concern has been raised, for example, by Steven Williamson:[228]

> Gold is an asset that people can flee to when the returns on financial assets are highly uncertain, and it possibly bears a premium above its "fundamental" value because people coordinate on it for that purpose. So maybe Bitcoin can serve the same function? But precious metals have the virtue of having no competitors. There is only so much of the stuff. Although Bitcoin is ultimately limited in supply, the supply of potential competitors is unlimited, and we are currently seeing a flood of close substitutes for it. Cryptocurrencies can be valued as a safe asset only if they are in limited supply. The code that governs the operation of a cryptocurrency is open source, i.e., it is publicly available at no cost and can therefore be costlessly replicated many times. Thus, there is nothing that limits the supply of cryptocurrencies so as to prop up their prices in the long term.

We agree that any store of value requires a limited supply. However, we disagree that the unlimited competition by Bitcoin clones must necessarily have a negative effect on Bitcoin's price.[a] As a case in point, let's look at the art market where famous paintings can be replicated at very low costs. For example, there are millions of copies of the Mona Lisa painting; anyone could go to a copy shop and print their own Mona Lisa. Yet these

---

3. Agents that use Bitcoin for illegal activities such as tax evasion and circumventing capital controls and as payment for goods on black markets may be willing to take a loss. However, because of the limited anonymity properties of Bitcoin, there is no substantial demand for Bitcoin units for such activities.

copies hardly influence the original's price because they can be easily distinguished from the original painting.

The same is true for Bitcoin units. It is impossible to copy Bitcoin units. It is only possible to copy the Bitcoin software and then to launch a new blockchain with an entirely new cryptoasset. This new cryptoasset can be easily distinguished from Bitcoin. In fact, identifying Bitcoin copies is much easier than in the art market where sometimes even experts are tricked into believing that a copy is the original.

a. To the contrary, Bitcoin clones may positively impact the interest in the original.

6.1.3 Volatility Analysis

For an asset to be useful as a medium of exchange or unit of account, it needs to have a low price volatility. A low price volatility, in turn, requires that its supply is elastic. Central banks in developed countries stabilize the value of their currencies by adjusting elastically the supply to accommodate changes in aggregate demand. In fact, the Federal Reserve System was explicitly founded "to provide an elastic currency" to mitigate the price fluctuations that arise from changes in the aggregate demand for the US dollar.

What distinguishes Bitcoin from these government currencies is the absence of a stability mechanism. Bitcoin's aggregate demand is driven by price expectations, and these expectations react in unpredictable ways to news, sentiments, and rumors. These highly volatile expectations affect aggregate demand, and since the Bitcoin supply path is fixed, Bitcoin's price volatility is high.

Table 6.1 summarizes Bitcoin's price volatility. The table shows the highest and lowest prices for the years 2009–2018 as well as the annualized volatility of the daily returns. The price volatilities are very large but decrease over time.

Figure 6.3 displays the rolling annualized price volatility on the basis of the standard deviation of the last 365 daily returns. The figure confirms the results presented in table 6.1. Bitcoin's price volatility is decreasing over time but is still much higher than the purchasing power volatility of the US dollar.

As discussed above, the reason for Bitcoin's high price volatility is the absence of a price stability mechanism in the Bitcoin protocol. Accordingly, it is very likely that the Bitcoin unit will forever display much higher short-term price fluctuations than government-operated fiat currencies. It is thus hardly surprising that various suggestions for creating a price-stable cryptocurrency have been developed.[33,70,120]

Table 6.1
Highest and lowest prices for the respective years and annualized volatility of the daily returns.

Jahr	Min	Max	$\sigma_{ann}(\Delta)$
2009	0.00	0.00	0.00
2010	0.00	0.50	∞
2011	0.30	35.00	1.96
2012	4.33	15.40	0.63
2013	13.40	1151.00	1.43
2014	310.74	953.29	0.75
2015	178.10	465.32	0.69
2016	364.33	998.33	0.48
2017	777.76	19497.40	0.95
2018	3236.76	17527.00	0.81
2019	3399.47	13016.23	0.68

Source: Data from Blockchain Explorer, n.d., https://www.blockchain.com/explorer; CoinMarket-Cap, website, n.d., https://coinmarketcap.com.

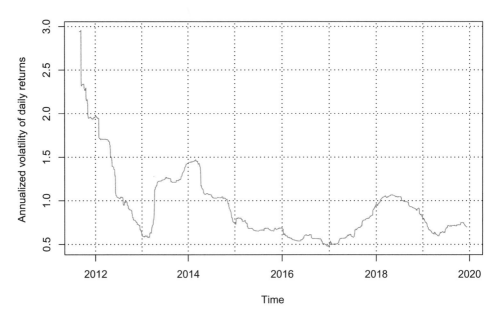

Figure 6.3
Annualized volatility of the daily returns of the Bitcoin price over the past 365 days.
Source: Data from Blockchain Explorer, n.d., https://www.blockchain.com/explorer; CoinMarket-Cap, website, n.d., https://coinmarketcap.com.

Table 6.2
Three types of stablecoins.

Target	Stability Mechanism	Type of Collateral	Examples
US$ Parity	Algorithmic	None	Basis
US$ Parity	Collateral	On-Chain (e.g., Ether)	DAI
US$ Parity	Collateral	Off-Chain (e.g., US$)	Tether

6.1.4 Stablecoins: The Quest for a Low-Volatility Cryptocurrency

A stablecoin is a cryptoasset that is developed with the aim of minimizing price volatility by embedding a stability mechanism.

The first stablecoins emerged in 2014 (e.g., BitShares, NuBits, Tether).[197,213] The report *The state of stablecoins* identifies and describes a total of fifty-seven live and prelaunch stablecoins.[4] The market capitalization of all stablecoins at the beginning of 2019 is roughly US$2.7 billion (which is roughly 2 percent of the total market capitalization of all cryptoassets). The largest one is Tether with a market capitalization of around US$2 billion.

There are three types of stablecoins that differ mainly in terms of the stability mechanism and the form of the collateral. The stability mechanism either is algorithmic or uses collateral. Collateral can be either off-chain or on-chain as explained further below. The three types are displayed in table 6.2.[5]

All stablecoins break the main value proposition of Bitcoin by adding some degree of centralization. The reason is that stability requires that the supply of a stablecoin adjusts to demand changes, which cannot be accomplished without introducing some degree of centralization. In some systems, this "only" requires price feeds; that is, *oracles* that inform a smart contract about the market price of the collateral and the stablecoin. In other systems, there is a centralized issuer who manipulates the supply of the stablecoin at his discretion. We will explain these mechanisms further below. Before we do so, it is worthwhile to have a look at how central banks stabilize their currencies.

---

4. We could not establish the exact publishing date for this report. Blockchain, *The State of Stablecoins*, Luxembourg: Blockchain, n.d., https://www.blockchain.com/ru/static/pdf/StablecoinsReportFinal.pdf.

5. The target is the reference asset to which the stablecoin is pegged. For most stablecoins, including the three examples that we discuss in this section (Basis, DAI, and Tether), this is the US dollar. However, a large part of our discussion also applies to stablecoins that use other currencies or a real asset such as gold.

Central Banking   There are two broad models of how central banks stabilize their currencies. Most central banks define a basket of goods and announce an inflation target with respect to this basket. Typically, the inflation target is around 2 percent inflation per year. Interestingly, there is no scientific evidence that a 2 percent inflation target is optimal, but most central banks nevertheless use it.

The problem with a "basket of goods" target is that central banks have no "direct" tools to influence its price. That is, they cannot simply buy and sell this basket to stabilize its price. To circumvent this problem, they have invented an arsenal of monetary policy tools such as open market operations, channel systems and floor systems, paying interest on money, negative interest rates, and reserve requirements, to name just a few. The interested reader can learn about these instruments in any monetary economics textbook. We mention these instruments here to emphasize that stabilizing the price of a "basket of goods" is not straightforward.

It is much easier to stabilize a currency against another currency or against any single asset for that matter. Some central banks use this stabilization mechanism. A currency board is a stability mechanism where the local currency is pegged to another currency, most often the US dollar.[6] A currency board creates only one unit of the local currency in exchange for one US dollar. It then holds the US dollar in its most liquid form as currency reserve. Consequently, the local currency is backed with 100 percent reserves at all time. The currency board redeems the local currency against the US dollar on demand. Such a peg cannot break since every unit of the local currency is backed by fully liquid US dollar reserves.

Nevertheless, monetary history is full of examples where currency pegs fail. The reason is politics. In a nutshell, exchange rate pegs fail for three reasons. First, under an exchange rate peg a country inherits the interest rates and the inflation rate from the country to which it pegs its currency. Unfortunately, these rates can become out of line and inflict severe damage to the national economy (for example, by generating high unemployment rates). This misalignment generates political pressure to abolish the peg. Second, under a currency peg, seigniorage income is small because currency reserves typically pay no or very low interest. For this reason, many countries do not hold fully liquid reserves, making them vulnerable to speculative attacks. Third, under a currency board a country cannot just print money when there is an emergency. This means, for example, that the central bank cannot assume the role of the "lender of last

---

6. The Hong Kong dollar is a good example of a national currency that is managed by a currency board.

resort" during a banking crisis. It is also not possible to finance the "government" during emergencies such as wars. As a result, currency boards are often abandoned during such crisis events.

In what follows, we discuss the three design types of stablecoins mentioned in table 6.2.

Algorithmic Stablecoins   The defining characteristic of a pure algorithmic stablecoin is the absence of collateral. Instead, the designer issues two assets (sometimes even three). One asset is the stablecoin, which we assume is pegged to the US dollar. The second asset is a bond that is redeemed for stablecoins at a future date.[7] We call this bond the "stablecoin bond."

The basic stability mechanism of an algorithmic stablecoin works as follows. If the demand for the stablecoin increases, its price also increases. To maintain the peg to the US dollar, the issuer creates additional stablecoins. These additional stablecoins are either airdropped or used to redeem any outstanding stablecoin bonds. Increasing the supply of an algorithmic stablecoin in such a way will eventually reduce its price.

If the demand decreases, the issuer creates additional stablecoin bonds and sells them against the stablecoin to reduce the quantity of stablecoins in circulation. The stablecoin bond is a promise to future stablecoins; that is, algorithmic stablecoins attempt to stabilize a falling price by promising to increase the stablecoin supply in the future.[190] To incentivize agents to buy the stablecoin bonds, they are sold at a discount. The discount is determined by market forces.

For example, assume a negative aggregate demand shock for the stablecoin occurs due to fake news. The price of the stablecoin falls below one US dollar. Because of severe doubts that the peg can be maintained, stablecoin bond buyers ask for a large discount—say, 50 percent. That is, they are willing to pay US$0.5 for a stablecoin bond that promises US$1 in stablecoins. This implies that, for every stablecoin that is removed from circulation, a promise to print two stablecoins is created. Prospective stablecoin bond buyers will take into account the future supply increase and might even ask for a larger discount than 50 percent. Increasing the discount would increase the future quantity of stablecoins even more. These dynamics can easily break the peg.[87]

---

7. To the best of our knowledge, the basic idea of an algorithmic stablecoin has been first proposed by Robert Sams.[190]

Box 6.2
Libra: Facebook's Stablecoin

In May 2019, Facebook announced that it intends to launch the Libra stablecoin. The coin will be pegged to a basket of currencies. The project is backed by the Libra Association and is headquartered in Switzerland, which includes many companies from the payment and technology sectors.

Given the large size of Facebook's network and the profound experience of some members of the Libra Association with payment technology, the Libra stablecoin may be quickly developed and adopted and become the first international privately issued virtual currency. However, the project faces severe regulatory hurdles. An "international currency" must be compatible with regulations in all countries in which it is offered. In some countries that would certainly require that the Libra Association obtains banking licenses and fulfill KYC and AML requirements in all countries. Further, given Facebook's many issues with user privacy and data leaks, lawmakers will ask tough questions with respect to data protection.

Moreover, the Libra blockchain is not decentralized and permissionless. Hence, access may be restricted as the Libra token is subject to counterparty risk. Accordingly, Libra has very little in common with Bitcoin and serves a different purpose.

Basis[2] is the most prominent algorithmic stablecoin. It raised US$133 million from various venture capital funds. The project was recently closed. The official explanation was regulatory issues;[8] however, we believe that the decision was partially influenced by the realization that the economics of the Basis stablecoin rested on shaky foundations. These weaknesses have been pointed out by Barry Eichengreen:[87]

> Here, too, the flaw in the model will be obvious to even a novice central banker. The issuer's ability to service the bonds depends on the growth of the platform, which is not guaranteed. If the outcome becomes less certain, the price of the bonds will fall. More bonds will then have to be issued to prevent a given fall in the value of the coin, making it even harder to meet interest obligations. Under plausible circumstances, there may be no price, however low, that attracts willing buyers of additional bonds. Again, the result will be collapse of the peg.

As suggested by Eichengreen, any designer of an algorithmic stablecoin should pay close attention to the vast economic literature on currency pegs. It is unclear how an algorithmic stability mechanism reacts to downward pressure and how long it can withstand such pressure. Who would be willing to the take the chance and

---

8. According to their website: "Unfortunately, having to apply US securities regulation to the system had a serious negative impact on our ability to launch Basis."[2]

buy stablecoin bonds if there is a panic? Nobody knows. For this reason, algorithmic stablecoins are prone to panics and sentiment-based swings. [109]

Our recommendation is to be very skeptical about algorithmic stablecoins. Among all the stability mechanisms that we discuss in this section, algorithmic stablecoins have the weakest foundations.

Collateralized Stablecoins: On-Chain   The working of a collateralized stablecoin with on-chain collateral is best explained by the DAI stablecoin, which is pegged to the US dollar. [211] The DAI stablecoin is an ERC-20 token and is based on a set of smart contracts on the Ethereum blockchain. Everyone can generate new DAI tokens. To do so, a user must send Ether—the native cryptoasset of the Ethereum blockchain—to one of the smart contracts. These funds serve as collateral for a loan in DAI. The interest rate is called the stability fee and a DAI loan is called a collateralized debt position (CDP).

Box 6.3
Demand and Supply in the DAI Stablecoin System

Fundamentally, agents with different risk attitudes are at the origin of the aggregate demand and the aggregate supply of the DAI stablecoin.

Aggregate supply of DAI. Agents who want to increase the risk of their portfolios of cryptoassets can use the DAI stablecoin to leverage their portfolios as follows. They can borrow DAI stablecoins and sell the newly created DAI for Ether or any other price-volatile cryptocurrency (leverage). This increases their risk exposures.

Aggregate demand for DAI. Agents who want to reduce the risk in their portfolios of cryptoassets can sell any price-volatile cryptocurrency for the DAI stablecoin. This decreases their risk exposures.

Thus, transfer of risk is at the origin of the aggregate demand and the aggregate supply of the DAI stablecoin. Since demand and supply can shift in unpredictable ways, there is a need for a mechanism that stabilizes the DAI price. This mechanism is explained in box 6.4.

Since a DAI loan is backed with Ether and the price of Ether is volatile, the loan has to be over-collateralized. Currently, the minimum collateral is 150 percent. That is, if a user locks Ether of value US\$150 in the smart contract, he can get a DAI loan of US\$100. It is strongly advised to hold much more collateral than 150 percent. The reason is that if the collateral value falls below 150 percent, the user's CDP is automatically liquidated—that is, the Ether held as collateral are automatically sold against DAI.

Box 6.4
DAI's Stability Mechanism

If the market price of DAI is above US$1, the stability mechanism must ensure that additional DAI stablecoins are created. This is indeed the case as the following arbitrage example demonstrates. Assume that the DAI market price is US$2. Then the following arbitrage opportunity exists. Get a loan of 1,000 DAI and sell them for US$2,000. The newly created DAI coins increase supply. If sufficiently many arbitrageurs follow this strategy, the higher supply will eventually reduce the DAI price. Once the price falls to US$1, buy 1,000 DAI for US$1,000 and pay back your debt. The only risk of this strategy is that the price of the Ether collateral may move in the wrong direction during the waiting period for this strategy to be profitable.

If the market price of DAI is below US$1, the stability mechanism must ensure that DAI stablecoins are removed from circulation. This is indeed the case as the following arbitrage example demonstrates. Assume that the DAI price has dropped to US$0.5, and consider an agent with a debt of 1,000 DAI. At this price, he can buy 1,000 DAI for US$500 and then use the 1,000 DAI to pay back his debt. This will unlock the Ether collateral and yield a profit of US$500.

The above description explains how the stability mechanism works in normal times when CDP owners expect the price of DAI to return to US$1. However, if in the second example they expect the price of DAI to fall further, they would have an incentive to wait even longer before they pay back their loans. In this case, the DAI price might continue to fall. [179]

The stability fee is one of the key monetary policy instruments of the DAI stablecoin. The stability fee is the interest rate that CDP owners have to pay on their outstanding DAI debts. An increase of the stability fee will reduce the incentive to open new CDPs and increase the incentive to close existing CDPs by paying back the DAI debt. An increase of the stability fee will therefore reduce the supply of DAI ceteris paribus. The DAI stability system is still fine-tuning how to use this instrument to increase the stability of the DAI.

There are additional mechanisms in place to ensure that the DAI price remains stable against the US dollar, even under high stress. To explain all of them goes beyond the scope of this section, but we would like to encourage readers to conduct their own research on this very interesting project.[a]

---

a. The DAI stablecoin has been developed and is governed by the Maker Platform, which is a decentralized organization.

The DAI stability mechanism is working so far, but only time will tell whether the DAI stablecoin is robust under all possible adverse events. Further, there are additional risks. First, it is possible that the DAI system of smart contracts is faulty and one day will behave in unexpected ways. This is the typical risk that applies to all smart contracts. Second, the DAI system requires price feeds. In particular, the smart contract needs to know the Ether price at any point in time. DAI has several distinct Ether price feeds and uses a weighted average of these feeds. Yet these price feeds add some centralization to an otherwise decentralized system and are a potential attack vector. Finally, the DAI stablecoin has kept its value during a time where the Ether price lost more than 90 percent. Nevertheless, it remains to be seen how the system would react when the Ether price falls by 50 percent or more in a very short time period.

Collateralized Stablecoins: Off-Chain Stablecoins based on off-chain collateral use regular bank accounts or other forms of centralized custody to hold the collateral. By far the largest and best-known stablecoin using off-chain collateral is Tether, which is pegged to the US dollar. It was founded in 2014[212] and is associated with the Hong Kong–based exchange platform Bitfinex. The history of the Tether stablecoin reveals the main issues that arise with off-chain collateral: namely, the lack of transparency, absence of censorship resistance, and lack of profitability.

First, from its inception there has been considerable uncertainty whether Tether has been fully backed with an adequate amount of US dollars. On the Tether website there are statements such as "Tether is always fully transparent" and "our reserve holdings are published daily." Unfortunately, we could not find an independent statement of their reserve holdings. The one on their website is from June 2018.

Second, holding reserves off-chain in a bank account is a central point of attack. Governments can simply shut down the Tether stablecoin by freezing the US dollar reserves. Interestingly, the issuer of the Tether stablecoin had to move its banking relations several times across various jurisdictions for undisclosed reasons.

Third, stability requires that a stablecoin is backed up at 100 percent of its value and that the assets held as reserves are liquid. Unfortunately, liquid assets such as cash pay no or very low interest. The main problem for an issuer of a stablecoin, therefore, is profitability. Tether, for example, charges fees on withdrawals and deposits. To make money, an issuer of a fully off-chain collateralized stablecoin is always tempted to engage in fractional reserve banking. This is not much different from the traditional banking sector where fractional reserve banking is the norm. The fact that transparency can be fully achieved only with expensive audits does not help profitability.

188

Chapter 6

Box 6.5
Fractional Reserve Banking

In the case of the US dollar and any other government-issued fiat currency, commercial banks create a large share of the aggregate money supply by engaging in fractional reserve banking (see section 1.5.1). Fractional reserve banking is also conceivable in the Bitcoin network. If Bitcoin users deposit their Bitcoin at a custodian, there is nothing in principle that would prevent this firm from keeping only a fraction of customer Bitcoin deposits in reserve. There are even concrete indications that some centralized exchanges and online wallets follow a business model of this kind. [115,116,205] Such business practices can potentially have devastating effects, in particular since there is currently very little regulation and no lender of last resort in Bitcoin's financial landscape.

Potential safekeeping services can be implemented using custodial options that are based on multisig solutions. This prevents the service provider from having exclusive control over the assets. Another option would be to use cryptographic proof to certify the level of reserves held in custody. [134,75]

Box 6.6
The Price History of Four Stablecoins

The following charts show the price history of NuBits, Tether, DAI, and USDC. Looking at the close-up figures on the right side, it becomes apparent that all stablecoins are subject to certain price fluctuations. However, there are vast differences, including the spectacular crash of NuBits. All stablecoins will be tested. The actual price development mainly depends on the implementation of the stability mechanism, the collateral, and the issuers' credibility.

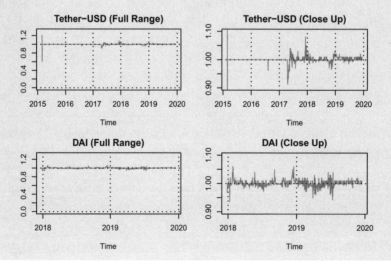

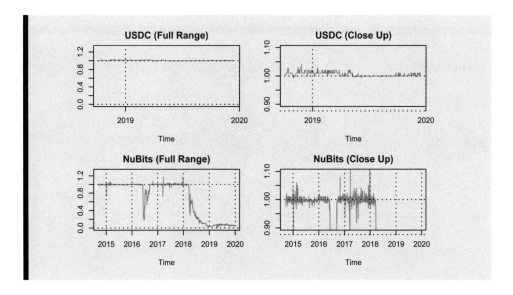

Stablecoin Outlook   Collateralized on-chain stablecoins such as DAI offer many benefits. They are useful for machine-to-machine payments, in smart contracts, and in some cases even atomic cross-blockchain transactions. Currently, we can see the first designs, and it is possible that many of them will fail. However, because a price-stable cryptoasset has so many benefits, blockchain enthusiasts will keep innovating relentlessly until they find a working design.

There are a few lessons that can be drawn today.[33] First, price stability requires collateral of at least 100 percent. For that reason, we discard the idea that stability can be attained solely through a fancy algorithm. Second, on-chain collateral has many benefits over off-chain collateral. With on-chain collateral, transparency is automatically given as demonstrated by the DAI stablecoin. Every user can verify that the collateral is effectively there. Further, off-chain collateral is a single point of attack and the threat of a sudden closure by an outside entity is clearly present. When the collateral is on-chain this threat is nonexistent. Finally, a stablecoin with off-chain collateral typically entails severe costs (e.g., audits) and is often issued with a profit motive. This results in a permanent desire to engage in fractional reserve banking as in the traditional banking world. Again, this desire is not present with a decentralized on-chain collateral solution like DAI.

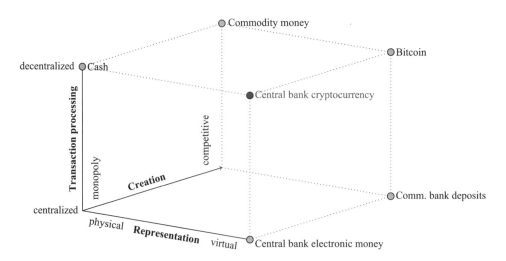

Figure 6.4
Central bank cryptocurrency.

6.1.5   Central Bank Digital Currency

There is the possibility that central banks will step in and offer a stable CBDC. There are two fundamentally distinct proposals for central bank digital currency: "central bank cryptocurrency" (a.k.a. Fedcoin) and "central bank electronic money for all." The distinction between the two can be easily identified if we extend figure 2.1 by adding "central bank cryptocurrency" as displayed in figure 6.4.

As shown in figure 6.4, the distinguishing characteristic of cryptocurrencies is the decentralized nature of transaction handling that enables users to trade Bitcoin units pseudo-anonymously without intermediaries and without having to ask anyone for permission.[9] Decentralization is essential for achieving the status of a censorship-resistant asset, which is the main selling point of Bitcoin.

Decentralization is a red flag for central banks.[10] The reputational risk of a decentralized national currency is simply too high.[31] Think of a hypothetical Fedcoin used by a drug cartel to launder money or a terrorist organization to acquire weapons. Moreover, commercial banks would rightfully start asking why they have to follow KYC ("know

---

9. For an alternative classification, see Bech and Garratt (2017).[22]
10. Why would a *central bank* issue a *decentralized virtual currency*? This is the crucial question that one needs to address when investigating central bank digital currency.

your customer") and AML ("anti-money laundering") regulations while the central bank is undermining any effects of this regulation by issuing an anonymous cryptocurrency with permissionless access. Further, any central bank that designs a permissionless cryptocurrency that circulates in other countries will be seriously challenged by its central bank peers. The Federal Reserve Bank of the United States or the People's Bank of China will likely not accept a hypothetical SNBcoin issued by the Swiss National Bank that is used by the citizens of these countries to a significant extent.

Box 6.7
Fedcoin

About five years after the publication of the Bitcoin white paper, the first calls for a Fedcoin emerged. As far as we know, the term Fedcoin was first mentioned in a blog post by J. P. Koning in 2013.[133] The idea was picked up by David Andolfatto in a blog post in 2015.[3] Interestingly, in this post, Andolfatto suggests that "because Fedcoin wallets, like cash wallets, are permissionless and free, even people without proper ID can utilize the product." Further, he suggests that it is an excellent idea that a "Fedcoin should be spared any KYC restrictions. ...The government seems able to live with not imposing KYC on physical cash transactions—why should it insist on KYC for digital cash transactions?"

In our view, his comparison ignores the fundamental difference between physical and virtual money. Due to its physical nature (see figure 6.4), cash users can remain anonymous and do not need to ask for permission to use it. There is no choice with cash; no central bank can issue physical cash where agents that use it in peer-to-peer transactions can be identified. In contrast, anonymity and access rules are choice variables when designing virtual money. It can be designed such that users remain anonymous or such that the buyer and the seller of every payment can be identified.

In Berentsen and Schär's article, "The case for central bank electronic money and the non-case for central bank cryptocurrencies,"[31] we (the article's authors) argue that central banks will opt for centralized virtual money to minimize reputational and political risks. With "central bank digital money for all" there is straightforward technology available that allows central banks to issue centralized virtual money that it can control tightly. This money does not require blockchain technology.

Box 6.8
An ERC-20 Fedcoin

In the previous note we argue that it makes no sense for a central bank to issue a decentralized currency. Nevertheless, from a technological point of view a central bank could easily introduce a central bank cryptocurrency. There exist technologies such as Ethereum's ERC-20 or ERC-223 token standards that can be used to create fungible tokens that are compatible with the Ethereum infrastructure.

Box 6.8 (continued)

To ensure parity between a crypto fiat unit and central bank reserves, the central bank must be willing to buy and sell any number of these tokens at par. The valuation will depend on the central bank's credibility, but if a central bank is determined to issue a central bank cryptocurrency, it would have the means to do so. In fact, the convertibility mechanism can be compared with different denominations of cash, where central banks make a similar claim.

Central Bank Electronic Money for All In the Berentsen and Schär article referenced in note 6.7,[31] we argue that there is a strong case for central bank money in electronic form (i.e., central bank electronic money in figure 6.4). Further, we argue that it would be very easy to implement. Implementation requires only that central banks would allow households and firms to open simple payment accounts with them. This would allow households and firms to make payments with central bank electronic money instead of commercial bank deposits.

There are many benefits. First, it satisfies the population's need for virtual money without facing counterparty risk. The reason is that, in contrast to private banks, a central bank cannot default on debt denominated in the national currency since it can always print money to pay its obligations.[31]

Second, there is substantial political pressure to reduce the use of cash and many countries have already restricted its use considerably.[11][30] The disappearence of cash would imply that households and firms will have no access to legal tender under the current monetary order. By offering simple payment accounts, central banks enable the public to hold legal tender in electronic form. A large part of the population will consider it a close substitute for cash, and this will make it easier to say goodbye to cash.

Third, "central bank electronic money for all" will increase financial stability. To continue to attract deposits, commercial banks would need to alter their business model or to increase interest payments on deposits to compensate users for the additional risk they assume. The disciplining effect on commercial banks will be reinforced by the fact that, in the event of a loss of confidence, customers' money can be quickly transferred to central bank electronic money accounts. To avoid this, the banks must make their business models more secure, for example, by taking fewer risks or by holding more reserves and capital.

---

11. The political pressure is based on the following views that we do not share. First, cash promotes crime and facilitates money laundering and tax evasion. Second, cash hinders monetary policy by limiting the central bank's ability to use negative nominal interest rates as a policy option.

Box 6.9
Bank Runs under "Central Bank Electronic Money for All"

With "central bank electronic money for all" there could be rapid shifts of large quantities of money from commercial bank deposits to central bank accounts that have no real causes (bank panics that are unrelated to fundamentals). This concern is emphasized in the Bank for International Settlement's 2018 report: [167] "the most significant and plausible financial stability risk of a general purpose CBDC is that it can facilitate a flight away from private financial institutions and markets towards the central bank."

A central bank has two instruments to address this issue. [31] First, the payment account can be capped. That is, it is possible to implement an upper bound on the quantity of money that an agent can hold in such an account. An upper bound is particularly recommended at the beginning for central banks and the private sector to gain experience with these types of accounts. Second, central banks must offer standing facilities where commercial banks can borrow against collateral in a fast and uncomplicated way.

Fourth, "central bank electronic money for all" simplifies monetary policy. The central bank could simply use the interest rate paid on these accounts as its main policy tool. If markets are not segregated—meaning that everyone has access to electronic central bank money—the interest rate on these accounts will be the lowest interest rate in the economy. The reason is that central bank electronic money will be the most liquid asset in the economy and holders of such money face no counterparty risk since a central bank cannot become illiquid.

Box 6.10
Exit Strategies

Many central banks are currently discussing the possibility of normalizing interest rates. Because of the massive amount of liquidity created in response to the financial crisis of 2008, standard monetary policy instruments such as open market operations are ineffective, and all instruments that are currently discussed have the characteristic that the central bank pays, in some form, interest on reserves. [27]

There is a political economy issue with these payments since, as of today, they are paid only to the few financial intermediaries that have access to central bank electronic money. The general public might not consider such large payments equitable or beneficial, and there is a high risk that it will trigger political controversies that have the potential to affect central bank independence. [28]

Central bank electronic money is an elegant way of avoiding possible political upheavals with regard to these interest payments by allowing the whole population to have access to these interest payments and not just a small group of commercial banks.

Fifth, implementing "central bank electronic money for all" is straightforward since these accounts can be used only for making payments. No credit can be obtained, and so almost no monitoring is needed (of course, some standard regulations would still apply). Further, it would be possible to mandate that commercial banks have to offer such accounts in the name of the central bank to their existing clients. The monetary units in these accounts would be excluded in the commercial banks' balance sheets to protect these assets in the case of a default.

There is an increasing number of academic papers that study issues around CBDC. A few have investigated the effect that CBDC has on the private banking sector[4,57] or have derived conditions under which the issuance of inside money and outside money are equivalent.[45] Some others focus on the societal benefits and welfare effects of introducing CBDC[43,124] or on the monetary policy implications.[24,124,162]

6.2 Scalability

The Bitcoin network can currently process fewer than ten transactions per second.[12] Sometimes this bottleneck expresses itself through high Bitcoin transaction fees and large pools of unconfirmed transactions, leading to an intense and fierce debate on how to scale Bitcoin and other cryptoassets. It is important to note that this debate has been ongoing for many years and that there are dozens of proposals on how to improve the overall performance of cryptocurrencies. For many of these solutions there are existing software packages, and some of them have already been implemented.[165] In this section, we will discuss the two most prominent scaling solutions: block size increases and payment channels, including the Lightning Network. Before doing so, we provide some data about the necessity to scale.

6.2.1 The Congestion Problem

Figure 6.5 depicts total Bitcoin transactions per day. From its inception in 2009, the number of transactions per day has constantly grown until peaking at the end of 2017. After the peak we observe a steep drop of almost 50 percent at the beginning of 2018. More recently, the number of transactions is around 200,000 transactions per day and appears to be increasing again.

In July 2010, the size of a block of the Bitcoin blockchain was capped at 1 MB. Over the past four years the average transaction size was between 400 and 600 bytes. This

---

12. The exact number depends on the type of transaction and the script size. Theoretically, ten transactions per second and slightly more would be feasible; however, in practice this number usually lies somewhere around four transactions per second.

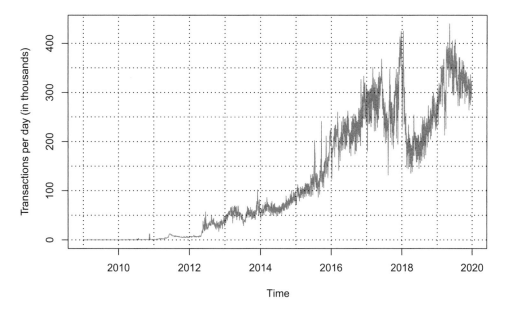

Figure 6.5
Number of Bitcoin transactions per day.

implies that a block can include between 1,600 and 2,500 transactions. [165] On average, a new block is added to the blockchain every ten minutes. Thus, the Bitcoin blockchain usually digests about three to four transactions per second. Depending on the type of the transaction and the corresponding script, there is room for improvement; however, even a number close to ten transactions per second would be no serious contender for a global payment network.

Centralized payment networks such as Visa and Mastercard achieve numbers in the hundreds or thousands. In 2016, PayPal processed 7.6 billion payment transactions, which comes down to about 240 transactions per second. The Visa network handled about 111.2 billion transactions in 2017, which is about 3,500 transactions per second. According to a Visa report, the maximum capacity of their network is 65,000 transactions per second. [165,172,220]

The low capacity of the Bitcoin network can lead to serious congestion. The first effect is that transaction fees spike during times of high activity. The second effect is a large increase in the mempool; that is, the pool of unconfirmed transactions. Figure 6.6 shows the known mempool. In particular, by the end of 2017, almost all blocks were very close to the 1 MB limit, and the mempool filled up quickly.

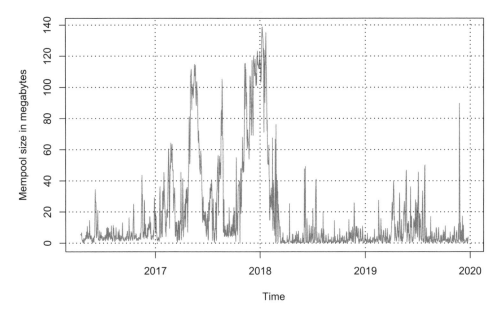

Figure 6.6
Unconfirmed Bitcoin transactions.
Data from Blockchain Explorer, n.d., https://www.blockchain.com/explorer.

The crypto community has been working on many solutions to these scaling problems, some of which have already been used in practice. In the following sections we discuss some of the most popular scaling approaches.

6.2.2   Block Size Limit Increase

Increasing the block size limit requires only small changes to the Bitcoin software, and it immediately increases the number of transactions per second that can be processed by the network. The change could be implemented through a one-time permanent increase, a predetermined growth path, or a dynamic block size, where the block size limit changes over time depending on the size of the last few blocks.

Despite the relatively small change in the code, such alterations should not be made lightly. Any increase of the block size limit corresponds to a change in the consensus rules, which is not backward compatible (i.e., a hard fork or forced fork). If some users disagree with the changes or forget to update their client, the change will lead to a fork (see section 2.5.3).

Moreover, a block size increase may make decentralization more difficult. If, for example, the block size limit were raised to 128 MB, the cost of running a full node would significantly increase, most likely leading to fewer full nodes and more centralization. Block size limit increases would also significantly prolong the time it takes to forward a block in the network, leading to more *block races* and higher orphan rates and thus adding uncertainty. Further, larger blocks foster centralization in mining. Accordingly, we do not think that block size limit increases should be thought of as the primary solution for scaling cryptoassets.[13] At best, they are accompanying measures to support other scaling approaches.

Box 6.11
The Scaling Debate

In the crypto community, there is much debate on the pros and cons of block size limit increases and other scaling solutions. Indeed, the opinions are so entrenched that Bitcoin split into two rival camps in August 2017. A large part of the Bitcoin community followed Bitcoin Core, which implemented SegWit; some people opted out for the alternative blockchain that is known today as Bitcoin Cash or B-Cash, increasing the size of their blocks to 8 MB, later increasing them to 32 MB, and currently considering further increases. Moreover, they decided not to implement SegWit (see section 4.7). As of today, the market value of the Bitcoin blockchain is much higher than the market value of the B-Cash blockchain. Recently the B-Cash community split into more camps, leading to a greater variety of smaller chains. In terms of market cap, community, and developer interest, these alternative camps are mostly negligible.

6.2.3   Payment Channels and the Lightning Network

So-called payment channels enable *off-chain* transactions; that is, transactions that are not propagated to the Bitcoin blockchain. They are shared exclusively between the two parties involved and later added to the Bitcoin blockchain in aggregated form. In this respect, off-chain transactions benefit from the security of the blockchain without burdening it.

Payment channels are based on multisig (pay-to-script-hash) unlocking conditions and allow two parties to perform almost any number of (micro)transactions. Such payments are secure and immediately valid and can be made between parties without an

---

13. Another quick fix to allow for more transactions per second is reducing the average time it takes to generate a block. Technically, this is very similar to a block size limit increase and can also be done by changing a parameter. In fact, most blockchains generate blocks much faster than Bitcoin. For example, Litecoin has an average time of 2.5 minutes to mine a block. The drawbacks of this approach are similar to the ones of a block size increase.

established relationship of trust. An additional advantage is that only two blockchain transactions are required to process any number of off-chain transactions. [174] In the following, we describe different types of payment channels and show how they can be linked via payment networks, such as the Lightning Network.

Unidirectional Payment Channels   In the simplest case, all payments within a payment channel are made in the same direction. If Tamara wants to make multiple payments to Brian over a period of time, they can open a unidirectional payment channel. For this they open a 2-of-2 multisig address (see section 4.5.3). Tamara creates a *funding transaction* in favor of the multisig address, which provides the Bitcoin balance for the payment channel. The higher the balance, the greater is the *capacity* of the payment channel.

Even before Tamara signs the funding transaction she composes a second transaction that returns the balance of the funding transaction from the multisig address back to her address. She sends this second transaction to Brian, who partially signs it and returns it to Tamara. This transaction is also known as a *refund transaction* and is subject to a nLockTime time lock. The time lock adds an additional condition to the transaction, which is that "I cannot be processed by the Bitcoin network before block T." This means that the refund transaction is processed by the Bitcoin network only after a certain point in time (usually measured in block height). It serves as a fallback if no other agreement has been reached by then and guarantees that Tamara will receive her balance back even if Brian is no longer available. Consequently, Tamara does not become dependent on Brian.

So far, two transactions have been prepared, but no message has yet been propagated to the Bitcoin network. All communication was strictly private between Tamara and Brian. This is now changing in a third step. Tamara propagates the funding transaction to the Bitcoin network. The payment channel is ready when the transaction is confirmed.

Tamara can now make her first (micro)payment using the payment channel. For this purpose, she creates a so-called *commitment transaction* that redistributes the Bitcoin balance of the multisig address. A commitment transaction is not propagated to the Bitcoin network for the time being but only shared between the two parties involved. Tamara creates a commitment transaction with two outputs: output 1 in favor of Brian and output 2 in favor of her own address. For example, if Tamara has opened a payment channel with 0.1 Bitcoin units and now wants to make a payment of 0.01 Bitcoin units to Brian, she will partially sign a transaction from the multisig address that will credit

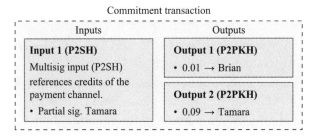

Figure 6.7
The output of the multisig address of the payment channel is used as input for the commitment transaction. Tamara signs the input and divides the balance between two outputs. The newly created outputs define the current state of the payment channel. The commitment transaction is only sent to Brian and not propagated to the Bitcoin network.

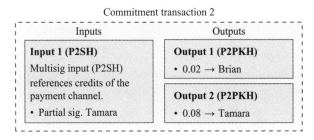

Figure 6.8
Commitment transaction 2 is created in the same way as its predecessor, partially signed by Tamara and sent to Brian. Its outputs define the new current state of the payment channel.

0.01 Bitcoin units to Brian's address and the remaining 0.09 Bitcoin units to her own address (see figure 6.7).[14]

If Tamara wants to send another 0.01 Bitcoin units to Brian later on, she creates a new commitment transaction with, again, two outputs—output 1 credits 0.02 Bitcoin units to Brian and output 2 credits the remaining 0.08 Bitcoin units to her own address (see figure 6.8).

Brian can close the payment channel at any time by adding his own signature to one of the partially signed commitment transactions and propagate it to the Bitcoin network. He has to choose between the various commitment transactions he received.

---

14. In fact, Tamara could transfer much smaller amounts. We decided to use relatively large numbers to make the examples easier to read.

They all use the same output as an input and are therefore competing. Brian will always choose the latest commitment transaction since it includes the largest payment for him. It is not possible for Tamara to cheat because, in order for her to propagate a transaction, she would require a signature from Brian. [36]

As long as the channel is open, Tamara can make any number of payments up to the initially deposited maximum amount. This maximum amount is called *channel capacity*. Since none of these payments are recorded in the Bitcoin blockchain, no transaction fees are due. Yet for the opening and closing of a payment channel, two transactions must be recorded in the Bitcoin blockchain and these two transactions are subject to a fee.

Possible use cases of payment channels include *pay-as-you-go* solutions such as per-second billing for Wi-Fi access or *pay walls* for content that can be unlocked through microtransactions. [217]

Bidirectional Payment Channels with Timelocks   Payment channels can also be used bidirectionally. However, once funds can flow in both directions, additional security measures need to be put in place. In particular, the goal is to prevent a person from publishing an old commitment transaction that was partially signed by the other party but no longer reflects the current state of the distribution of Bitcoin units.[15]

Let us follow up on our previous example where Brian received 0.02 Bitcoin units over the payment channel. Assume that he is now sending the 0.02 Bitcoin units back to Tamara with a third commitment transaction. The problem then becomes apparent. Brian holds two commitment transactions partially signed by Tamara with 0.01 (commitment transaction 1) and 0.02 Bitcoin units (commitment transaction 2) in his favor. Tamara holds commitment transaction 3, which is partially signed by Brian, with the entire channel balance of 0.1 Bitcoin units in her favor. Commitment transactions 1 and 2 are outdated and do not reflect the current state of the payment channel. Nevertheless, Brian could sign any one of them and propagate the old commitment transaction to the Bitcoin network.

The three commitment transactions (1–3) and the original refund transaction (0) are shown in table 6.3.

To prevent someone (in this case Brian) from propagating a transaction that does not correspond to the current state of the payment channel, each commitment transaction includes a `nLockTime` time lock. As discussed above, this restriction defines the earliest possible time at which a commitment transaction can be added to the blockchain.

---

15. In a unidirectional payment channel this problem does not exist. The person who receives the commitment transactions always has an incentive to propagate the latest transaction.

Table 6.3
Commitment transactions in bidirectional payment channel.

	Outputs		
#	Tamara	Brian	Partially signed
0	0.10	0.00	from Brian
1	0.09	0.01	from Tamara
2	0.08	0.02	from Tamara
3	0.10	0.00	from Brian

For each new commitment transaction the time lock is reduced by at least one block. If, for example, the payment channel was created at block t and the refund can be made at the earliest at block $t+1,008$, the first commitment transaction would have the time lock $t+1,007$ (or less), the second commitment transaction would have the time lock $t+1,006$ (or less), and the third commitment transaction would have the time lock $t+1,005$ (or less). This method ensures that the most recent commitment transaction can be propagated earlier than all other promises. The temporal sequence is illustrated in Figure 6.9.

Figure 6.9
Visualization of time locks.

Implementations using `nLockTime` have a drawback. The initial *refund transaction* creates an expiration date T for the channel. This leads to the necessity that the channel must be closed shortly before date T (at the latest at block $T-1$) and a new channel opened if required. Every closing and reopening requires two on-chain transactions with the corresponding transaction fees. If a larger value is selected for T, the payment channel does not need to be renewed as quickly, but at the same time there is the risk that the Bitcoin units will be locked in the payment channel for a longer period of time. This trade-off arises in both unidirectional and bidirectional payment channels.

In bidirectional implementations, the problem is exacerbated by the fact that with each commitment transaction, the expiration date is moved forward by at least one block. In a bidirectional payment channel with a timelock of $T=t+1,008$, a maximum of 1,007 commitment transactions can be created with the somewhat generous assumption that all `nLockTime` steps are one block only and that all transactions happen in a very short time period. This will rarely be the case. If the steps are larger than one block, the channel's life-span and the maximum number of commitment transactions will be reduced even further.[16]

Box 6.12
Various Time Locks

Time locks exist in various forms. They can be included in data fields at the transaction level or through the scripting language at the output level. Moreover, they exist in the form of absolute and relative time locks. An absolute time lock specifies a point in time or a block height at which the confirmed outputs can be referenced earliest. A relative time lock specifies a number of blocks that must elapse after the confirmation and before the newly created outputs can be referenced. An absolute time lock is comparable, for example, with the requirement "at 12 o'clock" while a relative time lock can be compared with the condition "in two hours." In the following, the four time locks are described.[177]

nLockTime. This is an absolute time lock at the transaction level that references a certain block height or a certain time. The field has existed since the beginning of Bitcoin and is considered the original time lock of Bitcoin.

CHECKLOCKTIMEVERIFY (CLTV). At the end of 2015 a new absolute time lock was introduced via BIP0065.[216] The difference to `nLockTime` is that this time lock is implemented as OP_CODE via the scripting language and thus refers to single outputs and not to a whole transaction. In this respect, the restriction can be used more flexibly.

nSequence. Analogous to `nLockTime`, this field has existed since the original implementation. However, it had a completely different meaning back then and was only later redefined so that it could be used as a relative time lock at the transaction level. The change is described in BIP0068[99] and was activated via a soft fork in mid-2016.

CHECKSEQUENCEVERIFY (CSV). This relative time lock dates back to BIP0112[145] and was activated via a soft fork in mid-2016. It is implemented as OP_CODE via the scripting language and thus refers to individual outputs.

---

16. Theoretically, it would be sufficient to reduce the time lock only for each change of direction of the cash flow. Several consecutive commitment transactions in the same direction can be seen as unidirectional cash flows and treated accordingly. Consequently, bidirectional payment channels could achieve significantly higher transaction numbers if they are subject to only a few directional changes. However, the fundamental problem of the limited life-span remains.

	Transaction level	Output level
	Consensus	Scripting language
Absolute time lock	nLockTime	CHECKLOCKTIMEVERIFY (CLTV)
Relative time lock	nSequence	CHECKSEQUENCEVERIFY (CSV)

It is important to note that due to the random block generation time and to the ever-changing total computing resources, the time a certain block height is reached is random.[a] Further, the timestamp of a block can be manipulated.[b]

a. The difficulty threshold is adjusted only every 2,016 blocks. In this respect, changes in computing resources can temporarily lead to a slightly faster or slower block creation rate. See also figure 6.1.
b. BIP0113 [125] tries to counteract this problem by using median values of the timestamps.

Bidirectional Payment Channels with Asymmetric Revocable Commitments The remarks in the last section suggest that in practice payment channels based on time locks are inefficient. A much better approach would be to invalidate old commitment transactions as soon as a newer commitment transaction is generated. This would prevent participants from propagating an old commitment transaction that no longer corresponds to the current state of the payment channel.

Unfortunately, commitment transactions cannot be easily withdrawn. A signed commitment transaction can be propagated to the blockchain at any time, and it becomes obsolete only if a competing transaction has been successfully added to the Bitcoin blockchain.[17] Luckily, a clever combination of special unlocking conditions and punishment mechanisms will create incentives such that no one wants to propagate an old state to the Bitcoin network. We are referring to *asymmetric revocable commitments*.

Let us expand our example so that Tamara and Brian open a new payment channel. This time both of them add 0.5 Bitcoin units, so the channel will have a total capacity of one Bitcoin unit. Instead of one refund transaction, two (asymmetric) refund transactions are now created. Let us first stick to Tamara's point of view. She receives a partially

---

17. The signature would still be valid even then, but since these are competing transactions, the commitment transaction would be ignored by the Bitcoin network as soon as a block containing the other transaction becomes part of the blockchain.

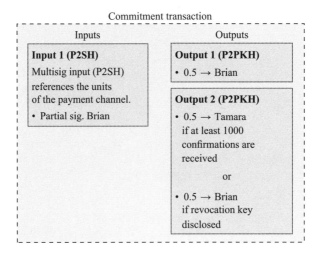

Figure 6.10
The output of the multisig address of the payment channel is used as input. This one is partially signed by Brian. If Tamara signs the transaction, output 1 is credited to Brian. Output 2 is credited to either Tamara or Brian, depending on whether Brian is in possession of the revocation key.

signed refund transaction with two outputs from Brian. Output 1 would give Brian 0.5 Bitcoin units and output 2 contains the 0.5 Bitcoin units for Tamara.

This is where it gets a little bit complicated. On the one hand, we want Tamara to be able to claim the amount she is entitled to and not be dependent on Brian. On the other hand, we must prevent her from publishing this *refund transaction* when it no longer reflects the current state of the payment channel.

To satisfy both requirements, the second output contains a `scriptPubKey`, which can be met by any one out of two conditions. Condition 1 is a time lock. Tamara can use output 2 as soon as the commitment transaction has a certain number of confirmations; that is, after a certain time delay, which is implemented via CHECKSEQUENCEVERIFY.

Condition 2 gives Brian the option to use output 2 before Tamara if he holds the revocation key for it. The revocation key is initially in Tamara's possession. But if Tamara creates a new commitment transaction, Brian will accept this new commitment transaction only if he receives the revocation key for the old commitment transaction. Once Brian is in possession of the revocation key, Tamara has no incentive to publish the old commitment transaction; otherwise Brian could use output 2 and thereby punish Tamara's fraud attempt. Figure 6.10 shows the relationships between inputs and outputs and the associated conditions.

From Brian's point of view, the situation is symmetric. He receives a partially signed transaction from Tamara with two outputs, where output 1 is in favor of Tamara and output 2 can be used by fulfilling any one of two conditions. Either Brian waits for a certain number of confirmations and can then use output 2, or Tamara is in possession of Brian's revocation key and can frontrun him using output 2 for herself. If it is the latest state of the payment channel, Brian can publish the transaction without constraint. However, if a more recent commitment transaction exists and Tamara is in possession of the associated revocation key, she is able to punish Brian for his fraudulent behavior.

This approach is an improvement over the exclusive use of time locks in section 6.2.3. In particular, payment channels with asymmetric revocable commitments do not have an expiration date. The drawback is that this mechanism requires the constant vigilance of both parties. For example, if Tamara propagates an old commitment transaction, Brian has to be online to be able to identify the attempted fraud. This requires Brian to constantly monitor the blockchain and look for potential violations. Consequently, this type of payment channel requires a 24/7 internet connection for both parties.

If a user cannot be online 24/7, he can delegate the monitoring to so-called *watchtowers*. These are service providers who constantly monitor the Bitcoin blockchain and punish the publication of old commitment transactions on behalf of the victim. As compensation, they receive part of the penalty paid by the fraudster. The use of multiple watchtowers prevents a potential fraudster from colluding with a watchtower. A person using the service only has to disclose very little information. In particular, the watchtower normally has no information about the identity of the persons involved or about the payment flow within the channel.

Lightning Network   Payment channels allow a very large number of (micro) transactions between two parties. However, they require a direct link between the two users. This is problematic once the network grows and the network participants want to be able to engage in transactions with anyone of the other particitpants. Let us assume, for example, that the network consists of n individuals. Then $\frac{n(n-1)}{2}$ blockchain transactions would be required to open a channel between any two users, and another $\frac{n(n-1)}{2}$ would be needed to close the channels. These blockchain transactions are of course subject to a transaction fee.

Moreover, each user would have to distribute its Bitcoin units among $n-1$ channels. It would, therefore, be ideal if we did not have to open a payment channel with every person but instead could forward the payments via a network of payment channels. This is where the Lightning Network comes in. [175]

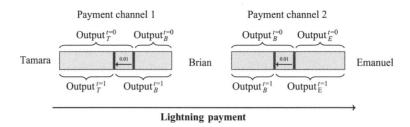

Figure 6.11
The payment is made via two payment channels. The balances in both channels get adjusted from
$t = 0$ to $t = 1$.

The Lightning Network is a so-called "second layer solution"; that is, an additional
network on top of the Bitcoin system that benefits from Bitcoin's security. Lightning
allows payments to be routed through multiple payment channels. It allows Tamara to
transfer Bitcoin units to Emanuel without opening a payment channel with Emanuel.
She could simply use an indirect connection through other payment channels. The
situation is shown in figure 6.11.

In the visualization in figure 6.11, Tamara uses the payment channel with Brian to
transfer him 0.01 Bitcoin units, and then Brian uses his channel with Emanuel so that
the 0.01 Bitcoin units will be credited to Emanuel. The problem with this approach is
that Brian may choose not to forward the payment in the second channel after having
accepted the payment in the first channel. To remove the need for trusting the other
party, the Lightning Network uses so-called *hash time-locked contracts* (HTLC).

HTLC links the use of an output to the disclosure of the preimage (input value) associated with a given hash value. The hash value is recorded in the script. Whoever can
provide the input value that leads to this hash value and meet any other criteria (like
signature requirements) may use the output.[18]

The easiest way to explain the concept is by providing an example. Figure 6.12 adds
an HTLC condition to figure 6.11. First, Emanuel creates a random number m. This random number serves as the input to the hash function and remains secret for the time

---

18. Originally, this method was developed in the context of atomic swaps between different
blockchains. The idea was that transactions on both blockchains depend on the disclosure of
the same input. This would guarantee that when confirming the transaction on blockchain A, the
corresponding transaction on blockchain B can also be propagated. However, HTLC can also be
used in the context of payment channels in such a way that either the Bitcoin units are adjusted
in all channels or in none of them.

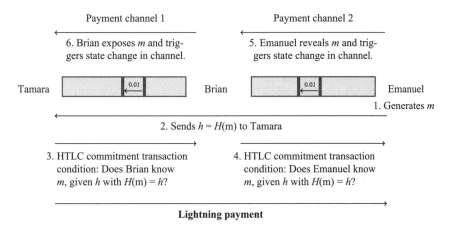

Figure 6.12
Linked payment channels with HTLC condition.

being. Second, Emanuel sends the associated hash value $h = H(m)$ to Tamara. Third, Tamara creates an HTLC commitment transaction. The state-changing output contains the unlocking condition that Brian (signature) must present the input m (hash-lock) within a certain number of blocks (CLTV time lock) to claim the output. Fourth, Brian creates an HTLC commitment transaction for the payment channel with Emanuel. Equivalently, Emanuel (signature) must present the input m (hash-lock) within a certain number of blocks (CLTV time lock) to be able to claim the output.

Up to this point in time, there has been no state change in any of the payment channels. Thus, if the CLTV time lock were to expire or if anything else went wrong, all commitment transactions would expire and the two payment channels would remain in their original states.

Before this happens, Emanuel has two choices. He could complement Brian's commitment transaction with his own signature and the input m and propagate it to the Bitcoin network. By disclosing m as part of `scriptSig`, Emanuel would gain access to the amount promised to him by Brian through the commitment transaction. At the same time, Brian, for his part, would learn input m and could therefore use it to complete Tamara's commitment transaction and then propagate it to the Bitcoin network. In this case, both payment channels would be closed and the Bitcoin units distributed according to the current state.

In many cases, however, the parties want to keep the payment channels open. If both parties agree that the channel should remain open, after Emanuel has disclosed *m*, Brian can simply create a new commitment transaction without the time lock. If Emanuel receives this new commitment transaction, he does not have to propagate the original HTLC commitment transaction before the expiry of the time lock, and the payment channel can continue to exist. Brian will then forward input *m* to Tamara and, if Tamara and Brian agree that this channel should also remain open, request a new commitment transaction without the time lock.

Now you might wonder why Brian would offer his payment channels as an infrastructure. The answer is transaction fees. Brian can disclose in advance under which conditions he is willing to make his channels available for use. Since this is a highly competitive business and the marginal costs are very low, transaction fees are currently in the range of a few satoshis.

In addition, Brian also has an interest in keeping his payment channels in balance. If he makes regular payments to Emanuel, the entire channel balance will eventually belong to Emanuel. To address this problem, Brian and Emanuel can offer their payment channels for reverse flows and thereby rebalance the distribution of funds in the channel.

Of course, Tamara, Brian, and Emanuel do not have to do all these steps manually. They have installed a lightning client on their computer that manages the payment channels and finds the most efficient routes for payments. Routing—that is, finding a path through the network—is technically the most challenging aspect of the Lightning Network and, accordingly, is the one that is currently undergoing major development. Several teams are working on implementations, agreeing on a common standard, and thus, ensuring compatibility between the various implementations.[121,189]

At this point it has to be mentioned that we have omitted two essential steps to make things less complicated. First, lightning payments can of course take paths that involve more than two payment channels; however, the principle remains the same. Second, it is essential for the security of the system that the time lock, starting from the last channel, is increased by at least one block for each step. In our example, the commitment transaction from Brian to Emanuel would have a time lock of t blocks and the commitment transaction from Tamara to Brian would have a time lock of $t+1$ blocks.

In conclusion, the Lightning Network is a young but very promising technology that could make Bitcoin suitable for mass adoption. One side effect is that lightning transactions are much harder to track. Depending on your political views this may be a selling point or cause for concern.

6.3   Adoption

Bitcoin units can already be exchanged for numerous goods and services. The market acceptance of Bitcoin, however, is nowhere near that of traditional government-issued fiat currencies. We already discussed the high price volatility and scalability issues that hold back Bitcoin's adoption as a medium of exchange.

One further reason is the complexity of this relatively new technology and the lack of user-friendly applications. In the long term, complexity need not be a problem. Few users understand the underlying technologies that they use on a daily basis. However, severe simplifications may introduce third-party dependencies and undermine some of Bitcoin's advantages. The next few years will demonstrate whether Bitcoin technology will succeed in reaching the mainstream by offering simplified products and services while keeping true to its permissionless nature.

In the following, we will first present the evolution of various activity metrics for the Bitcoin network. Thereafter, we consider some issues that may have a substantial impact on Bitcoin's adoption.

6.3.1   Transactions as an Indicator of Activity

Figure 6.5 shows the number of confirmed transactions on a daily basis. This number is an indication of the network's level of activity. Its explanatory power, however, should not be overestimated due to the diversity of transaction types that exist. If a person needs to make ten payments, he or she can do so by making one or ten transactions. Spam transactions or payments that transmit hundreds or even thousands of Bitcoin units to different people with a single transaction may distort the picture in either direction and may lead to an over- or underestimation of the actual activity level.

In figure 6.13 we address this problem by taking into account the total quantity of Bitcoin units transferred within a given day. But even this indicator of activity has a fundamental problem. It does not consider the fact that the value of a Bitcoin unit changes over time. These price changes mean that the data are not comparable across time.

In figure 6.14, we evaluate the Bitcoin transaction volumes using the respective daily conversion rate into US dollars. It immediately becomes clear that, from a real economic perspective, the spike at the end of 2011 (figure 6.13) is less important than the original visualization suggests.

Figure 6.14 must, however, be interpreted with some caution as well. Neither the number of transactions nor the transaction volumes say anything about the transactions' nature. People usually have numerous pseudonyms. A transaction could therefore

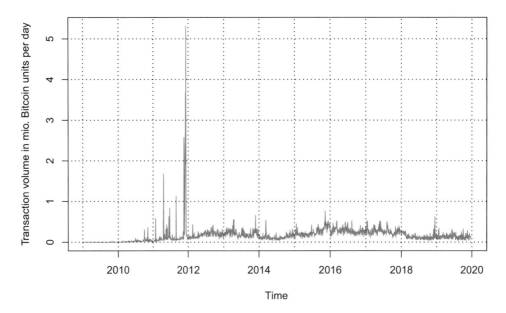

Figure 6.13
Estimated Bitcoin transaction volume per day (Bitcoin millions).
Source: Data from Blockchain Explorer, n.d., https://www.blockchain.com/explorer.

represent only a reorganization of a user's portfolio, in which Bitcoin units are allocated to other pseudonyms of the same person.

Moreover, the transactions included in figures 6.5, 6.13, and 6.14 are Bitcoin transactions that have been included in the Bitcoin blockchain. Transactions within centralized exchanges are not included in these statistics. Centralized exchanges update only the internal accounting of the respective customer claims for internal Bitcoin transactions. A blockchain transaction occurs only when a customer decides to withdraw the Bitcoin units from the exchange. Additionally, the measure omits any payments conducted through payment channels.

6.3.2   Bitcoin Inflation and Transaction Fees

Transaction fees are a potential reason why many people are reluctant to use Bitcoin. For the first few years of Bitcoin's existence, low transaction fees were one of the main arguments in favor of using Bitcoin for payments. This changed drastically during the bull run of 2017. The origin of the skyrocketing transaction costs was clearly due to the scalability issues discussed in section 6.2. Figure 6.15 displays the evolution of the average transaction fee in US dollars.

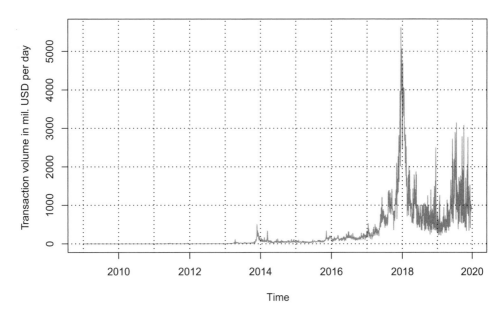

Figure 6.14
Estimated Bitcoin transaction volumes per day (US dollars millions).
Source: Data from Blockchain Explorer, n.d., https://www.blockchain.com/explorer.

Transaction fees represent only a fraction of the economic costs of a transaction. In addition to the fees, miners receive a fixed reward in the form of newly created Bitcoin units. This leads to an expansion in the money supply and to additional costs, which are transferred via inflationary pressure to existing Bitcoin holders. When additional Bitcoin units are mined—holding the aggregate demand for Bitcoin units constant—the Bitcoin price is reduced. Existing Bitcoin holders thus bear the costs of the Bitcoin "printing press." This is the same mechanism that applies to government-issued fiat currencies where printing additional money may reduce the real value of the existing money holdings. This cost is referred to in the literature as the "inflation tax."

Figure 6.16 displays the market price of a Bitcoin unit (dashed line) and the corresponding theoretical "no new creation" price (solid line). The "no new creation" price series is constructed as follows. For each date, we divide the market capitalization by the number of Bitcoin units that existed on January 1, 2013. Note that the "no new creation" price series is a theoretical price only. The true market price in the absence of additional Bitcoin creation is unknown. The difference between the two curves suggests that a person who owned Bitcoin units from the beginning of 2013 until the end of 2019, paid an inflation tax of approximately US$5,000 per unit.

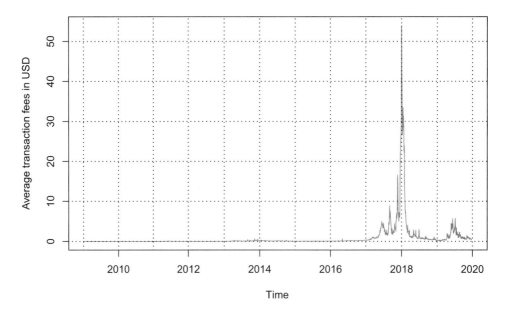

Figure 6.15
Average transaction fees paid in US dollars. Daily averages.
Source: Data from Blockchain Explorer, n.d., https://www.blockchain.com/explorer.

The creation of new Bitcoin units is decreasing and will ultimately converge to zero. Accordingly, the inflation tax will become less important over time. However, it also implies that the miners' revenues from newly created Bitcoin units decrease. If this reduction is not compensated with higher transaction fee income (or some other income source), it will reduce the hashing power applied to mining and, hence, the security of the Bitcoin network.[19]

Figure 6.17 displays the fee as a fraction of the economic cost of a transaction. The sharp increase at the end of 2012 is the result of the block reward halving that took place on November 28, 2012.[20] The block reward decreased from fifty to twenty-five Bitcoin units per block. A further decrease from twenty-five to 12.5 Bitcoin units per block occurred at block 420,000 on July 9, 2016. At block 630,000 there will be another block reward decrease to 6.25 Bitcoin units. Block 630,000 will most likely be reached shortly before the release of this book.

---

19. There are voices that claim that the Bitcoin network is producing a surplus of security because of the block rewards. [196]

20. See Blockchain, Block height 210000, webpage, 2017, https://blockchain.info/block-height /210000.

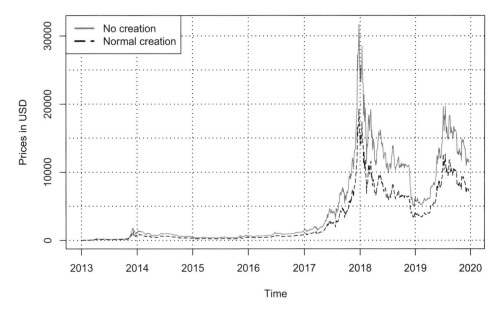

Figure 6.16

Comparison of price data per Bitcoin unit, with (dashed line) and without (solid line) the inflation tax.

Source: Data from Blockchain Explorer, n.d., https://www.blockchain.com/explorer.

The low fraction of transaction fee income relative to the block reward adversely affects the miners' incentive to add transactions to block candidates. Transaction fees increase their income only marginally. In contrast, adding transactions to a block increases the block's size and the time it takes for it to be relayed to other nodes. This increases the risk that miners may lose their block reward to a competitor who has almost simultaneously generated and propagated a smaller block that can spread across the network more quickly (see section 5.3.4). [114]

Interestingly, the problem is not as common in practice as a theoretical analysis would suggest. This is probably due to the fact that large mining pools are not anonymous and control such a large proportion of the overall computing resources of the network that they have an incentive to maintain the credibility of the Bitcoin system and thus the value of their block rewards.

6.3.3 Denomination

People may have difficulties reading decimal numbers and interpreting the information correctly. The high price of Bitcoin entails that the prices of many goods and services

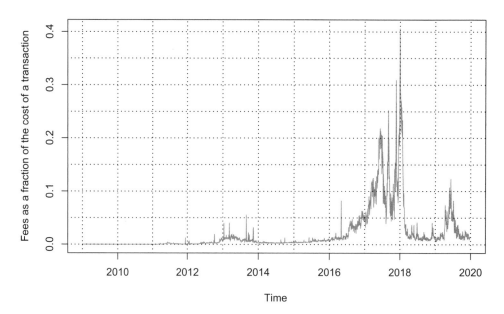

Figure 6.17
Transaction fees as a fraction of the economic cost of a transaction. Daily average in US dollars.
Source: Data from Blockchain Explorer, n.d., https://www.blockchain.com/explorer.

have to be expressed in fractions of a Bitcoin unit and that users are therefore forced to
use decimal places.

This problem is a direct consequence of Bitcoin's success. In our chronology of Bitcoin's price development in section 2.5.4, we described the first documented Bitcoin
market price when two pizzas were traded in exchange for 10,000 Bitcoin units. Today,
the price of a pizza in Bitcoin involves many decimal places due to the immense increase
in the value of the Bitcoin unit.

Such prices are problematic because various marketing studies show that consumers
have difficulties in correctly interpreting and comparing numbers that include decimal
places. [150] For example, many consumers would not be able to immediately recognize
that 0.0531 is almost six times the value of 0.0089329.

The criticism is, however, only partially justified because the reference unit could
be easily adapted. Bitcoin prices could be referenced in fractions of Bitcoin units—that
is, in bits, which correspond to one millionth of a Bitcoin unit. [235] Table 6.4 shows
different denominations of the Bitcoin unit.

Table 6.4

Possible denominations of a Bitcoin unit.

Sub unit	In Bitcoin units
1 Bitcoin	1 Bitcoin
1 Deci-Bitcoin	0.1 Bitcoin
1 Centi-Bitcoin	0.01 Bitcoin
1 Milli-Bitcoin	0.001 Bitcoin
1 Bit (Micro-Bitcoin)	0.000001 Bitcoin
1 Satoshi	0.00000001 Bitcoin

6.3.4 Confirmation Time

A further issue is the time it takes for transactions to get confirmed. Since new blocks are usually generated every ten minutes, the average time it takes to confirm a transaction will also be in this range. Further, the probabilistic nature of block generation makes these waiting times unpredictable. It is therefore possible that confirmations are received almost immediately or only several hours later.

In the case of online shopping, such delays rarely pose a problem. In the case of purchases at point-of-sale terminals, however, long, unpredictable waiting times are unacceptable. A common example of this is a transaction in a coffee shop. [235]

There are several approaches that address this issue. With regard to waiting times, first it must be noted that, when dealing with small amounts, unconfirmed transactions can offer a sufficiently high degree of security. In particular, if a merchant has solid network connections and waits a few seconds, a customer transaction will be included in the blockchain with a very high probability. [19] Moreover, there are service providers that require the transactions to be signed not only by the customer but also by the respective payment service provider. This enables the customer to plausibly show that, without the aid of the payment service provider, he or she would not be able to publish a competing transaction. Such a payment can be considered valid immediately because double spend attacks are not possible under these conditions. [37] Last but not least, payment channel and Lightning Network transactions are immediately valid (see section 6.2.3).

6.3.5 Distribution of Bitcoin

A study conducted in 2014 showed that a maximum of 1.2 million people owned Bitcoin. [117] This figure is based on the number of Bitcoin addresses that had significant Bitcoin balances. Since a user can own several Bitcoin addresses, this estimate of Bitcoin

Table 6.5

Distribution of wealth within the Bitcoin network.

Category	Address			Aggregated Credit Balances		
Bitcoin	Number	%	↑ Σ%	Bitcoin	%	↑ Σ%
0–0.001	11,258,106	48.57%	100.00%	2,269	0.01%	100.00%
0.001–0.01	5,188,202	22.38%	51.43%	21,128	0.12%	99.99%
0.01–0.1	4,156,992	17.93%	29.05%	136,881	0.78%	99.87%
0.1–1	1,852,902	7.99%	11.12%	587,735	3.35%	99.09%
1–10	572,704	2.47%	3.12%	1,506,996	8.58%	95.74%
10–100	134,271	0.58%	0.65%	4,397,511	25.05%	87.16%
100–1,000	14,745	0.06%	0.07%	3,719,447	21.19%	62.11%
1,000–10,000	1,709	0.01%	0.01%	4,320,975	24.61%	40.92%
10,000–100,000	102	0.00%	0.00%	2,289,181	13.04%	16.31%
100,000–1,000,000	5	0.00%	0.00%	573,958	3.27%	3.27%

Source: BitInfoCharts, Cryptocurrency statistics, website, February 26, 2019, bitinfocharts.com.

addresses constitutes an upper limit for the number of possible users. Table 6.5 presents the results from a similar analysis that uses a data set from February 2019.[38] It is striking that at that time almost 20 percent of all the Bitcoin units were owned by only 115 addresses. Other analyses even go as far as computing the Gini coefficient to measure the distribution of wealth within the Bitcoin network.[210] Table 6.5 shows that that a large number of Bitcoin units are distributed among relatively few addresses. Because these addresses cannot be linked to any custody service provider, it has to be assumed that the Bitcoin units corresponding to these addresses belong to one person (pay-to-public-key hash) or a few (pay-to-script-hash) persons.

All these studies must be viewed with caution. The basic problem is that these studies use pseudonyms to assign the respective Bitcoin balances to a person. However, because most Bitcoin users employ many pseudonyms, it is impossible to accurately assign Bitcoin units to the individuals who actually own them.[21] Moreover, some addresses belong to exchanges, meaning that the Bitcoin units are owned by a large number of persons. Also, many addresses are not controlled by a single user. Pay-to-script-hash addresses with multisig unlocking conditions, as an example, could be controlled by more than one party (see section 4.5.4). Finally, there are blockchain transactions of very low value, which were carried out as part of stress tests or attacks on the network. The transaction values are often lower than the transaction costs and therefore remain

---

21. There are some algorithms that permit attributions/assignations to be approximated under certain circumstances.[184]

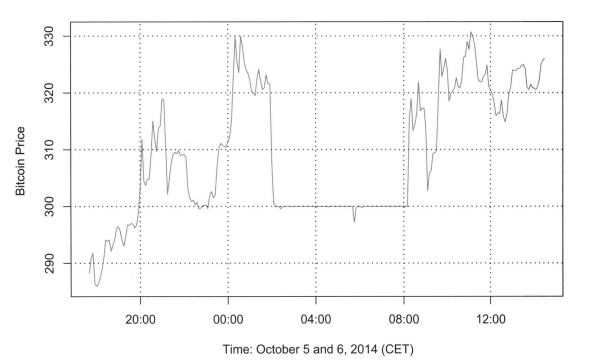

Figure 6.18
Bitcoin price on the BitStamp exchange when the *Bearwhale* appeared. Time period from October 5 to October 6, 2014.
Source: BitInfoCharts, Cryptocurrency statistics, website, October 5–6, 2014, bitinfocharts.com.

as Bitcoin dust (small fractions of Bitcoin units) on a very high number of different addresses.

Although we discourage the uncritical use of these metrics, table 6.5 suggests that there are some persons who own significant amounts of Bitcoin units. Such persons are known as *Bitcoin whales*. Bitcoin whales may either be financially powerful individuals who have made large investments or users who became involved in Bitcoin early on and were able to amass a large number of Bitcoin units through purchases or mining activities.

Large sell orders can have a significant impact on the Bitcoin price. An example of such an event could be observed on October 6, 2014, when approximately 26,000 Bitcoin units were transferred to an exchange and offered for sale. Bitcoin's market price immediately slid by approximately 10 percent.[186] This event, which is illustrated in figure 6.18, has become known in the Bitcoin community as *Slaying the*

Bearwhale,[22] which is a symbolic event for the huge price impact that a single individual can have.

> **Box 6.13**
> **Satoshi Nakamoto's Wealth**
>
> The person who was in the best position to amass a very large number of Bitcoin units is Satoshi Nakamoto. His fortune is estimated at approximately one million Bitcoin units. [140] It is interesting that his Bitcoin holdings have never been moved despite the fact that they had a value of almost US$20 billion when the Bitcoin price was at its peak.
>
> Many users of the Bitcoin system assume that the private keys for managing these Bitcoin units were discarded. Nevertheless, one should always be aware of the possibility that these coins could suddenly hit the market and exhibit a large downward pressure on the Bitcoin price. Further, if the inventor of Bitcoin would suddenly sell, this would most likely have a strong negative psychological impact on the market.

6.4   Political Challenges

Bitcoin faces not only technological and economic challenges but also political challenges. The main critique is the large use of electricity for mining, its potential use for illegal activities such as money laundering and tax evasion, and regulatory uncertainties.

6.4.1   Electricity Use

Proof-of-work mining uses a large quantity of electricity. Let us address this observation by first calculating the electricity use of Bitcoin mining. In this section, we provide only an overview about the main parameters that are required to calculate Bitcoin's electricity use, and we make a very coarse calculation for the year 2018. A more detailed estimate is presented in Alex de Vries's 2018 article. [74]

A straightforward way to calculate the electricity used in Bitcoin mining is to realize that, in a competitive market, the expected marginal cost of producing a block is equal to marginal revenue; that is,

$$MR = MC.$$

---

22. *Bear* and *whale* are animals used as metaphors to describe a type of Bitcoin market trader, where *bear* refers to trader behavior on the stock market when prices are falling (*bear market*) and *whale* refers to a trader who has a huge stock of Bitcoin units.

The marginal revenue of Bitcoin mining is the sum of the block reward and the transaction fee earned from mining a block. In 2018, the block reward was 12.5 Bitcoin units and, for simplicity, we shall ignore the transaction fee income. Most expenses of a miner have to be paid in fiat currencies, so we need to calculate the US dollar value of the block reward. For simplicity, we assume that in 2018 the Bitcoin price was constant and equal to US$4,000.[23] Under these assumptions, the marginal revenue per block is US$50,000.

There are fixed costs and variable costs of mining. To keep it simple, we ignore the fixed costs and assume that the only variable cost is electricity. In a competitive market, there is free entry into the business of mining. This implies that entry and exit of miners occurs until the expected marginal cost of mining a Bitcoin equals the marginal revenue of mining a Bitcoin; that is, $MC = MR = $ US$4,000.

We are now ready to calculate the electricity consumption of the Bitcoin network per year. On average, every ten minutes a block is created. This implies 144 blocks per day and consequently 52,560 blocks per year. Since every block earns 12.5 Bitcoin units, 657,000 Bitcoins are created during the course of this year. Assuming a constant Bitcoin price of US$4,000, the total revenue is US$2,628,000,000. Under our many simplifying assumptions, the same amount is spent on electricity.

To calculate the electricity consumption in kilowatts we need to make an assumption about the price of electricity. Since electricity is an important cost component for a miner, most miners locate in areas with low electricity costs. For this reason, we impute ten cents per kilowatt hour (kWh), which, according to our calculations, implies that the electricity use is 26,280,000,000 kWh.

What is left to do is to look up a table where the electricity use of different countries is registered. Such data can be found, for example, on Wikipedia, and is summarized in table 6.6.[226]

The data in this table is from 2014. However, we have made so many shortcuts for our calculation that this timing mismatch is an unimportant detail. The purpose of our example is to show the basics of how to calculate and compare the electricity consumption of Bitcoin with other electricity-consuming entities. In fact, more sophisticated estimates arrive at similar values.[74]

Our calculation demonstrates that it is easy to get an estimate of Bitcoin's electricity consumption. In contrast, it is much more difficult to evaluate the result from a normative point of view. Is this electricity consumption a problem? Should Bitcoin be

---

23. We invite the interested reader to make his own more precise calculations.

Table 6.6
Electricity use of different countries.

Rank	Country	kWh/Year	Year	Source	Population
63	Slovakia	28,360,000,000	2014	CIA	5,445,802
64	Serbia	26,910,000,000	2014	CIA	7,143,921
65	Bahrain	25,000,000,000	2014	CIA	1,378,904
66	Ireland	25,000,000,000	2014	CIA	4,952,473
67	Oman	25,000,000,000	2014	CIA	3,355,262

Wikipedia, List of countries by electricity consumption, webpage, 2014, https://en.wikipedia.org/wiki/List_of_countries_by_electricity_consumption.

abolished for environmental reasons? The answer to this question is a matter of personal opinion. From our perspective, the societal benefit of a censorship-resistant database and a permissionless cryptoasset is very high. Further, it also matters what type of electricity is used. Is the electricity produced through renewable resources? How much does it contribute to global warming? These are issues for future research.

Finally, we want to remind the interested reader that centralized payment systems are also very resource hungry. Besides infrastructure and operating costs, one would have to calculate the explicit and implicit resource use of all financial entities that are involved in maintaining the existing payment infrastructure of a country or even the world, considering that Bitcoin is an asset without borders. Salary and infrastructure costs should be counted among the explicit costs and the option of a misuse of a centralized payment infrastructure among the implicit costs.

Unfortunately, we are not aware of any data that estimate the cost of maintaining a payment infrastructure for a country or even for the world. Nevertheless, we can provide a hint by providing some data for the European Central Bank (ECB). In 2017, the ECB's total operating costs, including depreciation and banknote production costs, was 1,075,000,000 euros. [20] According to our calculations, in US dollars this is roughly 50 percent of the cost of maintaining the Bitcoin system in its current form.[24] The ECB, of course, is not the only actor in the euro area payment system. To obtain a comprehensive picture, we would have to include the cost of private banks and other

---

24. The actual costs are subject to price changes and to the reward halving. For any given Bitcoin price, the electricity consumption drops by 50 percent with the reward halving, meaning that Bitcoin will only require more resource if its price increases by more than 100 percent within four years.

private financial institutions that are involved in the payment system. Once we add the private sector, we will easily surpass the cost of maintaining the Bitcoin network. Moreover, this rough estimate does not include any of the implicit costs mentioned above.

How should we compare these operating costs to Bitcoin's electricity consumption? We do not know. What we do know for sure is that there are thousands of men and women working in the payment sector, and all of these people use electricity, fly to meetings and conferences, and commute to work. It would be interesting to calculate the energy use of maintaining the current payment system. This is left for future research.

6.4.2 Regulatory Uncertainty and Illegal Activities

To our knowledge, there exists no reliable data about Bitcoin's use for illegal activities such as money laundering or tax evasion. Nevertheless, even at a very early stage in the life of the Bitcoin system, politicians and regulators have expressed concerns that Bitcoin could become the number one choice for criminals to hide their financial activities. A case in point was the opening of the marketplace Silk Road in 2011. It rapidly gained popularity among darknet users who could trade items ranging from weaponry to illegal drugs. To ensure anonymity for its customers, Silk Road accepted only Bitcoin as a payment instrument.

A few years later, these concerns remain, but it has also become clear that Bitcoin is a very bad choice as a payment instrument for illegal activities. The reason is that the Bitcoin blockchain is a public ledger. Transaction information is stored forever, and users have to be very careful if they want to remain anonymous. In fact, forensic methods that investigate payment flows on the Bitcoin blockchain have become increasingly sophisticated and allow for better connections of multiple Bitcoin addresses and sometimes even to the identity of the owner. We expect these forensic methods to improve significantly over time and, for this reason, we strongly recommend not using Bitcoin for illegal activities.

Nevertheless, Bitcoin will remain a focal point for regulators worldwide. As of today, there is no common international approach to the regulation of Bitcoin. In some countries its use is illegal while in other countries standard anti-money laundering laws apply. In most countries regulatory authorities are still discussing how to incorporate Bitcoin into their existing regulatory framework. We therefore expect that there will be additional regulations imposed over time.

6.5   Exercises

Exercise 6.1: Name three types of stablecoin projects, including an example, and show how they try to peg the token to another asset.

Exercise 6.2: Show the differences between central bank digital currencies and central bank cryptocurrencies and discuss why a central bank may be reluctant to use a public blockchain with a decentralized consensus protocol.

Exercise 6.3: Describe the idea behind a commitment transaction and how the concept is used in the context of payment channels.

Exercise 6.4: Explain why Bitcoin may not be a good choice for illegal activities. Consider the transaction architecture you have studied in chapter 4. Do you expect this to change with the Lightning Network? Why or why not?

7 Further Applications

The Bitcoin blockchain provides an infrastructure that enables many non-monetary applications. Back in 2014, the venture capital firm Ledra Capital, for example, published a list with eighty-four use cases for blockchain technology.[138] It is, however, not in the scope of this book to cover specific industries. Instead, we want to familiarize the reader with core concepts that highlight the advantages of public blockchains and show how they can be used in an industry-agnostic way. As such, the following examples are representative of the technology's potential but are by no means exhaustive.[1]

Moreover, we deliberately restrict our attention to non-monetary applications. Monetary innovations such as *machine-to-machine payments* in the context of the Internet of Things (IoT), stablecoins, or global microtransactions have already been dealt with in previous chapters.

7.1 Decentralized Verification and Attestation

The Bitcoin blockchain can be viewed as a public pinboard that is managed in a decentralized way. It can be used to safeguard any type of information. In contrast to a normal pinboard, the information cannot subsequently be removed or changed. The time at which the information was added to the blockchain is recorded alongside the information and the pseudonym of the author.

Null data transactions can include any information via the OP_RETURN operation code (see section 4.5.5). While the size of data that can be added is relatively small, it is sufficient to include a hash value (see section 4.2). Once a hash value has been added to

---

1. There are voices who are less optimistic about the use cases for the blockchain technology. [5]

the blockchain, it cannot be deleted or changed. Immutable hash values allow anyone to prove the existence, authenticity and integrity of data.

7.1.1 Existence

A so-called *proof of existence* certifies that a document existed at a specific point in time. The document does not have to be disclosed. For a proof-of-existence, it is sufficient to calculate its hash value and include it in a transaction. Eventually the transaction gets confirmed in a block and thereby linked to a specific point in time.

Let us assume, for example, that Michèle has been asked by a firm to work out a new business strategy. After completing the work, she presents her ideas to the firm's management and provides a paper containing her plans. To prevent the managers from claiming at some future date that her ideas were developed internally, Michèle can add the hash value of the draft to the blockchain. This would allow her to prove that her paper already existed at the point in time when the block was added to the blockchain. She could disclose the draft to any third party and thereby enable them to compute and verify its hash value, proving that it corresponds with the hash value recorded in the blockchain.

A cryptographic hash function (see section 4.2) makes it computationally infeasible to generate a document that has a specific hash value. This implies that matching hash values are sufficient proof that a document existed at the time its hash value was recorded in the blockchain. Although proof-of-existence does not offer legal protection analogous to a patent, it does have many interesting areas of application.

7.1.2 Integrity

Another possible application is protecting the integrity of some data. If, for instance, someone wishes to ensure that the content of a contract will not be altered, they can embed the hash value of the contract in the blockchain. Every change to the contract will inevitably trigger a change of its hash value so that it no longer corresponds to the hash value that is recorded in the blockchain. Any manipulations would thus be immediately apparent.

This method for protecting data can be integrated in business processes. The hash values of documents relating to controlling and compliance, for example, can be regularly added to a public blockchain. The confidentiality of the documents would still be guaranteed because the hash value does not reveal the content of the data.

7.1.3 Authenticity

If it is possible to associate a public key with a company, an organization, or a person, then it will also be possible to verify the authenticity of documents. If the hash of a document is signed by an organization, it can be reasonably assumed that the document was also issued or signed by this organization.

In a joint project, the University of Basel and BlockFactory have begun to secure academic credentials on a public blockchain.[201,98] Students who pass blockchain-related classes get a publicly verifiable certificate. When a potential employer receives the document, he or she can compute its hash value and check whether the University of Basel has added it to the blockchain. Potential employers can therefore verify the existence, authenticity, and integrity of the certificates on the basis of blockchain entries. This approach substantially reduces the risk that manipulated certificates could circulate undetected. Cryptographically secure hash values (and some randomness in the certificate's creation process) ensure that, despite the public nature of the blockchain, data protection is a nonissue.[2]

7.2 Tokens and Colored Coins

The Bitcoin blockchain permits only transactions in the native Bitcoin unit. However, since the scripting language of the Bitcoin network allows additional information to be tied to a transaction, a promise of payment can be attached to a fragment of a Bitcoin unit. The Bitcoin fragment serves only as a wrapper that allows the promise of payment to be traded over the Bitcoin network.

The economic value of a such a Bitcoin fragment derives from the attached promise of payment. Such promises, of course, are subject to issuer risks. If the party who issues the promise is unable or unwilling to fulfill it, the promise has no value. The Bitcoin blockchain cannot enforce such external promises; it can only keep track of who owns the Bitcoin fragment.

So-called *colored coins* are Bitcoin fragments that are "colored" with additional data that represent a promise of payment. A colored coin can promise, for example, that the issuer will pay the owner US$1,000 on December 31, 2030. Depending on the issuer's credibility, credit rating, and reputation, the market will ascribe an additional value to this Bitcoin fragment (see section 1.4).

---

2. Similar projects based on the Bitcoin blockchain exist. The University of Nicosia, for example, uses the Bitcoin blockchain to safeguard diplomas for the master lecture series on digital currencies.[219]

The attached data can contain any type of promise. Precious metals, company shares, or debt are only a few examples. Basically, any type of asset can be formed and traded on the Bitcoin blockchain in this way. Technologically, the Bitcoin blockchain could therefore be used as a basic infrastructure to record and track ownership rights of all sorts. However, scalability and regulatory concerns, particularly in the domain of security law, impose certain limitations.

While colored coins were of some importance in the early days of Bitcoin, they are rarely used today. They have been replaced by *tokens* that are mainly created on the Ethereum blockchain. These tokens are usually based on the ERC-20 [221] token standard. The main difference between colored coins and tokens is that tokens are issued via so-called *token contracts*. Token contracts are databases managed on the blockchain.[3]

Although ERC-20 is currently by far the most widely used token standard, we would like to mention that there are many alternatives. On the Ethereum blockchain, the ERC-223 [78] and ERC-777 [72] standards, for example, solve some of the issues that can occur when transferring ERC-20 tokens, and the ERC-721 [88] token standard allows the issuance of nonfungible assets such as collectibles. Outside the Ethereum ecosystem, NEO offers the NEP-5 [218] token standard. Many more blockchains have their own token standards. Token contracts are not possible on the Bitcoin blockchain due to its limited scripting language. It is, however, possible to issue tokens on a Bitcoin sidechain or second layer such as Liquid, [79] Rootstock, [141] or Omni [227] (formerely Mastercoin). Table 7.1 shows the popularity of various token standards. We have only included listed tokens.

7.3 Smart Property

Smart property is an external, nonnative promise that is attached to a Bitcoin fragment or issued as a token and thereby able to be traded over a blockchain. However, the term smart property is restricted to physical objects; that is, movable property and real estate. Smart property binds the use of the physical object to cryptographic signatures. The physical object sends a cryptographic challenge to the person who wants to use it and only grants access if the person is able to solve this challenge.

---

3. The interest in these tokens has been skyrocketing in 2017 and early 2018, when so-called initial coin offerings (ICOs) or token sales saw a sharp increase in popularity. [166] Unfortunately, many of these tokens are entirely useless, and some are even outright scams.

Table 7.1

Listed tokens per platform.

Rank	Platform	Number		Market capitalization	
		Absolute	Relative	Absolute	Relative
1	Ethereum	1,108	89.43%	8,695,655,366	77.91%
2	Neo	27	2.18%	83,100,800	0.75%
3	Waves	24	1.94%	34,593,249	0.31%
4	Stellar	15	1.21%	97,214,953	0.88%
5	BitShares	13	1.05%	21,896,211	0.20%
6	Qtum	10	0.81%	15,434,624	0.14%
7	Omni	7	0.57%	2,007,734,292	19.11%
8	Nem	6	0.48%	31,442,156	0.29%
9	Counterparty	6	0.48%	7,629,517	0.07%
10	EOS	5	0.40%	16,772,483	0.15%
	Other	18	1.45%	20,488,711	0.19%

Source: Data from CoinMarketCap, website, February 26, 2019, https://coinmarketcap.com; Tether, website, February 26, 2019, tether.to.

A common example of such an object is a smart car. The car's doors will open and its engine will start only for a person who can prove ownership of the private key that belongs to the address that currently has control over the colored coin or token representing this asset. [207]

Key systems based on similar cryptographic principles are already in use today. However, the cryptographic challenges are usually static, meaning that they are tied to a specific key pair. A sale means that the keys must be handed over to the new owner physically, and this entails the risk that the seller made copies of the keys. With blockchain technology, the owner can choose a new key, an option that would allow cars to be traded virtually. Moreover, it would be able to grant temporary access, creating new business models for the sharing economy.

Although the ownership of smart property is not subject to counterparty risk, it requires the existence of a functioning legal system. Any physical protection for an object can be circumvented by force. Analogous to mechanical house doors, cryptographic locks are only partially effective access barriers, which additionally need to be safeguarded by the legal system. Further, if physical access is denied, the physical object, despite the cryptographically guaranteed change of ownership, will offer the new owner no value.

> **Box 7.1**
> **Disequilibrium Owing to Colored Coins and Tokens**
>
> Bitcoin and Ether units are secured by a simple, yet very sophisticated system of incentives. When the price rises, the miners' real remuneration automatically increases. As a consequence, the hash rate will also rise, which will make the blockchain more secure. In contrast, when nonnative assets are attached to the Bitcoin blockchain, its security requirements increase, but the remuneration of the miners remains constant. Consequently, colored coins and tokens can theoretically cause a disequilibrium between the remuneration of miners and the incentive to attack.

7.4   Blockchain Contracts (Smart Contracts)

There exists a large number of contradicting attempts to define the term *blockchain contract*. Even more confusing is that the more popular term, *smart contract*, is misleading. We will therefore concentrate on a minimal, very broad definition that covers only those aspects of the term that are agreed on in the majority of the existing literature.

Blockchain contracts or smart contracts are scripted sequences that link at least one outcome to specific requirements and/or events. The completion of these sequences is secured by the blockchain; that is, by the ledger and the consensus protocol.

7.4.1   UTXO as Blockchain Contracts

According to this definition, every unspent transaction output (UTXO) can be considered to be a blockchain contract. [44] Every transaction output is secured by unlocking conditions (see section 4.5). The first person who presents a solution can freely dispose of the Bitcoin units that are tied to that output.

The specific conditions of UTXO contracts vary depending on the script. Pay-to-public-key and pay-to-public-key-hash require a signature with a private key that satisfies specific requirements. Multisig requires *m*-of-*n* signatures, and pay-to-script-hash allows a certain level of flexibility in shaping the contract. The technical details relating to the unlocking conditions are given in section 4.5. It is important to note that an UTXO satisfies the definition of a blockchain contract and that many simple contracts can be deployed on the Bitcoin blockchain using these standard scripts.

7.4.2   State Machines and Contract Accounts

Although UTXOs meet our definition of blockchain contracts, many people would argue that Bitcoin does not support smart contracts. To understand where this claim is coming from, we have to analyze some of the differences between Bitcoin and more complex blockchain implementations such as Ethereum.[89]

Ethereum is similar in many ways to Bitcoin. It is a distributed public ledger that (currently) employs the proof-of-work consensus protocol. Transactions are signed with a private key, propagated in a network, and eventually confirmed in a block. There are, however, some key differences.

Ethereum does not use Bitcoin's UTXO model. Instead it relies on accounts. Each account is controlled either by a private key (externally owned account or EOA) or by code (contract account or CA). An EOA is not very different from a Bitcoin address. There are some technical differences, but on an intuitive level it functions in similar ways. Whoever is in control of the private key of an address can make transfers from that account. CAs are more complex and do not exist in the Bitcoin system. A CA is an account that is not controlled by a private key. Instead it is governed by its bytecode. It gets deployed by an EOA (or other CAs) that propagates a contract creation transaction including the code on the Ethereum blockchain. A simple example would be a contract that accepts payments and immediately forwards them according to a predefined (and precoded) distribution schedule. Whenever someone sends a transaction to the contract, it is triggered and its code is executed.

This is of course a very simplistic example of a CA. Thanks to Ethereum's Turing completeness and its capability to store and operate on state variables, more complex CAs can be designed that govern entire organizations, replicate complex financial instruments, or create decentralized marketplaces. Even the token contracts mentioned in section 7.2 are based on CAs. The flexibility unlocks great potential. Yet, the increased complexity also introduces new attack vectors and may make the system more vulnerable and harder to maintain. It remains to be seen if the benefits of the flexibility outweigh potential security trade-offs.

7.4.3   Transaction Design and Off-Chain Contracts

It is possible to significantly extend the scope of blockchain contracts by using clever transaction design. In section 6.2 we learned about the use of state channels in the context of micropayments. Similar concepts can be employed for other use cases. Although the goals can be very different, all of these contracts depend on clever transaction design and on the possibility to use the blockchain for dispute resolution in case of conflict.

Two examples in which we use transaction design to emulate contracts before they even enter the blockchain are "conditional purchase agreements" and "collateralized loans." We will now introduce these contracts.

Conditional Purchase Agreements   We begin our analysis with conditional purchase agreements and consider a specific example where Claudia wishes to purchase a colored coin from Jake with Bitcoin units. Moreover, we assume that the colored coin was issued by the authors and can be redeemed for a physical copy of this book.

This trade harbors certain risks for both parties. Claudia wants Jake to hand over the colored coin first, but Jake wants to receive Claudia's Bitcoin units first. In traditional systems, problems of this kind are solved by a centralized service that temporarily holds on to the payment and then releases it once the promised good has been transferred. A centralized solution to this problem is unsatisfactory in the context of a public blockchain. Instead, there is an alternative approach that has the power to solve this problem in a much more elegant way.

The two transactions can be combined in a single Bitcoin transaction to make use of the fact that Bitcoin transactions are executed either completely or not at all. This eliminates the possibility that one of the two parties obtains ownership of both objects. Technically, a conditional purchase agreement is implemented using a transaction with two inputs and two outputs.

In our example, Claudia first generates the transaction "wrapper" including all the inputs and outputs. The first input comprises the Bitcoin units that Claudia has to transfer to Jake. The second input references the colored coin from Jake. The newly created outputs lock the Bitcoin units in favor of Jake and the colored coin in favor of Claudia. In a second step, Claudia signs the transaction and thereby fulfills the unlocking condition of the first input with the Bitcoin units. Recall that the transaction is not yet valid, as only one of the two nonseparable inputs contains a valid signature. The transaction will be considered valid by the Bitcoin network only when Jake has signed the transaction as well so that both inputs contain a valid signature. The transfer of the Bitcoin units and the colored coins will then be executed simultaneously as part of the same transaction, effectively removing any counterparty risk from the exchange.

Collateralized Loans   Let us consider a situation in which Claudia wishes to take out a Bitcoin loan and Brian is willing to offer the loan against collateral. [110,207] Claudia's collateral is a cryptoasset; for example, a colored coin that is tradable on the Bitcoin blockchain.

A conditional purchase agreement, analogous to the last example, would be problematic because the collateral usually has a higher value than the loan. In this case, Brian would have an incentive to keep the collateral. Claudia is aware of this problem and would therefore agree to such a contract only on the condition that she has a guarantee that she will regain possession of the pledged asset subject on her timely repayment of the loan. The situation is a classic example of a hold-up problem.

Luckily, there is a technical solution to this problem that can be implemented by cleverly linking various components of the Bitcoin system. In the first step, Claudia and Brian jointly generate a 2-of-2 multisig address, subsequently termed M. The address serves as a decentralized escrow account that collectively safeguards both parties' securities, analogous to a shared account with joint signatures. Before Claudia transfers the colored coin to the new address, a few further steps have to be taken to guarantee that the loan transaction is processed smoothly.

Claudia generates a transaction that transfers the colored coin from M to Brian. She embeds a time restriction (nLockTime) in it, preventing the transaction from being confirmed before a specific date. She then signs the transaction message and sends it to Brian. The transaction will be processed by the Bitcoin network only when the appointed date t has been reached, Brian will be able to add his signature and successfully relay the transaction to the network.

In a second step, Brian generates a transaction that transfers the colored coin from the multisig address M to Claudia. In addition, the transaction contains a second output crediting Brian's Bitcoin address. This second output is set to equal the loan amount, and it is formulated so that any number of inputs amounting in total to that sum can be used (see section 4.6). He then signs the transaction message and sends it to Claudia. Here again, the transaction will be processed by the Bitcoin network only when Claudia supplements the transaction with inputs amounting in total to the respective sum and cosigns the message.

In the third and final step, both parties generate and sign the transaction that is based on the two inputs and the two outputs that transfer the colored coin to M and the loan to Claudia.

Claudia can now complete the transaction anytime and broadcast it to the Bitcoin network. If she does this, Brian will receive the loan repayment (including interest), and Claudia will regain the collateral that she deposited. If Claudia fails to repay the loan by the appointed date, Brian can complete the first transaction message by cosigning it and then use the collateral as he wishes.

7.4.4 Oracles

Blockchains can easily handle native data. However, if a contract includes conditions that depend on external data, things get more difficult. Examples of external data include sports results, stock market prices, or meteorological observations. These data points obviously cannot be observed on-chain and require so-called *oracles*—that is, trusted interfaces who provide the data.

While the provision of this type of data enables many interesting applications like betting or insurance contracts, the execution depends on the *oracles*. It therefore can hardly be called decentralized.

Contracts using oracles can be implemented in different ways. For example, both contracting parties can transfer the units of value stipulated in the contract to the address of an oracle and record the precise conditions that have to be met for the transactions to be released. The organizational structure of this type of oracle is de facto a centralized authority that controls the assets and contract execution. In this case, the oracle has the authority to decide unilaterally on the outcome of the contract but also has control over the assets.

An implementation that is as naïve as this leads to the four following problems:[144]

1. The oracle presents a central point of attack and thereby undermines the main advantage of the Bitcoin system.

2. The oracle's method for levying data and its decision-making process might not be transparent and could deliver false results.

3. The oracle may disappear before the contract is processed. This can happen if the server that is hosting the oracle is no longer accessible. Further, if the private key is lost, the assets would be tied up in a contract that could never be processed or executed.

4. The oracle may be corruptible. One could offer bribes to influence contract execution or withhold the asset.

An implementation that uses a 2-of-3 multisig address offers a marginally better level of protection. Here, the three private keys are distributed among the two contract parties and the oracle. With this setting, contract execution is still dependent on a single centralized service. The oracle can therefore still exclusively determine the outcome of the contract, but it no longer has the power to withhold or expropriate the assets. The restriction prevents the oracle, for example, from being able to send the Bitcoin units to a totally different Bitcoin address. In addition, both contract parties can try to reach an agreement and jointly manage the tied asset. If for some reason the oracle can no longer be reached, the Bitcoin units could therefore be reclaimed from the oracle's custody. This implementation solves problem 3 completely and problem 4 partially.

An even better solution is the use of several oracles—for example, seven oracles and an 8-of-15 multisig[4] unlocking condition. Four private keys are assigned to the two contract parties respectively. The other seven keys are owned by the oracles. Both of the advantages of the previous implementation also apply here. If more than half of the oracles were unavailable, both contract parties would still be able to release the assets. On the other hand, the oracles do not control and therefore cannot confiscate the assets. Such partial decentralization makes corruption more difficult and eliminates vulnerabilities associated with a single point of attack. Theoretically, the oracles could still collude and thereby change the outcome. However, this would require a large number of third parties to work together and risk their reputation.[144]

To implement a system of this kind with m-of-n multisig unlocking conditions, one can freely modify the number of oracles as long as the following constraints hold. Each of the two contract parties holds $\frac{m}{2}$ private keys. In addition to this, there are $m - 1$ oracles, each of which hold one private key. This type of implementation usually involves of a m-of-$2m - 1$ multisig implementation, subject to the restriction that m must correspond to an even number.

The use of oracles may be seen as circumventing the original intention of blockchain contracts. Considering the extremely diverse and interesting range of possible applications, these types of contracts nevertheless may have a bright future.[10]

7.5 Exercises

Exercise 7.1: During the process of writing this book, the authors used the Bitcoin blockchain to safeguard their ideas and texts. Outline the procedure that would need to be followed to safeguard such information and identify the benefits that the authors derive from it.

Exercise 7.2: Give an example of a situation where each of the following non-monetary Bitcoin-blockchain applications can be used: (1) proof of existence, (2) proof of integrity, and (3) proof of authenticity.

Exercise 7.3: Explain the concept of counterparty risk in the context of colored coins and tokens.

---

4. Recorded in a pay-to-script-hash unlocking condition.

Exercise 7.4: Smart property, by definition, is not subject to counterparty risk in its classic sense. Explain where you see potential risks and how smart property differs from native protocol assets like Bitcoin.

Exercise 7.5: Name a few examples of blockchain contracts and identify the advantages of blockchain contract processing compared with non-blockchain-based processes.

Exercise 7.6: Explain why contracts that are based on external circumstances can only partly be regarded as blockchain contracts.

8 Practical Guidelines for Bitcoin

In this chapter, we provide some practical advice on how to get started using Bitcoin. We will consider several possibilities for procuring and safeguarding Bitcoin units and indicate some of the risks and errors that users should avoid. After this, we will discuss how to make and receive payments using Bitcoin units.

> **Exclusion from liability.** Cryptoassets are highly speculative and can result in a total loss of the user's invested capital. All activities undertaken—such as the procurement, the handling, and safeguarding of cryptoassets—are performed at the reader own risk. The authors are not legally liable for any losses—including losses that are a direct consequence of following the descriptions in this book. This is not financial/investment advice.

8.1 Procurement

To gain experience with Bitcoin units, it is necessary to procure them first. There are numerous methods for doing this, and they can roughly be divided into three categories: You can either (1) find someone who is willing to gift you Bitcoin units, (2) try to obtain them through mining, or (3) purchase them.

8.1.1 Gifts
Some Bitcoin owners are willing to give you some fractions of a Bitcoin unit for trial purposes. Good locations for coming into contact with Bitcoin users are meetups, conferences, and presentations given on the topic of Bitcoin. However, be careful. There are many people who will try to scam you. In particular, do not trust anyone who promises to gift you a significant amount.

If you simply want to gain experience you might also want to consider Bitcoin's test network. Through a so-called faucet, you can get test coins that do not carry any value but are a great option for testing purposes and to gain some experience.

8.1.2 Mining

Newcomers to Bitcoin often consider mining to be the natural activity to obtain Bitcoin units. However, in many cases, this is an extremely unprofitable method of procurement. The mining market has changed enormously over the last few years and has become professional. Processors (CPUs) and graphics cards (GPUs) have been replaced by chips that have application-specific integrated circuits (ASICs). These chips have been developed specifically for Bitcoin mining and are mainly used by large mining operations. These companies have established a competitive advantage based on returns to scale, low electricity prices, and low cooling costs.

The short product life cycle of the hardware is a further problem. This makes it very difficult to amortize the acquired hardware. Old mining hardware is often offered at online auction houses for absurdly high prices. Before purchasing hardware, users are advised to find out whether the purchase of the device will be cost-effective. Any profitability calculation should be made on the basis of actual prices and without considering possible speculative profits. If mining is not profitable at the current price, then a direct purchase of Bitcoin units is preferable to mining.

To summarize: for most people, Bitcoin mining can only be recommended for educational purposes.

> **Box 8.1**
> **Cloud Mining**
>
> Some service providers allow investors to buy shares in mining equipment. The respective provider supplies and maintains the hardware. The investor receives a part of the mining income. In return, the provider charges a one-off fixed sum for the share certificate as well as a periodic fee, which is intended to cover the cost of hardware maintenance and electricity. Some providers also charge a membership fee.
>
> We strongly discourage the purchase of any cloud-mining shares. Cloud-mining is generally only profitable for the provider. The payout is often opaque, and investors have no control over the physical hardware. In many cases, the hardware does not even exist, and the system is run as a Ponzi scheme. [178]

8.1.3 Purchase

Over-the-Counter Purchases (OTC) Bitcoin units can be purchased from other people or companies by means of a bilateral transaction. These purchases are called over-the-counter (OTC) transactions and can be settled in a face-to-face meeting or via any type of communication channel. Naturally, the appropriate precautionary measures have to be taken in both cases.

Regular Bitcoin events (so-called Bitcoin meetups) are a good starting point for purchasing smaller amounts. Before engaging in purchases of this kind, it is crucial that you check the current exchange rate. Moreover, insist that the transaction includes an acceptable transaction fee and wait for at least one confirmation to reduce the risk of a double spend (see section 5.3.5). For larger amounts, it is advisable to wait for several confirmations. Three to six confirmations are generally considered sufficient to ensure that the transaction is irreversible. This takes on average between thirty and sixty minutes. For small amounts, one confirmation is perfectly fine.

For purchases that do not involve a face-to-face meeting, it is strongly recommended to use a trusted platform. A trusted platform offers a reputation system and fulfills a fiduciary role. Face-to-face meetings can be arranged for cash payments, or transactions can be carried out using wire transfers. In the case of a wire transfer, one should take account of the fact that some commercial banks will block payments with a reference mentioning "Bitcoin" or "crypto" for no apparent reason. This problem is so deep-rooted that some banks even refuse to offer accounts to officially regulated Bitcoin companies.

Normally, you will be able to purchase smaller amounts of Bitcoin units without proving your identity. However, for larger amounts, the seller is obliged to satisfy the so-called know-your-customer (KYC) regulation, which requires, among other things, that the customer must be identified.

> **Box 8.2**
> **Never Purchase a Private Key**
>
> Never purchase a private key from another person. The person may have copies of this key and would therefore be in the position to control the associated Bitcoin units. A legitimate OTC purchase must therefore always be carried out using a Bitcoin blockchain transaction that credits the Bitcoin units to one of your Bitcoin addresses.
>
> To ensure that you have exclusive control over the corresponding private key, you must personally generate the key/address pair. Private keys that are communicated or transferred to you via other people are unsafe.
>
> If a person wishes to offer you help when installing a wallet or your client, you must prevent this person from seeing your key or your mnemonic seed (see box 4.3). The disclosure of this information can lead to the total loss of your Bitcoin units.

Centralized Exchange Platforms   The most common way to obtain Bitcoin units is to buy them at one of the many centralized Bitcoin exchanges. A user can simply open an account and then transfer fiat currency to it. The account holder can then use these funds to buy Bitcoin units or one of the many other cryptoassets. The pricing on large exchanges is competitive with relatively small bid-ask spreads. Most exchanges provide cryptocurrency order books and relatively sophisticated financial tools that make the trading process transparent. However, it is still recommended to compare the various fee structures and to do your research on the business practices and reputation of a particular exchange. In particular, when selecting a centralized exchange, one should also consider the trading volumes, the offered services, and security.

Most importantly, users of centralized exchanges must be aware that they do not control the private keys to their assets. This can lead to substantial security issues (see section 8.2.2). It is therefore recommended that the user transfers his cryptoassets as quickly as possible to one of the addresses for which he is in exclusive possession of the private key.

Some centralized exchanges have a registration process that is fully compliant and comparable to the KYC requirements for opening an account with commercial banks. These requirements include domicile and passport checks as well as the respective anti-money laundering rules. A few cryptocurrency exchanges implement none of these requirements and operate in a legal vacuum. We strongly recommend not to use exchanges that are both centralized and nonregulated.

Box 8.3
Brokers

If you do not want to worry about acquiring Bitcoin units yourself, there are some companies that offer brokerage services. These brokers trade on your behalf against a fee. When contracting brokers, you must be vigilant and wary of the risks. Further, the fees for brokerage are only worthwhile when buying larger amounts of Bitcoin units.

Before you can trade, you must deposit either cryptoassets or government-issued fiat currency to the exchange. For a Bitcoin transaction, the exchange provides you with a Bitcoin address. Currencies can generally be transferred to the exchange's bank account and normally will be credited within a few days.

A faster alternative is to use a credit card payment. Since credit card payments can be reversed, centralized exchanges who offer credit card payments face a high level of risk. Consequently, only exchanges that verify their customers' identities offer this option. Moreover, a surcharge is imposed to cover the credit card fees and chargeback risk.

Bitcoin ATM Bitcoin ATMs are appearing to be similar to standard banking ATMs. With regard to the spectrum of functions that they provide, however, these machines have little in common with traditional cash dispensers. They allow users to buy Bitcoin units in exchange for fiat currency – and some models function as two-way currency converters. The counterparty is normally the ATM's operating company.

In order to buy Bitcoin units, the customer feeds the desired banknote into the Bitcoin ATM. The Bitcoin units are then credited to a Bitcoin address that the customer has previously generated. To execute the Bitcoin payment, the customer must present a QR code containing the beneficiary Bitcoin address in front of the machine's integrated camera.

Some machines generate new addresses and issue a paper receipt on which the public address and the corresponding private key are printed. This method again poses the threat that the private key might remain in the machine's memory and thus can be copied by the provider or a malicious third party (see section 8.2).

Physical Bitcoin Units Some companies embed Bitcoin units within physical objects so that they can be circulated in the form of coins, certificates, bars, or other objects. The private key for managing the respective assets is physically hidden within the object itself. The public address is externally visible.

The problem regarding these objects is that the purchaser must trust the producer. First, he does not know whether the corresponding private key has actually been placed beneath the seal. Once he has broken the seal to find out, the Bitcoin units are no longer attached to the object, defeating the original purpose. Second, the same key might have been used for several objects, or it might be in the possession of the producer or a third party. Physical objects of this kind therefore fall within the category that we warned against in box 8.2 and should only be acquired with caution.

> **Box 8.4**
> **Physical Objects Without Bitcoin Content**
>
> In addition to the objects that contain a private key, there are other physical objects in circulation that are solely ornamental. These objects are sold under the label "Bitcoin," although they contain no Bitcoin units.
>
> Some of these objects even exist in various versions. The early versions of the physical Bitcoin issued by physical Bitcoin manufacturer Casascius contained a seal that concealed a private key that safeguarded the respective Bitcoin (BTC) nominal value of the coin (BTC 1, 0.5, or 0.1). Owing to regulatory difficulties, the second iteration of these coins has been sold without the seal and therefore without Bitcoin content. [52]

8.2   Storage

As we shall see below, private keys can be stored in many ways. Irrespective of the method of safekeeping, there are two important principles to follow. First, private keys must be stored in such a way that they will not get lost. The loss of a private key means the irrecoverable loss of the associated Bitcoin units. Second, no other person should ever be given access to your private key because, if a person has possession of a private key, he or she also obtain unrestricted control over the assets on the corresponding address.

All storage options have specific advantages and disadvantages. In particular, there is an unavoidable trade-off between convenience and security. Wallets of the category *hot storage* are directly linked to the internet and have the capacity to initiate transactions. Wallets of the category *cold storage* consist of wallets that do not have a network connection.

8.2.1   Selecting a Private Key

If you wish to store your Bitcoin units independently, you will need at least one Bitcoin address and the corresponding private key. A basic functionality of practically all *software wallets* is the generation of new addresses. The wallet generates the private key in the background and, in most cases, displays a mnemonic seed that you can use to restore your Bitcoin units (see box 4.3). This convenient way of generating a key is adequate for most applications.

As an alternative, there are websites that can be used to generate private keys. Extreme caution is required when using such services. Websites that have fraudulent motives will generate a private key and keep a copy of it to access your funds later on. It is important that you only use websites whose codebase is disclosed so that you can ensure they use a cryptographically secure random number generator. Further, the process employed for selecting the private key must only be performed on your personal computer. Ideally, you should download the whole website and open it on a computer that has no internet connection. In this way, you will prevent any third party from accessing your data.

Box 8.5
Caution Regarding Random Number Generators

Random numbers that are generated by computers are not random in the strict sense of the term. They are based on functions whose outputs, although appearing to be random, are actually generated deterministically. Simple pseudo-random number generators are therefore predictable.

> Consequently, the use of simple pseudo-random number generators to obtain private keys can lead to serious problems. The outputs often exhibit certain patterns, undermining the security of the private key. Cryptographically secure pseudo-random generators can counteract this problem.
>
> If you use one of the well-established wallets to generate your key, you will not have to confront this problem. The selection is made automatically on the basis of cryptographically secure pseudo-random number generators.

True random numbers can be generated on the basis of physical phenomena. Keys can be selected, for example, by throwing dice or coins. Box 4.4 provides a comprehensive description of how to generate private keys using dice and coins. This can be considered the most secure option. However, please make sure that you have access to your address before sending any cryptoassets to it.

> **Box 8.6**
> **Mycelium Entropy**
>
> Mycelium Entropy is a device in the form of a universal serial bus (USB) stick that can be used to generate private keys. The integrated random number generator is based on three sources of entropy that facilitate the random selection of private keys. At the same time, the device is extremely user-friendly.
>
> A further advantage is its independence from computers. Mycelium Entropy can be connected directly to a printer that has a USB Port. This method eliminates attack vectors via computers (see box 8.7 for a detailed discussion on the choice of a printer).
>
> The device is primarily used for generating *paper wallets* (see section 8.2.3). The generated private key and the mnemonic seed can also be imported into other storage options.

8.2.2   Hot Storage

When private keys are stored on devices that are directly or indirectly connected to the internet, the term hot storage is used. This type of storage offers convenience of access, but wallets of this kind are more vulnerable to attacks than the cold storage alternatives, which will be dealt with in section 8.2.3.

Software Wallets   *Software wallets* are usually very user-friendly and, when connected to the internet, can be used not only for storage purposes but also to transfer Bitcoin units. We distinguish between *desktop wallets* for computers and *mobile wallets* for mobile devices such as smart phones or tablets.

Owing to the network connection, software wallets are vulnerable to a variety of attacks. Most smartphones and tablets isolate individual apps and thereby provide better protection against malware. In contrast, desktop computers are vulnerable in this respect because applications are usually deeply anchored within the system and interact with each other without any significant restrictions; as well, there are substantial differences between the various operating systems.

It is always advisable to encrypt the private keys in the software wallet. Almost all popular software wallets offer this option. However, even encryption only provides partial protection. If a computer has been infected with a *key logger*—that is, a program that reads and registers all keystrokes—the wallet's encryption will be ineffective.

In addition, there is a considerable risk of losing the private keys. This might occur, for example, as a result of hard drive failure. Backups of the key (mnemonic phrase) can partially counteract this problem, but they should never be stored in digital form. Software wallets are generally unsuitable for the long-term storage of larger Bitcoin holdings. They should be used instead as a kind of everyday wallet to access smaller Bitcoin holdings quickly and conveniently.

A software wallet can be operated either as a full node client, as a *simplified payment verification (SPV) client*, or on the basis of a centralized subnetwork (see section 3.2). Full nodes are able to autonomously validate transactions but require a continuous internet connection. In addition, it initially takes a few days on average for the complete blockchain to be downloaded and processed. SPV clients and centralized subnetworks have substantially shorter loading times and fewer system requirements but have to rely on third-party information to validate transactions. For many applications, SPV clients are sufficient. Wallets based in centralized subnetworks should be used with caution.

Many standard software wallets leave their users in full control of their private keys. This is a welcome development, but it also means that you alone, without exception, are responsible for backups and the safekeeping of your Bitcoin units. An alternative approach consists in splitting the control so that outbound transactions have to be signed by both the user and the wallet operator's centralized service. These services are usually based on multisig (see section 4.5.3), where the second signature is triggered by the *two-factor authentication* (2FA) of the user. Normally, systems of this kind provide an alternative method which would allow you to continue using your assets if the service provider were to disappear.

Storage on Centralized Exchanges Bitcoin units can be stored on centralized exchanges. This is usually very convenient. Nevertheless, we must strongly urge you not to use this type of service for storing your Bitcoin units. The major problem with centralized exchanges is the fact that the user is not in possession of the private keys and therefore has no control over his or her Bitcoin units. If the centralized exchange is unable to or does not wish to sign a transaction, the user cannot regain control over his or her funds. Further, centralized exchanges present a lucrative target for hacker attacks. Section 2.5.4 describes a number of attacks on centralized exchanges in which Bitcoin users lost significant amounts.

8.2.3   Cold Storage

Cold storage wallets consist of wallets that do not have a network connection. The storage of your private keys in strict isolation from the internet prevents hacker attacks and is the best option for long-term safekeeping.

The objective of cold storage is to ensure the safety of your Bitcoin units. This comes at the cost of convenience. To initiate a transaction, either a pre-signed transaction or the private keys need to be imported into a hot storage wallet. In the following, we will discuss the main cold storage solutions, such as *hardware wallets*, *paper wallets*, and *brain wallets*.

Hardware Wallet   Hardware wallets are devices that are exclusively intended for storing private keys.

For simple hardware wallets without additional functionalities, a secure digital (SD) card, an external hard drive, or a USB stick is sufficient. Private keys can be stored on these media and kept somewhere away from the computer. If you want to store your Bitcoin units in this way for a longer period, it is worthwhile finding out how long the respective medium's expected life-span is. It is, in any case, advisable to keep copies on another medium.

So-called *offline wallets* are computers without internet access, which are set up exclusively as a software wallet. The great advantage of these offline wallets, compared with simple storage media, is that you can independently generate new private keys and addresses. In addition, transactions can be generated and signed offline. The signed transaction then only has to be exported to an *online wallet* to be propagated. The signed transaction contains no information that would allow inferences to be drawn about the private key. It corresponds exactly to the transaction message that will be propagated in the network anyway.

When Bitcoin became more popular, specialized hardware wallets emerged. These devices combine high security standards with simple and convenient handling. The devices can be connected to a computer to trigger the transactions. They only allow the exchange of transaction data but ensure that private keys always remain in the secure module of the hardware wallet.

When you buy such a device, it is crucial to ensure that you order it directly from the manufacturer or from a trusted retailer and that you receive it in its original packaging— sealed, that is. If you buy a used hardware wallet, it is advisable to reset the device prior to first use and to reinstall the official firmware from the manufacturer's website.

Paper Wallet   Paper wallets are paper-based notes that contain private keys. Alternatively, paper notes can also contain the mnemonic seed that can be used to derive several private keys. Paper wallets offer such advantages that they are easy to store and are the most economical cold storage option.

The notes can be either written by hand or printed. In both cases, it is advisable to write the private key several times on the same paper so that, in the case of partial damage, the complete key can still be restored. Often, the corresponding QR codes are also printed in addition to the private key.

Box 8.7
The Choice of a Suitable Printer

Paper wallets are a good option for storing private keys over the long term. However, when printing, you should be extremely careful. In addition to the possibility that your computer may be infected with malware, the printer may also present new attack vectors and expose your private keys to additional risks.

Printing jobs are usually stored in the printer's RAM and remain readable there for a long period of time. This is particularly a problem if the printer is connected to a network. Connect your printer directly via USB and ensure that no network cable is plugged in and that your printer's Wi-Fi function is disabled. Ideally, both your computer and your printer should have no contact with the internet at any point in time. As an additional security measure, it is recommended to disconnect the printer from its power supply after printing.

The software wallet Armory uses the Secure Print™ mechanism to protect the private key. The printout has to be supplemented with hand-written notes. This protects the private key even if an attacker has managed to read the printer's RAM.

For long-term storage, it is imperative that you consider the printing quality. It is advisable to use a laser printer as the documents that it produces cannot be smudged and are less sensitive to light and dampness. The durability of the paper wallet can be further enhanced by laminating the notes. Finally, do not use thermal paper.

Storing private keys in a physical form protects them from hacker attacks. At the same time, you carry the responsibility for ensuring that no one can view your private keys. If a third party managed to gain access to your paper wallet, this person would obtain control over all your assets. In particular, it is advisable to print only encrypted private keys and store the password in another location.

In addition, you should ensure that your paper wallet does not get lost or destroyed. Elemental forces such as fire or water could destroy your note and cause you to lose all your Bitcoin units.

Box 8.8
Protecting Private Keys from Loss

Time and again, warnings appear in the press about hacker attacks and Bitcoin thieves. However, most users who lose their Bitcoin units do so through the loss of the private key.

One possible way to solve this problem would be, for example, to generate several copies of the private key. The same private key could then be kept in several places. But as the number of copies increase, so do the number of potential attack vectors; this creates a certain trade-off between availability and security against third-party access.

A sophisticated approach for creating availability without compromising security is to split the key. For example, consider a setting where two out of three paper wallets are required to access the assets. If one note is lost, the assets could still be restored without a problem by using the other two notes. At the same time, if a third party has gained physical access to one of the three paper wallets, the attacker will still not be able to gain control over the assets.

Key systems of this kind can be structured by using multisig or a procedure called *Shamir's Secret Sharing*. The difference between these two procedures is only technical. With multisig, several keys exist, a subset of which are necessary to satisfy the unlocking condition. In contrast, Shamir's Secret Sharing uses traditional Bitcoin addresses with a single private key but splits this private key into several fragments. Here again, at least two fragments are necessary to derive the private key.

As already mentioned in section 8.2.1, numerous websites exist that can be used to generate paper wallets. These tools are user-friendly and often have very attractive printed layouts.

8.2.4   Brain Wallet

Private keys do not need to be written down anywhere. It may be sufficient to memorize the private key to ensure that you will remember it in the future. This type of safekeeping is called a *brain wallet*—a wallet that exists in your memory.

Only a few people will have the capacity to remember a 256-digit binary number. A much more practical procedure is to choose any combination of words and use a hash function (for example, `SHA256`) to generate a private key. This deterministic procedure is replicable, so you only have to remember the original combination of words. It is crucial that the sentence or the combination of words is produced randomly. Sentences from publicly accessible media, such as books, films, or songs, are a bad choice and will very likely lead to the loss of the Bitcoin units. Alternatively, you can also memorize the mnemonic seed to derive your key.

A further aspect that should be considered in connection with brain wallets is estate planning. If you want your Bitcoin units to pass to someone else in the event of your death, you should plan accordingly. Obviously, the use of brain wallets is highly problematic in this case.

8.3 Payments

Bitcoin units were developed as "a peer-to-peer electronic cash system." [158] In this respect, it is important to learn how to pay with Bitcoin units and how to take them in payment.

8.3.1 Paying with Bitcoin Units

Technically, it is easy to pay with Bitcoin. However, because the number of shops that accept Bitcoin units is still limited, you have to do some research and adapt your shopping to the limited options available. There are curated lists that record the available points of acceptance.

While real-world locations are limited, you can easily find a large variety of online shops that accept Bitcoin for many goods and services. An interesting starting point is *OpenBazaar*, a decentralized e-commerce platform that uses Bitcoin units as its main currency. [168]

The precise sequence of the payment process depends on the type of wallet that has been installed. The general process is always the same. Figure 8.1 shows the typical payment process.

After you have selected your goods and/or services, inform the retailer that you wish to start the payment process (1). The retailer then gives you a request for payment (2). This contains a Bitcoin address and a description or invoice number as well as the amount that you owe in Bitcoin units. The bill can be sent to your wallet either via Bluetooth, near-field communication (NFC), or a similar technology, or it can be alternatively displayed in the form of a QR code for scanning. In any case, your wallet will show the information on-screen and ask you for your confirmation (3). When you authorize the payment (4), a transaction message is generated, signed, and broadcasted to the Bitcoin network (5). As soon as the retailer receives the transaction message, he will send you an acknowledgement of your payment (6). The time that it takes until you receive the final confirmation (7) will depend on the network connection and on

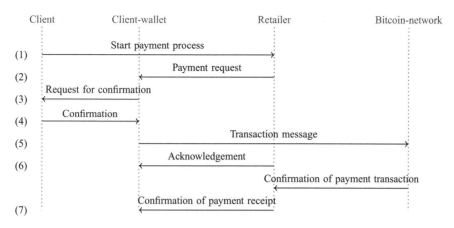

Figure 8.1
Standardized payment process according to BIP0070.
Source: Gavin Andresen and Mike Hearn. Payment protocol. GitHub, July 29, 2013. [11]

the retailer's specific acceptance criteria and the transaction fee. Usually, a confirmation takes between three seconds and one hour. [11]

Figure 8.1 highlights the simplicity of a Bitcoin payment. As a client, you do not have to do anything other than scan a QR code and confirm the payment request. All the other processes are performed automatically. The technical details from the previous sections are essential for understanding specific features of the Bitcoin system, but an end user does not need to know these details.

8.3.2 Acceptance of Bitcoin Payments

Accepting Bitcoin payments gives retailers numerous advantages. First, the transaction fees are low in comparison with credit card payments—especially when using second layer solutions like the Lightning Network. Second, customers cannot reverse their payments once they have received the goods or services. Third, acceptance of Bitcoin payments provides an opportunity to attract a new segment of customers.

There are various methods for accepting Bitcoin payments, and these can be split roughly into two categories: acceptance via a self-managed system or via the intermediation of a payment service provider.

Self-Managed Systems In analogy to cash, Bitcoin units can be accepted without the need for an intermediary. You can simply generate a Bitcoin address and forward it with a request for payment to your customer.

Figure 8.2
Payment request in QR code.

Simple requests for payment are valid as soon as they contain (at the very least) the Bitcoin address. The payment request is usually formatted as follows: `bitcoin:<Bitc oin_Adresse>?`. Many wallets also recognize QR codes without the Bitcoin prefix.

The standardization according to proposal BIP0021 [195] offers the possibility to specify further parameters such as the payment amount, the retailer's name, or the payment purpose description. The encoding is done using predefined meta-tags where the Bitcoin address is followed by a "?", and further parameters are separated from each other using "&".

The following example of a payment request references the Bitcoin address that was generated on the basis of the private key in box 4.1. The invoiced amount was set at 0.0005 Bitcoin units. In addition, the transaction message contains the owner information "Book" and the payment purpose description "Test payment."

```
bitcoin:1E8jc2eRXmjF2FKebTZwAsxwaRWeDvEwDj?amount=0.0005&label=Book
%20Address&message=Test%20Payment
```

The information can also be presented as a QR code so that the customer only has to scan the code. An example of a request for payment of this kind is shown is figure 8.2. Try to scan this code using your wallet, and you will see how simple it is to pay with Bitcoin units.[1]

You can either send the customer the payment request via Bluetooth, NFC, or similar connections or show the QR-code. If the customer uses a wallet, which also applies the standard procedure, the wallet will recognize the payment request, insert the information, and ask the customer for confirmation.

---

1. Do not send Bitcoin units to the "book" address since every reader of this book has access to the corresponding private key. You will most likely lose any funds that are sent to this address.

If you wish to implement the payment request yourself, you should follow BIP0071[8] or BIP0072.[9]

Payment requests are usually straightforward to manage, and there are no additional fees. This method is particularly attractive for smaller companies. However, further business requirements, such as accounting, online shop implementations, or point-of-sale systems, can make independent management considerably more complex. In addition, it is advisable to thoroughly evaluate the security risks. You should, for example, wait for at least one confirmation (on average, ten minutes) before you consider a payment to be valid. With larger payments, you should wait for several confirmations. So-called block explorers are good tools for evaluating the safety of a transaction. In particular, many block explorers offer early warning systems that are able to quickly identify any double spending attempts made by your customers.

A further point that you should consider is the volatility of the Bitcoin price (see section 6.1). In addition, take care to ensure that you generate a new, unique payment address for each of your customers. Although it is possible to have all your customers' payments credited to the same Bitcoin address, this has two major disadvantages. First, it will become increasingly difficult to distinguish among your customers' transactions. This is true in particular if you deal with many similar transactions. Analogous to the reference numbers on payment slips, Bitcoin addresses can be assigned to individual customers. Second, you must be aware of the fact that the Bitcoin transactions, although not identifiable by name, can be publicly observed. If you always use the same Bitcoin address, people who know this address (i.e., all your customers) will be able to monitor all your incoming payments.

Self-managed systems are primarily suitable for small companies that do not expect to have large sales volumes and are looking for the most economical system. For such cases, a simple wallet without any additional functions will be sufficient. However, if you expect to receive many Bitcoin payments, it may be worthwhile engaging a payment service provider.

Box 8.9
The Use of *xpub*

If you want to store your private keys in cold storage but at the same time want to be able to generate new Bitcoin addresses directly at a point-of-sale terminal or on the server of the online shop, the process offered by BIP0044[170] is an option. This proposal describes the standard that is used to derive *hierarchical deterministic wallets* and to generate new addresses without the corresponding private key.

Box 8.9 (continued)

The technical details are presented in section 4.1.5 in greater detail. The hardware wallet Trezor or the software wallet Armory are both very user-friendly and facilitate the simple export of the xpub data file that is necessary for a user to independently derive new Bitcoin addresses. In addition, both wallets have integrated functions that enable addresses to be generated in the absence of the private key.

Payment Service Providers Payment service providers offer a large number of tools that substantially simplify the implementation of Bitcoin payments at point-of-sale terminals and in online shops. These tools usually include all features needed throughout the payment life cycle—from the issue of the payment request to its receipt and temporary custody of the Bitcoin units.

In addition, the retailer has the possibility to immediately convert a Bitcoin payment into the local currency and thereby protect himself against Bitcoin's price volatility.

Further, many payment service providers will assume liability for any malfunctions. If, for example, a double spending attack is successful after the payment service provider has accepted the payment, the retailer will be reimbursed in most cases.

Even though the fees are usually much lower than for credit cards, these services are not free. It is worthwhile to compare the offers, as the fees may depend on the scope of the services desired.

8.4 Exercises

Exercise 8.1: Name three methods for procuring Bitcoin units. Which procurement method would you consider using for a sum amounting to: (1) 0.0005 Bitcoin unit, (2) 0.5 Bitcoin unit, and (3) 50 Bitcoin units?

Exercise 8.2: Outline the various storage possibilities along with their advantages and disadvantages.

Exercise 8.3: Install a software wallet of your choice and note the private key or the mnemonic seed (physically on a piece of paper) as a safety copy.

Exercise 8.4: For trial purposes, procure a small number of Bitcoin units, and put them in your Bitcoin wallet.

Exercise 8.5: Generate a paper wallet, and make a trial payment to credit this Bitcoin address. Check the procedure of the transaction using your wallet and a block explorer.

References

[1] ABC 10 News. 2013. World's first ever Bitcoin ATM unveiled in San Diego. YouTube, May 2. https://youtu.be/ZqEdBCKFPAo.

[2] Nader Al-Naji, Josh Chen, and Lawrence Diao. 2017. Basis: A price-stable cryptocurrency with an algorithmic central bank. White Paper, June 20. https://www.basis.io.

[3] David Andolfatto. 2015. Fedcoin: On the desirability of a government cryptocurrency. MacroMania, February 3. http://andolfatto.blogspot.com/2015/02/fedcoin-on-desirability -of-government.html.

[4] David Andolfatto. 2018. Assessing the impact of central bank digital currency on private banks. Working Paper 2018-026C, Federal Bank of St. Louis, Research Division, St. Louis, MO, October. https://research.stlouisfed.org/wp/more/2018-026.

[5] David Andolfatto. 2018. Blockchain: What it is, what it does and why you probably don't need one. *Federal Reserve Bank of St. Louis Review*, 100:87–95.

[6] Gavin Andresen. 2011. M-of-n standard transactions. GitHub, October 18. https://github .com/bitcoin/bips/blob/master/bip-0011.mediawiki.

[7] Gavin Andresen. n.d. Blockchain rule update process. GitHub. https://gist.github.com /gavinandresen/2355445.

[8] Gavin Andresen. 2013. Payment protocol MIME types. GitHub, July 29. https://github.com /bitcoin/bips/blob/master/bip-0071.mediawiki.

[9] Gavin Andresen. 2013. Uri extensions for payment protocol. GitHub, July 29. https:// github.com/bitcoin/bips/blob/master/bip-0072.mediawiki.

[10] Gavin Andresen. 2014. Bit-thereum. GavinTech, June 9. http://gavintech.blogspot.ch/2014 /06/bit-thereum.html.

[11] Gavin Andresen and Mike Hearn. 2013. Payment protocol. GitHub, July 29. https://github .com/bitcoin/bips/blob/master/bip-0070.mediawiki.

[12] Andy Skelton. 2012. Pay another way: Bitcoin. The WorldPress.com Blog, November 15. https://en.blog.wordpress.com/2012/11/15/pay-another-way-bitcoin/.

[13] Andytoshi. 2013. The birthday paradox. Paper, January 8. https://download.wpsoftware .net/bitcoin-birthday.pdf.

[14] Andreas Antonopoulos. 2015. *Mastering Bitcoin*. Newton, MA: O'Reilly Media.

[15] Martin A. Armstrong. 2015. The origins of money. In *Monetary history of the world* ArmstrongEconomics.com. http://www.armstrongeconomics.com/research/monetary-history-of -the-world/historical-outline-origins-of-money.

[16] Moshe Babaioff, Shahar Dobzinsky, Sigal Oren, and Aviv Zohar. 2011. On bitcoin and red balloons. *ACM SIGecom Exchanges*, 10(3):5–9.

[17] Adam Back. 1997. [Announce] hash cash postage implementation. http://www.hashcash .org/papers/announce.txt Email, March 28.

[18] Adam Back. 2002. Hashcash—a denial of service counter-measure. Paper, August 1. http:// www.hashcash.org/papers/hashcash.pdf.

[19] Tobias Bamert, Christian Decker, Lennart Elsen, Roger Wattenhofer, and Samuel Welten. 2013. Have a snack, pay with bitcoins. In *Proceedings of the 13th IEEE International Conference on Peer-to-Peer Computing*, Trento, Italy, September 9–11.

[20] European Central Bank. 2018. *ECB Annual Report 2017*. Franfurt am Main: ECB. https:// www.ecb.europa.eu/pub/pdf/annrep/ecb.ar2017.en.pdf.

[21] Vladimir Basov. 2015. How top gold producers margins are being squeezed. Mining.com, March 17. http://www.mining.com/top-gold-producers-margins-squeezed/.

[22] Morten Bech and Rodney Garratt. 2017. Central bank cryptocurrencies. *BIS Quarterly Review*, September.

[23] Mike Belshe, Wences Casares, Jihan Wu, Jeff Garzik, Peter Smith, and Erik Voorhees. 2017. Segwit2x final steps. LinuxFoundation.org Mailing List, November 8. https://lists .linuxfoundation.org/pipermail/bitcoin-segwit2x/2017-November/000685.html.

[24] Aleksander Berentsen. 1998. Monetary policy implications of digital money. *Kyklos*, 51(1): 89–118.

[25] Aleksander Berentsen. 2006. On the private provision of fiat currency. *European Economic Review*, 50:1683–1698.

[26] Aleksander Berentsen. 2017. Bitcoin, blockchain und geldpolitik. In Ernst Baltensperger, *Festschrift zu Ehren von Ernst Baltensperger*, edited by Schweizerische Nationalbank. Zurich: Orell Fussli.

[27] Aleksander Berentsen, Sébastien Kraenzlin, and Benjamin Müller. 2018. Exit strategies for monetary policy. *Journal of Monetary Economics*, (99):20–40.

[28] Aleksander Berentsen, Alessandro Marchesiani, and Christopher J. Waller. 2014. Floor systems for implementing monetary policy: Some unpleasant fiscal arithmetic. *Review of Economic Dynamics*, 17(3):523–542.

[29] Aleksander Berentsen and Guillaume Rocheteau. 2002. On the efficiency of monetary exchange: How divisibility of money matters. *Journal of Monetary Economics*, 49(8):1621–1649.

[30] Aleksander Berentsen and Fabian Schär. 2016. The fallacy of a cashless society. In *Cash on Trial: SUERF Conference Proceedings 2016/1*, edited by C. Beer, E. Gnan, and U. W. Birchler. Vienna: SUERF–The European Money and Finance Forum.

[31] Aleksander Berentsen and Fabian Schär. 2018. The case for central bank electronic money and the non-case for central bank cryptocurrencies. *Federal Reserve Bank of St. Louis Review*, 100:97–106.

[32] Aleksander Berentsen and Fabian Schär. 2018. A short introduction to the world of cryptocurrencies. *Federal Reserve Bank of St. Louis Review*, 100:1–16.

[33] Aleksander Berentsen and Fabian Schär. 2019. Stablecoins: The quest for a low-volatility cryptocurrency. In *The Economics of Fintech and Digital Currencies*, edited by A. Fatas. Washington, DC: CEPR Press.

[34] Aleksander Berentsen and Joachim Setlik. 2016. Mein gegenvorschlag. Vollgeld-initiative.com. https://vollgeld-initiative.com/Gegenvorschlag.html.

[35] Peter Bernholz. 2003. *Monetary Regimes and Inflation*. Northampton, MA: Edward Elgar.

[36] Mike Hearn. 2019. Contract: Example 7: Rapidly-adjusted (micro)payments to a pre-determined party. Bitcoin Wiki, February 25. https://en.bitcoin.it/wiki/Contract#Example_7:_Rapidly-adjusted_.28micro.29payments_to_a_pre-determined_party.

[37] BitGo. 2016. BitGo instant, the on-chain solution for instant bitcoin commerce surpasses 10,000 BTC transacted per week, equivalent to $7M USD. Official BitGo Blog, December 6. https://blog.bitgo.com/bitgo-instant-the-on-chain-solution-for-instant-bitcoin-commerce-surpasses-10-000-btc-transacted-65040cd48d3a.

[38] BitInfoCharts. 2016. Top 100 richest bitcoin addresses. In Bitcoin Rich List, webpage. https://bitinfocharts.com/top-100-richest-bitcoin-addresses.html.

[39] bitpay. 2012. BitPay exceeds 1,000 merchants accepting bitcoin. News release, September 11. https://blog.bitpay.com/bitpay-exceeds-1000-merchants-accepting-bitcoin/.

[40] Burton H. Bloom. 1970. Space/time trade-offs in hash coding with allowable errors. *Communications of the ACM*, 13(7):422–426.

[41] Stephanie Bodoni and Amy Thomson. 2015. EU's top court rules that bitcoin exchange is tax-free. Bloomberg.com, October 22. http://www.bloomberg.com/news/articles/2015-10-22/bitcoin-virtual-currency-exchange-is-tax-free-eu-court-says-ig21wzcd.

[42] Coralie Boeykens. 2007. Papiergeld, eine chinesische erfindung. National Bank of Belgium. http://www.nbbmuseum.be/de/2007/09/chinese-invention.htm.

[43] Michael Bordo and Andrew Levin. 2017. Central bank digital currency and the future of monetary policy. NBER Working Paper No. 23711, National Bureau of Economic Research, Cambridge, MA, August. http://www.nber.org/papers/w23711.

[44] Richard Gendal Brown. 2015. Bitcoin as a smart contract platform. Richard Gendal Brown (blog), March 30. http://gendal.me/2015/03/30/bitcoin-as-a-smart-contract-platform/.

[45] Markus Brunnermeier and Dirk Niepelt. 2019. On the equivalence of private and public money. White Paper, January 1. https://scholar.princeton.edu/sites/default/files/markus/files/equivalenceprivatepublicmoney.01jan2019.pdf.

[46] Johannes Buchmann. 2010. *Einführung in die Kryptografie*. Heidelberg: Springer.

[47] Swiss Parliament, The Federal Assembly. 2013. 13.5177: Quels sont les coûts de fabrication de l'argent suisse? Parliamentary Business, June 10. https://www.parlament.ch/en/ratsbetrieb/suche-curia-vista/geschaeft?AffairId=20135177.

[48] Vitalik Buterin. 2012. Bitcoin, decentralization and the Nash equilibrium. *Bitcoin Magazine*, 1(1):19–21.

[49] Vitalik Buterin. 2013. Selfish mining: A 25% attack against the bitcoin network. *Bitcoin Magazine*, November 4. https://bitcoinmagazine.com/7953/selfish-mining-a-25-attack-against-the-bitcoin-network/.

[50] Phillip D. Cagan. 1956. The monetary dynamics of hyperinflation. In *Studies in the Quantity of Money*, edited by Milton Friedman. Chicago, IL: University of Chicago Press.

[51] Gabriele Camera, Marco Casari, and Maria Bigoni. 2013. Money and trust among strangers. *Proceedings of the National Academy of Sciences*, 110(37):14889–14893.

[52] Casascius. n.d. Physical bitcoins by Casascius. Website. https://www.casascius.com/.

[53] Bruce Champ, Scott Freedman, and Joseph Haslag. 2011. *Modeling Monetary Economics*. New York: Cambridge University Press.

[54] Flavien Charlon. 2015. Change the default maximum op_return size to 80 bytes. GitHub, February 3. https://github.com/bitcoin/bitcoin/pull/5286.

[55] David Chaum. 1982. Blind signatures for untraceable payments. *Advances in Cryptology: Proceedings of Crypto 82*, edited by D. Chaum, R. L. Rivest, and A. T. Sherman. New York: Plenum. http://www.hit.bme.hu/~buttyan/courses/BMEVIHIM219/2009/Chaum.BlindSigForPayment.1982.PDF.

[56] Adrian Chen. 2011. The underground website where you can buy any drug imaginable. Gawker, June 1. http://gawker.com/the-underground-website-where-you-can-buy-any-drug-imag-30818160.

[57] Jonathan Chiu, Seyed Davoodalhosseini, Janet Jiang, and Yu Zhu. 2019. Central bank digital currency and banking. White Paper, February 8. https://papers.ssrn.com/sol3/papers.cfm ?abstract_id=3331135.

[58] Bhagwan Chowdhry. 2015. I (shall happily) accept the 2016 Nobel Prize in Economics on behalf of Satoshi Nakamoto. *Huffington Post*, November 6. http://www.huffingtonpost.com /bhagwan-chowdry/i-shall-happily-accept-th_b_8462028.html.

[59] Roger Clarke. 1997. Europay Switzerland's SVC project. Paper, Canberra, May 22. http:// www.rogerclarke.com/EC/SVCSwitz.html.

[60] Roger Clarke. 1997. Smart cards in banking and finance. *Australian Banker* 111(2). http:// www.rogerclarke.com/EC/SCBF.html.

[61] CNBC. 2018. Bitcoin is the "mother of all scams" and blockchain is most hyped tech ever, Roubini tells Congress. CNBC, October 11. https://www.cnbc.com/2018/10/11 /roubini-bitcoin-is-mother-of-all-scams.html.

[62] Coinbase. 2014. Dell.com partners with Coinbase to become the largest ecommerce merchant to accept bitcoin. The Coinbase Blog, July 18. https://blog.coinbase.com/2014/07 /18/dell-com-partners-with-coinbase-to-become-the/.

[63] Coinbase. 2014. Expedia.com partners with Coinbase for hotel payments via bitcoin. The Coinbase Blog, June 11. https://blog.coinbase.com/2014/06/11/expedia-com-partners-with -coinbase-for-hotel/.

[64] CoinDesk. 2015. Bitcoin venture capital investments. http://www.coindesk.com/bitcoin -venture-capital/.

[65] Committee on Homeland Security and Governmental Affairs, United States Senate. 2013. *Beyond silk road: Potential risks, threats, and promises of virtual currencies.* Hearing, 113th Congress, 1st Session, November 13. https://www.gpo.gov/fdsys/pkg/CHRG-113shrg86636 /pdf/CHRG-113shrg86636.pdf.

[66] Committee on Homeland Security and Governmental Affairs, United States Senate. 2013. Beyond silk road: Potential risks, threats, and promises of virtual currencies. Hearing, 113th Congress, 1st Session, November 13 (video). https://www.youtube.com/watch ?v=bKYkN2xDoZc.

[67] Andrea Corbellini. 2015. Elliptic curve cryptography: A gentle introduction (series). Andrea Corbellini (website), May 17. http://andrea.corbellini.name/2015/05/17/elliptic -curve-cryptography-a-gentle-introduction/.

[68] Bitcoin Core. 2016. Segregated witness benefits. Blog post, January 26. https://bitcoincore .org/en/2016/01/26/segwit-benefits/.

[69] Sébastien Couture and Brian Fabian Crain. 2015. Emin Gün Sirer & Ittay Eyal: From selfish miners to the miner's dilemma. Epicenter Bitcoin. Podcast, episode 76, April 27.

https://letstalkbitcoin.com/blog/post/epicenter-bitcoin-76-emin-gun-sirer-and-ittay-eyal
-from-selfish-miners-to-the-miners-dilemma.

[70] Sébastien Couture and Brian Fabian Crain. 2015. Robert Sams: Bitcoin, volatility and the
      search for a stable cryptocurrency. Epicenter Bitcoin. Podcast, episode 60, January 4. https://
      epicenterbitcoin.com/podcast/060/.

[71] Cryptyk. 2013. Why aren't hacked bitcoins blacklisted? Reddit, Bitcoin subreddit,
      April 28. https://www.reddit.com/r/Bitcoin/comments/1d9vz7/why_arent_hacked_bitcoins
      _blacklisted/.

[72] Jacques Dafflon, Jordi Baylina, and Thomas Shababi. 2017. EIP 777: ERC777 token standard.
      Ethereum Improvement Proposal, November 20. https://eips.ethereum.org/EIPS/eip-777.

[73] Wei Dai. 1998. B-money. Wei Dai (website). http://www.weidai.com/bmoney.txt.

[74] Alex de Vries. 2018. Bitcoin's growing energy problem. *Joule*, 2:801–805.

[75] Christian Decker, James Guthrie, Jochen Seidel, and Roger Wattenhofer. 2015. Making bit-
      coin exchanges transparent. In *Computer Security—ESORICS 2015, Part II*, edited by G. Pernul,
      P. Ryan, and E. Weippl. Berlin: Springer.

[76] Christian Decker and Roger Wattenhofer. 2013. Information propagation in the bitcoin net-
      work. In *Proceedings of the 13th IEEE International Conference on Peer-to-Peer Computing*, Trento,
      Italy, September 9–11.

[77] Christian Decker and Roger Wattenhofer. 2014. Bitcoin transaction malleability and MtGox.
      Computer Security—ESORICS 2014, edited by M. Kutylowski and J. Vaidya, 313–326. Berlin:
      Springer.

[78] Dexaran. n.d. ERC223-token-standard. GitHub, n.d. https://github.com/Dexaran/ERC223
      -token-standard.

[79] Johnny Dilley, Andrew Poelstra, Jonathan Wilkins, Marta Piekarska, Ben Gorlick, and Mark
      Friedenbach. 2017. Strong federations: An interoperable blockchain solution to central-
      ized third party risks. White Paper, Cornell University, January 30. https://blockstream.com
      /assets/downloads/strong-federations.pdf.

[80] Dish. 2014. Dish to accept bitcoin. Press release, May 29. http://about.dish.com/press-release
      /products-and-services/dish-accept-bitcoin.

[81] Joan Antoni Donet, Cristina Pérez-Solá, and Jordi Herrera-Joancomartí. 2014. The bitcoin
      P2P network. In *Financial Cryptography and Data Security*, edited by R. Bohme, M. Brenner,
      T. Moore, and M. Smith, 87–102. Berlin: Springer.

[82] Emily Dreyfuss. 2016. Craig Wright ends his attempt to prove he created Bitcoin: "I'm
      sorry." *Wired*, May 5. https://www.wired.com/2016/05/craig-wright-ends-attempt-prove
      -created-bitcoin-im-sorry/.

[83] DutchBrat. 2014. MTGox: Addressing transaction malleability. Bitcoin Forum, February 10. https://bitcointalk.org/index.php?topic=458082.

[84] dwdollar. 2010. New exchange (bitcoin market). Bitcoin Forum, January 15. https:// bitcointalk.org/index.php?topic=20.0.

[85] Cynthia Dwork and Moni Naor. 1992. Pricing via processing or combatting junk mail. *Lecture Notes in Computer Science*, 740:139–147.

[86] Fred Ehrsam, Brian Armstrong, Jesse Powell, Nejc Kodric, Bobby Lee, Nicolas Cary, and Jeremy Allaire. 2014. Joint statement regarding Mt. Gox. Blockchain Blog, February 24. https://blog.coinbase.com/2014/02/25/joint-statement-regarding-mtgox/.

[87] Barry Eichengreen. 2018. Opinion: Highly touted "stable coins" are anything but. *Caixin*, September 13. https://www.caixinglobal.com/2018-09-13/opinion-highly-touted-stable -coins-are-anything-but-101325668.html.

[88] William Entriken, Dieter Shirley, Jacob Evans, and Nastassia Sachs. 2018. EIP 721: ERC-721 non-fungible token standard. Ethereum Improvement Proposals, January 24. https://eips .ethereum.org/EIPS/eip-721.

[89] Ethereum. 2016. A next-generation smart contract and decentralized application platform. White paper. https://github.com/ethereum/wiki/wiki/White-Paper.

[90] European Central Bank. 2012. *Virtual Currency Schemes*. Frankfurt am Main: ECB, October. https://www.ecb.europa.eu/pub/pdf/other/virtualcurrencyschemes201210en.pdf.

[91] Ittay Eyal and Emin Gün Sirer. 2014. Majority is not enough: Bitcoin mining is vulnerable. White Paper, Cornell University. In *Financial Cryptography and Data Security*, edited by N. Christin and R. Safavi-Naini, 436–454. Berlin: Springer. http://www.cs.cornell.edu/ie53 /publications/btcProcFC.pdf.

[92] Rick Falkvinge. 2014. Major bitcoin exchange not executing withdrawals; now owes clients $38m in disappeared money. Falkvinge on Liberty, February 4.http://falkvinge.net/2014/02 /04/major-bitcoin-exchange-not-executing-withdrawals-now-owes-clients-38m-in-disapp eared-money/.

[93] Federal Bureau of Investigation (FBI). 2012. Bitcoin virtual currency: Unique features present distinct challenges for deterring illicit activity. Washington, DC: FBI, April 24. http://www .wired.com/images_blogs/threatlevel/2012/05/Bitcoin-FBI.pdf.

[94] Jesus Fernandez Villaverde. 2018. Cryptocurrencies: A crash course in digital monetary economics. *Australian Economic Review*, 51: 514–526.

[95] Jesus Fernandez-Villaverde and Daniel Sanches. 2016. Can currency competition work? NBER Working Paper No. 22157, National Bureau of Economic Research, Cambridge, MA., April. https://www.nber.org/papers/w22157.

[96]   Hal Finney. 2005. n.d. Reusable proofs of work. NakamotoInstitute.org. http://nakamoto institute.org/finney/rpow/index.html.

[97]   Hal Finney. 2013. Bitcoin and me (hal finney). Bitcoin Forum, March 19. https://bitcointalk .org/index.php?topic=155054.0.

[98]   Center for Innovative Finance. 2018. Certificates based on blockchain technology. University of Basel, Faculty of Business and Economics Blog, April 30. https://cif.unibas.ch/en /blog/details/news/certificates-based-on-blockchain-technology/.

[99]   Mark Friedenbach, BtcDrak, Nicolas Dorier, and kinoshitajona. 2015. Relative lock-time using consensus-enforced sequence numbers. GitHub, May 28. https://github.com/bitcoin /bips/blob/master/bip-0068.mediawiki.

[100] Milton Friedman. 1991. *The Island of Stone Money*. Working Papers in Economics, no. E-91-3. Hoover Institution, Stanford, CA.

[101] William Henry Furness. 1910. *The Island of Stone Money: Uap of the Carolines*. Philadelphia, PA: J. B. Lippincott.

[102] Rodney Garratt and Neil Wallace. 2018. Bitcoin 1, bitcoin 2, ...: An experiment in privately issued outside monies. *Western Economic Association International*, 56:1887–1897.

[103] Leah McGrath Goodman. 2014. The face behind bitcoin. *Newsweek*, March 6. http://www .newsweek.com/2014/03/14/face-behind-bitcoin-247957.html.

[104] David Graeber. *Debt: The First 5000 Years*. Brooklyn, NY: Melville House, 2011.

[105] Andy Greenberg and Gwern Branwen. 2015. Bitcoin's creator Satoshi Nakamoto is probably this unknown Australian genius. *Wired*, December 8. http://www.wired.com/2015/12 /bitcoins-creator-satoshi-nakamoto-is-probably-this-unknown-australian-genius/.

[106] Skye Grey. 2013. Satoshi Nakamoto is (probably) Nick Szabo. LikeInAMirror, December 1. https://likeinamirror.wordpress.com/2013/12/01/satoshi-nakamoto-is-probably-nick -szabo/.

[107] Skye Grey. 2014. Occam's razor: Who is most likely to be Satoshi Nakamoto? LikeInAMirror, March 11. https://likeinamirror.wordpress.com/2014/03/11/occams-razor-who-is-most -likely-to-be-satoshi-nakamoto/.

[108] Steve H. Hanke and Nicholas Krus. 2013. The hanke-krus hyperinflation table. Cato Institute, May. https://www.cato.org/research/world-inflation-and-hyperinflation-table (scroll to "Download the Hanke-Krus World Hyperinflation Table").

[109] Qureshi Haseeb. 2018. Stablecoins: Designing a price-stable cryptocurrency. Hacker Noon, February 9. https://hackernoon.com/stablecoins-designing-a-price-stable-cryptocurrency -6bf24e2689e5.

[110] Mike Hearn. 2018. Smart property. Bitcoin Wiki, July 16. https://en.bitcoin.it/wiki/Smart _Property.

[111] Mike Hearn and Matt Corallo. 2012. Connection bloom filtering. GitHub, October 24. https://github.com/bitcoin/bips/blob/master/bip-0037.mediawiki.

[112] Ethan Heilman. 2014. One weird trick to stop selfish miners: Fresh bitcoins, a solution for the honest miner. In *Financial Cryptography and Data Security*, edited by R. Bohme, M. Brenner, T. Moore, and M. Smith, 161–162. Berlin: Springer. https://eprint.iacr.org/2014 /007.pdf.

[113] Bradley Hope. 2015. A bitcoin technology gets Nasdaq test. *Wall Street Journal*, May 10. https://www.wsj.com/articles/a-bitcoin-technology-gets-nasdaq-test-1431296886.

[114] Nicolas Houy. 2014. The bitcoin mining game. Paper, March 11. https://ssrn.com/abstract =2407834. https://halshs.archives-ouvertes.fr/file/index/docid/958224/filename/1412.pdf.

[115] David Howden. 2014. Bitcoin bank run. Mises Wire, February 8. https://mises.org/blog /bitcoin-bank-run.

[116] David Howden. 2014. Bitcoin bank run, take 2. Mises Wire, February 11. https://mises.org /blog/bitcoin-bank-run-take-2.

[117] Brandon Hurst. 2014. Here's how many people actually own Bitcoin. *Business Insider*, March 29. https://www.businessinsider.com/heres-how-many-people-actually-own-bitcoin -2014-3.

[118] SIX Group. n.d. Inquiry IBAN. Website. https://www.six-group.com/interbank-clearing/en /home/standardization/iban/inquiry-iban.html.

[119] Anna Irrera. 2015. UBS to open blockchain research lab in London. *Wall Street Journal*, April 2. http://blogs.wsj.com/digits/2015/04/02/ubs-to-open-blockchain-research-lab-in -london/.

[120] Mitsuru Iwamura, Yukinobi Kitamura, Tsumotu Matsumotu, and Kenji Saito. 2014. Can we stabilize the price of a cryptocurrency? Understanding the design of bitcoin and its potential to compete with central bank money. Discussion Paper Series A No. 617, Institute of Economic Research, Hitotsubashi University, November. http://www.ier.hit-u.ac.jp/Common /publication/DP/DPS-A617.

[121] Mats Jeratsch. 2016. n.d. Thunder network. Website. https://matsjj.github.io/.

[122] Charles Kahn. 2018. Payment systems and privacy. *Federal Reserve Bank of St. Louis Review*, Fourth Quarter: 337–344. https://doi.org/10.20955/r.100.337-44.

[123] Jonathan Katz and Yehuda Lindell. 2015. *Introduction to Modern Cryptography Second Edition*. Boca Raton, FL: CRC Press.

[124] Todd Keister and Daniel Sanches. 2018. Should central banks issue digital currency? Paper presented at the Conference on "Economics of Payments IX," Bank for International Settlements, Basel, Switzerland, November 15–16. https://www.bis.org/events/eopix_1810 /keister_paper.pdf.

[125] Thomas Kerin and Mark Friedenbach. 2015. Median time-past as endpoint for lock-time calculations. GitHub, August 10. https://github.com/bitcoin/bips/blob/master/bip-0113.mediawiki.

[126] Thomas Kerin, Jean-Pierre Rupp, and Ruben de Vries. 2015. Deterministic pay-to-cript-hash multi-signature addresses through public key sorting. GitHub, February 8. https://github.com/bitcoin/bips/blob/master/bip-0067.mediawiki.

[127] Khan Academy. 2016. The euclidean algorithm. From Modular arithmetic in *Journey into cryptography*. https://www.khanacademy.org/computing/computer-science/cryptography/modarithmetic/a/the-euclidean-algorithm.

[128] Nobuhiro Kiyotaki and Randall Wright. 1989. On money as a medium of exchange. *Journal of Political Economy*, 97(4):927–954.

[129] Nobuhiro Kiyotaki and Randall Wright. 1993. A search-theoretic approach to monetary economics. *The American Economic Review*, 83(1)(1993):63–77.

[130] Narayana R. Kocherlakota. 1996. Money is memory. Research Department Staff Report 218, Federal Reserve Bank of Minneapolis, Minneapolis, MN, October.

[131] J. P. Koning. 2013. Ghost money: Chile's unidad de fomento. *Moneyness* (blog), September 23. http://jpkoning.blogspot.ch/2013/09/ghost-money-chiles-unidad-de-fomento.html.

[132] J. P. Koning. 2013. Separating the functions of money—the case of Medieval coinage. *Moneyness* (blog), September 13. http://jpkoning.blogspot.ca/2013/09/separating-functions-of-moneythe-case.html.

[133] J. P. Koning. 2013. Why the Fed is more likely to adopt bitcoin technology than kill it off. *Moneyness* (blog), April 14. http://jpkoning.blogspot.com/2013/04/why-fed-is-more-likely-to-adopt-bitcoin.html.

[134] Kraken. 2016. Kraken proof-of-reserves audit process. Webpage. https://www.kraken.com/security/audit.

[135] Joshua A. Kroll, Ian C. Davey, and Edward W. Felten. 2013. The economics of bitcoin mining, or bitcoin in the presence of its adversaries. In *Proceedings of the Twelfth Workshop on the Economics of Information Security 2013*, Washington, DC, June 11–12.

[136] Leslie Lamport, Shostak Robert, and Marshall Pease. 1982. The byzantine generals problem. *ACM Transactions on Programming Languages and Systems*, 4(3): 382–401.

[137] laszlo. 2010. Pizza for bitcoins? Bitcoin Forum, May 18. https://bitcointalk.org/index.php?topic=137.0.

[138] Ledra Capital. 2014. Bitcoin series 24: The mega-master blockchain list. Ledra Capital Blog, March 11. http://ledracapital.com/blog/2014/3/11/bitcoin-series-24-the-mega-master-blockchain-list.

[139] Axel Leijonhufvud. 1981. *Information and Coordination*. New York: Oxford University Press.

[140] Sergio Lerner. 2013. The well deserved fortune of Satoshi Nakamoto, bitcoin creator, visionary and genius. Bitslog, April 17. https://bitslog.wordpress.com/2013/04/17/the -well-deserved-fortune-of-satoshi-nakamoto/.

[141] Sergio Demian Lerner. 2015. *RSK White Paper Overview*, November 19. Montevideo: IOV Labs, RSK, November 19. Rsk whitepaper. https://docs.rsk.co/RSK_White_Paper-Overview .pdf.

[142] Adam B. Levine. 2013. The controlled demolition of Cyprus. Let's Talk Bitcoin! Podcast, episode 1. https://soundcloud.com/mindtomatter/the-controlled-demolition-of.

[143] Adam B. Levine. 2015. Exciting possibilities. Let's Talk Bitcoin! Podcast, episode 272, December 12. https://letstalkbitcoin.com/blog/post/lets-talk-bitcoin-272-exciting-possibilities.

[144] Anthony Lewis. 2014. Orisi white paper. GitHub, September 15. https://github.com/orisi /wiki/wiki/Orisi-White-Paper.

[145] Eric Lombrozo and Mark Friedenbach. CHECKSEQUENCEVERIFY. GitHub, August 10, 2015. https://github.com/bitcoin/bips/blob/master/bip-0112.mediawiki.

[146] Eric Lombrozo, Johnson Lau, and Pieter Wuille. 2015. Segregated witness (consensus layer). GitHub, December 21. https://github.com/bitcoin/bips/blob/master/bip-0141.mediawiki.

[147] P. H. Madore. 2015. Satoshi Nakamoto not eligible for Nobel prize. CCN.com, November 17. https://www.cryptocoinsnews.com/satoshi-nakamoto-not-eligible-nobel-prize/.

[148] Jon Mantonis. 2013. Why bitcoin fungibility is essential. CoinDesk, December 1. http:// www.coindesk.com/bitcoin-fungibility-essential/.

[149] Gregory Maxwell. 2011. Deterministic wallets. Bitcoin Forum, June 18. https://bitcointalk .org/index.php?topic=19137.0.

[150] Gregory Maxwell. 2015. (nullc) Bitcoin scale tests by (alleged) Satoshi! 340gb blocks, 568k transactions! Reddit.com, Bitcoin subreddit (comment), December 9. https://www .reddit.com/r/Bitcoin/comments/3w07lq/blockchain_scale_tests_by_alleged_satoshi_340 _gb/cxsfhxb.

[151] Timothy C. May. 1992. The crypto anarchist manifesto. Email, November 22. http://www .activism.net/cypherpunk/crypto-anarchy.html.

[152] Robert McMillan. 2015. IBM adapts bitcoin technology for smart contracts. *Wall Street Journal*, September 16. http://www.wsj.com/articles/ibm-adapts-bitcoin-technology-for-smart -contracts-1442423444.

[153] Jacques Melitz. 1974. *Primitive and Modern Money*. Boston, MA: Addison-Wesley.

[154] Carl Menger. 1892. On the origins of money. *Economic Journal* 2:239–255.

[155] Microsoft. 2014. Now you can exchange bitcoins to buy apps, games and more for Windows, Windows Phone and Xbox. Press release, December 11. http://blogs.microsoft.com /firehose/2014/12/11/now-you-can-exchange-bitcoins-to-buy-apps-games-and-more-for -windows-windows-phone-and-xbox/.

[156] Microsoft. 2016. Microsoft store doesn't accept bitcoin. Press release, March. http:// windows.microsoft.com/en-us/windows-10/microsoft-store-doesnt-accept-bitcoin.

[157] mtgox. 2010. New bitcoin exchange (mtgox.com). Bitcoin Forum, July 18. https://bit cointalk.org/index.php?topic=444.0.

[158] Satoshi Nakamoto. 2008. Bitcoin: A peer-to-peer electronic cash system. Paper.

[159] Arvind Narayanan, Joseph Bonneau, Edward Felten, Andrew Miller, and Steven Goldfeder. 2016. *Bitcoin and Cryptocurrency Technologies*. Princeton, NJ: Princeton University Press.

[160] New Liberty Standard. 2010. 2009 exchange rate. February 5. http://newlibertystandard .wikifoundry.com/page/2009+Exchange+Rate.

[161] N.Y. Fin. Serv. Law § 200 (2015). http://www.dfs.ny.gov/legal/regulations/adoptions/dfsp 200t.pdf.

[162] Dirk Niepelt. 2018. Reserves for all? central bank digital currency, deposits, and their (non)- equivalence. CESifo Working Paper 7176, CESifo Group, Munich, Germany.

[163] Anders Nilsson. 2014. The troublesome history of the bitcoin exchange mtgox. Anders.io, February 12. https://anders.io/the-troublesome-history-of-the-bitcoin-exchange-mtgox/.

[164] Ed Nosal and Guillaume Rocheteau. 2011. *Money, Payments and Liquidity*. Cambridge, MA: The MIT Press.

[165] Remo Nyffenegger. 2018. Scaling bitcoin. Master's thesis, University of Basel, August 9.

[166] Remo Nyffenegger and Fabian Schär. 2018. Token sales: Eine analyse des blockchain- basierten unternehmensfinanzierungsinstruments. *Corporate Finance*, 5–6:121–125.

[167] Bank for International Settlements (BIS), Committee on Payments and Market Infrastructures and the Markets Committee. 2018. Central bank digital currencies. Basel: BIS, March. https://www.bis.org/cpmi/publ/d174.pdf.

[168] OpenBazaar. n.d. Website. https://openbazaar.org/.

[169] Overstock. 2014. Overstock.com first online retailer to accept bitcoin. Press release, January 9. http://investors.overstock.com/phoenix.zhtml?c=131091&p=irol-newsArticle _print&ID=1889670.

[170] Marek Palatinus and Pavol Rusnak. 2014. Multi-account hierarchy for deterministic wallets. GitHub, April 24. https://github.com/bitcoin/bips/blob/master/bip-0044.mediawiki.

[171] Marek Palatinus, Pavol Rusnak, Aaron Voisine, and Sean Bowe. 2013. Mnemonic code for generating deterministic keys. GitHub, September 10. https://github.com/bitcoin/bips /blob/master/bip-0039.mediawiki.

[172] Paypal. 2018. Paypal reports fourth quarter and full year 2017 resultst. Business Wire, January 31. https://www.businesswire.com/news/home/20180131006195/en/PayPal -Reports-Fourth-Quarter-Full-Year-2017.

[173] Yessi Bello Perez. 2015. Bitcoin's price rise explained by industry insiders. CoinDesk, October 31. http://www.coindesk.com/bitcoins-price-rise-explained-by-industry-insiders/.

[174] James Poole. 2014. Http based bitcoin micropayment channel demo—microtrx. YouTube, September 25. https://www.youtube.com/watch?v=HmYP-7pcdhM.

[175] Joseph Poon and Thaddeus Dryja. 2016. The bitcoin lightning network: Scalable off-chain instant payments. Lightning Network Paper, January 14. https://lightning.network /lightning-network-paper.pdf.

[176] Nathaniel Popper. 2015. Decoding the enigma of satoshi nakamoto and the birth of bit-coin. *New York Times*, May 15. http://www.nytimes.com/2015/05/17/business/decoding-the -enigma-of-satoshi-nakamoto-and-the-birth-of-bitcoin.html.

[177] James Prestwich. 2017. Bitcoin's time locks. The Balance Wheel, October 13. https://prestwi .ch/bitcoin-time-locks/.

[178] Puppet. 2014. Cloudmining 101 (ponzi risk assessment). Bitcoin Forum, November 30. https://bitcointalk.org/index.php?topic=878387.0.

[179] Bittmex Research. 2018. A brief history of stablecoins (part 1). BitMEX, July 2. https://blog .bitmex.com/a-brief-history-of-stablecoins-part-1/.

[180] Reuters. 2015. China to cap overseas cash withdrawals to curb outflows—sources. September 29. https://www.reuters.com/article/china-economy-unionpay-idUSL3N11Z2TH20150929.

[181] Charles Riley and Zhang Dayu. 2013. China cracks down on bitcoin. CNN, December 5. http://money.cnn.com/2013/12/05/investing/china-bitcoin/.

[182] Ronald L Rivest, Adi Shamir, and Len Adleman. 1978. A method for obtaining digital signatures and public-key cryptosystems. *Communications of the ACM*, 21(2):120–126.

[183] Rob Price. 2015. The mysterious creator of bitcoin has been nominated for the nobel prize in economics. Business Insider, November 9. http://www.businessinsider.com /bitcoin-inventor-satoshi-nakamoto-nominated-nobel-prize-economics-bhagwan-chodry -2015-11.

[184] Dorit Ron and Adi Shamir. 2013. Quantitative analysis of the full bitcoin transaction graph. In *Financial Cryptography and Data Security*, edited by A. R. Sadeghi, 6–24. Berlin: Springer.

[185] Dorit Ron and Adi Shamir. 2014. How did Dread Pirate Roberts acquire and protect his bitcoin wealth? In *Financial Cryptography and Data Security*, edited by R. Bohme, M. Brenner, T. Moore, and M. Smith, 3–15. Berlin: Springer.

[186] Everett Rosenfeld. 2014. Bitcoin's 'BearWhale' and the future of a cryptocurrency. CNBC, October 9. https://www.cnbc.com/2014/10/09/bitcoins-bearwhale-and-the-future-of -a-cryptocurrency.html.

[187] Michael Rosing. 1999. *Implementing Elliptic Curve Cryptography*. Greenwich, CT: Manning.

[188] Jakob Roth, Fabian Schär, and Aljoscha Schöpfer. 2019. The tokenization of assets: Using blockchains for equity crowdfunding, August 27. http://dx.doi.org/10.2139/ssrn.3443382.

[189] Paul Russell. 2016. c-lightning: A specification compliant Lightning Network implementation in C. GitHub, January 21. https://github.com/ElementsProject/lightning.

[190] Robert Sams. 2015. A note on cryptocurrency stabilisation: Seigniorage shares. GitHub. https://github.com/rmsams/stablecoins.

[191] Daniel Sanches. 2016. On the welfare properties of fractional reserve banking. *International Economic Review*, 57:935–954.

[192] Thomas Sargent and Francois Velde. 2003. *The Big Problem of Small Change*. Princeton, NJ: Princeton University Press.

[193] Linda Schilling and Harald Uhlig. 2019. Some simple bitcoin economics. *Journal of Monetary Economics*, 106:16–26.

[194] Klaus Schmeh. 2013. *Kryptografie*. Heidelberg: dpunkt Verlag.

[195] Nils Schneider and Matt Corallo. 2012. Uri scheme. GitHub, January 29. https://github .com/bitcoin/bips/blob/master/bip-0021.mediawiki.

[196] Jonas Schnelli. 2016. What's new in bitcoin core 0.12. YouTube, January 22. https://youtu .be/RWeIEFBrItE (minute 48).

[197] Fabian Schuh and Daniel Larimer. 2015. Bitshares 2.0: Financial smart contract platform. Paper. http://docs.bitshares.eu/_downloads/bitsharesfinancial-platform.pdf.

[198] Schweizerische Eidgenossenschaft. 1934. Dreizehnter Abschnitt: Einlagensicherung (Art. 37). In Bundesgesetz über die Banken und Sparkassen. https://www.admin.ch/opc/de /classified-compilation/19340083/index.html.

[199] Schweizerische Eidgenossenschaft. 1999. Bundesgesetz über die Währung und die Zahlungs-mittel. December 22. https://www.admin.ch/opc/de/classified-compilation/19994336 /201601010000/941.10.pdf.

[200] Fabian Schär. 2020. Cryptocurrencies: Miner heterogeneity, botnets and proof-of-work efficiency. *Frontiers in Blockchain* (forthcoming).

[201] Fabian Schär and Fabian Mösli. 2019. Blockchain diplomas: Using smart contracts to secure academic credentials. *Journal of Higher Education Research*, 41.

[202] Ken Shirriff. 2014. Mining bitcoin with pencil and paper: 0.67 hashes per day. Ken Shirriff's Blog, September 28. http://www.righto.com/2014/09/mining-bitcoin-with-pencil -and-paper.html.

[203] Kristian Slabbekoorn. 2014. The Willy report: Proof of massive fraudulent trading activity at Mt. Gox, and how it has affected the price of bitcoin. The Willy Report, May 25.

https://willyreport.wordpress.com/2014/05/25/the-willy-report-proof-of-massive-fraudu
lent-trading-activity-at-mt-gox-and-how-it-has-affected-the-price-of-bitcoin/.

[204] Daniel Stuckey. 2013. A working bitcoin ATM is in San Diego, but its most vocal backer
is gone. Vice, May 3. http://motherboard.vice.com/blog/a-working-bitcoin-atm-is-in-san
-diego-but-its-most-vocal-backer-is-gone.

[205] Peter Surda. 2014. Mt. Gox and fractional reserve banking. Economics of Bitcoin, February
11. http://www.economicsofbitcoin.com/2014/02/mt-gox-and-fractional-reserve-banking
.html.

[206] Tim Swanson. 2014. The anatomy of a money-like informational commodity: A study
of bitcoin. Seattle, WA: Amazon Digital Services. https://s3-us-west-2.amazonaws.com
/chainbook/The+Anatomy+of+a+Money-like+Informational+Commodity.pdf.

[207] Nick Szabo. 1997. The idea of smart contracts. Paper. http://www.fon.hum.uva.nl/rob
/Courses/InformationInSpeech/CDROM/Literature/LOTwinterschool2006/szabo.best.vwh
.net/idea.html.

[208] Nick Szabo. 2005. Bit gold. Unenumerated, December 27. http://unenumerated.blogspot
.ch/2005/12/bit-gold.html.

[209] Amir Taaki. 2011. BIP purpose and guidelines. GitHub, August 19. https://github.com
/bitcoin/bips/blob/master/bip-0001.mediawiki.

[210] Paolo Tasca. 2015. A market analysis of the bitcoin economy. Presentation at the Finance
2.0 Crypto Conference, Zurich, Switzerland, September 23. http://www.finance20.ch/wp
-content/uploads/2015/09/Crypto15_PaoloTasca.pdf.

[211] The Maker Team. 2017. The Dai stablecoin system. White Paper, Maker DAO, Santa Cruz,
CA, December. https://makerdao.com/en/whitepaper.

[212] Tether. Tether: Fiat currencies on the bitcoin blockchain. White Paper, 2016. https://tether
.to/wp-content/uploads/2016/06/TetherWhitePaper.pdf.

[213] Tether.io. 2015. Tether: Fiat currencies on the bitcoin blockchain. White Paper. https://
tether.to/wp-content/uploads/2015/04/Tether-White-Paper.pdf.

[214] The Economist. 2014. Bitcoin's future hidden flipside: How the crypto-currency could
become the internet of money. March 13. https://www.economist.com/finance-and-econo
mics/2014/03/13/hidden-flipside.

[215] Time Inc. 2014. Time Inc. partners with Coinbase to become the first major magazine
publisher to accept bitcoin payments. Press release, December 16. http://www.timeinc
.com/about/news/press-release/time-inc-partners-with-coinbase-to-become-the-first-major
-magazine-publisher-to-accept-bitcoin-payments/.

[216] Peter Todd. 2014. OP_CHECKLOCKTIMEVERIFY. GitHub, October 1. https://github.com
/bitcoin/bips/blob/master/bip-0065.mediawiki.

[217] Kyle Torpey. 2014. A solution for trustless bitcoin microtransactions is here. CCN, September 24. https://www.ccn.com/solution-trustless-bitcoin-microtransactions/.

[218] Tyler Adams, Luodanwg, and Tanyuan. 2017. Neo NEP-5 token standard. GitHub, August 10. https://github.com/neo-project/proposals/blob/master/nep-5.mediawiki.

[219] University of Nicosia. 2019. Free MOOC DFIN: 511: Introduction to Digital Currencies. Course, Cyprus. https://www.unic.ac.cy/blockchain/free-mooc/.

[220] Visa. 2017. *Annual Report 2017*. San Francisco, CA: Visa Inc. https://s1.q4cdn.com /050606653/files/doc_financials/annual/2017/Visa-2017-Annual-Report.pdf.

[221] Fabian Vogelsteller and Vitalik Buterin. 2015. EIP 20: ERC-20 token standard. Ethereum Improvement Proposals, November 19. https://eips.ethereum.org/EIPS/eip-20/.

[222] Erik Voorhees. 2016. Looting of the fox. Money and State. http://moneyandstate.com /looting-of-the-fox/.

[223] Kurt Wagner. 2013. World's first bitcoin ATM opens in Vancouver, Canada. Mashable, October 30. http://mashable.com/2013/10/30/bitcoin-atm-2/.

[224] Drew Weisenberger. 2015. How many atoms are there in the world? Jefferson Lab Science Education. http://education.jlab.org/qa/mathatom_05.html.

[225] Wikipedia. 2019. M-Pesa. Wikimedia Foundation, last updated October 16. https://en .wikipedia.org/wiki/M-Pesa.

[226] Wikipedia. 2014. List of countries by electricity consumption. Webpage. https://en.wiki pedia.org/wiki/List_of_countries_by_electricity_consumption.

[227] J. R. Willett. 2012. Mastercoin v. 0.5, January.

[228] Stephen Williamson. 2018. Is Bitcoin a waste of resources? *Federal Reserve Bank of St. Louis Review*, 100:107–115.

[229] Pieter Wuille. 2012. Hierarchical deterministic wallets. GitHub, February 11. https://github .com/bitcoin/bips/blob/master/bip-0032.mediawiki.

[230] Pieter Wuille. 2013. Alert: Chain fork caused by pre-0.8 clients dealing badly with large blocks. Bitcoin Forum, March 12. https://bitcointalk.org/index.php?topic=152030.0.

[231] Pieter Wuille. 2015. Strict der signatures. GitHub, January 10. https://github.com/bitcoin /bips/blob/master/bip-0066.mediawiki.

[232] Pieter Wuille. 2017. Base32 address format for native v0-16 witness outputs. GitHub, March 20. https://github.com/bitcoin/bips/blob/master/bip-0173.mediawiki.

[233] Pieter Wuille. 2017. New address type for SegWit addresses. YouTube, March 28. https:// youtu.be/NqiN9VFE4CU.

[234] Addy Yeow. 2015. Bitnodes incentive program. Bitnodes. https://bitnodes.21.co/nodes /incentive/.

[235] David Yermack. 2015. Is bitcoin a real currency? An economic appraisal. In *Handbook of Digital Currency*. edited by David Lee and Kuo Chuen, 31–45. London: Academic Press.

[236] Tyler Durden. 2017. Bitcoin tumbles after Jamie Dimon calls it a fraud: "would fire anyone trading it." ZeroHedge, September 12. https://www.zerohedge.com/news/2017-09-12 /bitcoin-tumbles-after-jamie-dimon-calls-it-fraud-would-fire-anyone-trading-it.

Index